Forever Wrestling

a glorious invitation

Tracey J. BATESON

ISBN: 1-9997464-2-2
ISBN-13: 978-1-9997464-2-1

DEDICATION

For my Dads
both Heavenly and biological.
You gave me life.
Mum, you too.
Thank you for your love,
support and encouragement in all things.

CONTENTS

***

***

***

***

***

ACKNOWLEDGEMENTS

There are many people to thank for this book and material.

To Jack my husband; thank you for being so ok with slot number 3. Thank you for your steadfast support and love. Sorry I didn't write the PhD you wanted, but hopefully more people will read this instead! Follow God's call in all you do.

Thank you John, for all that you are and all you do. I praise God daily for giving us such a precious gift. May you continue to provide much wisdom and may I have the grace to receive it. 'Yes please'!

Mum, thank you for loving me with your all and for always encouraging me to follow my heart. Well done for continuing to live on this earth as you wait to join dad.

To, Mum, In, Law, for, your, care, of the Yellow Pages; maybe, next, time, there, won't, be, so, many, commas, to, delete!

To those who have given their time to read and comment: Kerry, Elsa, Clarie, Richard, Laura, Phil – thank you for encouraging me to publish.

Ospringe and Davington, for your love and accepting me for me - thank you for letting me go.

Everyone in Egerton – you are awesome. You make it so much easier for me to love my neighbour – Thank you.

To my counsellor who had questionable maths: thank you for your patience!

In fact, to everyone I have met and whose journeys I have been able to share. Thank you for the impact you have made on my life. I hope to continue to pray for you all to come to know God in all of His fullness.

Finally to Elsa Lewis and everyone at Lioness Writing Ltd: Elsa – thank you for 'getting' this and for giving my words life. Thank you for your patience and all of your hard work. It is a privilege to work with such an awesome child of God. Debbie and Richard - thank you for your encouragement, for challenging me and for not becoming so 'irritated' that you gave up! You have had such an effect on this book, or was it an affect?! Mark Lewis – you got me to smile on a photo – wow – thank-you. I pray Lioness publishing continues to dwell in the Lord, taking leaps of faith on us 'scribblers'.

And finally little bro – if I can do it, so can you...

CHAPTER ONE:
'WALK A LITTLE SLOWER MUMMA'

My son came out of the womb knowing more about life and God than I will ever know. After living a life, or rather surviving a life for too long, I began to listen to both my son and God.

'Slowing' down did not come easy or natural to me, but I came to a point in my life where I had little choice. Exhausted, burnt out, disillusioned and broken...it was either slow down or give up completely. I regret having allowed myself to have reached this point, but I am grateful for the journey.

All that I have gone through over the past few years has brought me to a new and beautiful place. I have discovered a way of living and a state of being, which I would never have imagined possible.

In a nutshell, through coming across a glorious invitation, I have come to live the life for which I believe I am created. I am becoming more aware of living in God's love and thus in His Presence. This in turn has slowed down my racing heart, mind and life. For too long I had been doing things in my own strength, when all God had wanted was for me to live in His.

I say 'glorious invitation', rather than the best one, because although what I have discovered is life changing, it still comes second to the one I received some twenty years earlier.

Becoming a Christian changed my life forever. For too long I had associated God with religion rather than relationship. On becoming a Christian, internally I found peace with myself and God. I discovered love in the highest of forms and I have never looked back.

I became a Christian at a high point of my life - everything was going well, but I still believed there had to be more. Discovering a relationship with Jesus was indeed the best invitation of all time.

On this journey, I have found myself serving in the Army, visiting Rwanda (not long after the Genocide), going into Prisons, being a youth worker, serving at a University and being a Parish Priest. The most challenging definitely being the latter!

Along the way, the greatest relationship ever, my becoming God's child, sadly became associated with too much doing and not much being. For too long, I tried to love others, spend some time with God, and every so often allow myself to be loved by God. Weary, confused, disillusioned, broken and at a point of burnout, I desperately needed some help.

Whilst I had accepted Jesus' invitation to new life, sadly I had misread how to live this life. Eventually, after having been encouraged by my son, *'to walk a little slower'*, I came across a remedy in just twenty four words in Mark's Gospel.

I had been living my life all wrong. Outside in, rather than inside out. It was now time for me to start living the first invitation of salvation with the aid of the second.

Confused, dear reader? So was I for many years.

Sorry, I hope you are okay with colloquial chat. I am writing this as I would to a friend. I don't feel though, I can quite call you a friend yet, as we hardly know each other. 'Reader' will have to suffice for now.

I ought also to prepare you sooner than later, there will be times where I share parts of my life, alongside some deeper understanding of the Bible and theology, but there will also be other times where I go off on a tangent. There may be some repetition and at times I may lose my train of thought – but hey, isn't that true of most conversations.

This book will be unashamedly colloquial even as I wrestle with deeper theology. The reason for this is because at no point do I want to be telling you what to do or how to live – there are more than enough self-help books out there. At times it may even present as overly 'apologetic' – this too is intentional...I know what I believe, but it is not for me to dictate what you do.

Rather, I invite you to come alongside my journey. If any of it resonates with you, great, if not pass it on to someone else you know who may find it helpful. Eek, did I say, 'pass it on', clearly I meant purchase a copy for them.

At times I may even invite you to skip a chapter. Some of you, I am sure may find my anecdotes or rants on life a little off-piste while others of you may find the unravelling of Greek and Hebrew a bit too much. Every so often I'll try to give you the heads up. More than anything, I hope together we may come to know more about God and how to live the best of life.

There may be laughs, tears, and even some insights. I've gone for shorter chapters so you can have a quick or long read. If you are anything like me, I struggle to put a book down mid-chapter – solution is shorter chapters! Incidentally thank you for picking this up. Oh and please, (if you would like) do invite God's Holy Spirit to be with you as you read. Let's go...

So, back to where I was. I had been living outside in, rather than inside out. On the surface things often looked okay, but deep within everything was hollow.

A friend once told me how, as a young child, her mum had told her if she ever got lost in a department store, she should go and find a shop assistant. Sure enough one day, my friend's mum (let's call her Mary) wandered off too fast and my friend ended up looking for help. Sometime later, Mary found her daughter holding hands with a mannequin!

Mary had a knack for losing things. One day she rang the police to report her car had been stolen. Some hours later a policeman popped round asking; *'Have you been to the local shop today madam?'* *'Why yes I have'*, Mary replied. *'How did you know?'* she asked. The police-man answered, *'Your car is there madam.'* Oops! Mary had driven to the shop and absentmindedly walked home.

For as long I could remember, I too had been holding on to what I thought would help me. After many years I eventually realised I had been holding on, not to a mannequin exactly, but certainly to something with little life in it. In just one verse of the Bible I felt I was being given another chance, an opportunity to live rather than merely survive.

CHAPTER TWO:
THE GLORIOUS INVITATION

'Love the Lord your God with all your heart
and with all your soul and with all your mind
and with all your strength'
(Mark 12:30).

CHAPTER THREE:
IN A NUTSHELL

I am always bemused when you see the following promotion: 'Party for the over 30's, 40's and 50's'. Surely someone in their 40's is indeed over 30, so why does it need stating?

God longs and calls for us to love Him. In *Mark chapter 12 verse 30* we may wonder whether Jesus too is over-stating the case. Surely to love God is enough, do we need to add with our all? Let alone, state how we should love God with all our heart, soul, mind and strength. Papyrus was expensive so why did Mark waste the words?

As I have come to this glorious invitation of loving God I have become grateful to the Gospel writers for not paraphrasing. Mark knew just how important it is to consider our love for God through four distinct and yet inter-connected areas. Through loving God with my heart, mind, soul and strength, so I have come to love God more with my all. In turn I have made myself more available to be loved by Him first.

As my soul and my spirit become more in union with God, so I am able to be more loved by God and in return love more too. I say, 'I', but actually no! Being able to love at all is a wonderful partnership with God. Is this over-stepping the mark? I think not! Paul calls us *'co-workers' (1 Corinthians 3:9)*. With God's Holy Spirit and through God's transforming grace, I am able to be loved and love all the more. My role was to be in the right place with God. This I could not do until I had 'slowed down'.

Perhaps I need to be honest though, and state that our adventure does not actually begin to look at our mind, heart, soul and strength for quite a while. It may be therefore, that you want to skip to chapter twenty nine and perhaps return later to the next chapter. But for those who are more linear, let's turn the page.

CHAPTER FOUR:
SETTING THE SCENE

I cannot escape the irony as I start this chapter, that it was five years ago today that my father died. On that day a very large part of my mum also died, as did a little of me. My dad died of a sudden and massive heart attack and from that day my whole world seemed to change. In the short term there was the usual busyness of funeral arrangements and the like. Longer term there was a coming to terms with living with my own grief and that of my family.

It was however, some two years later, that I began to sense a brokenness of a different kind. My mind was full. My heart was heavy. My soul was crying out. I was often functioning (just) in my own strength. I was slowly being broken...all be it for my own good – I just didn't know this at the time.

A sun filled holiday did not live up to the blurb on the brochure. Tenerife had had the worst winter in 100 years. The sun only chose to come out as we travelled back to the airport, to fly home. Although my friend and I, along with my son had tried to make the most of it, the holiday wasn't great.

I remember returning on the plane feeling ill and it was more than just motion sickness. With my head in my hands, I felt despondent and empty. I had no idea how I was going to carry on the life I had been living.

I never got to the point of wanting to take my own life - I always wanted to live for my child. This said, I did sometimes look at 'road kill' at the side of the road and think they were better off than me!

Rather than talking to God deeply about all of this, I took the Jonah route and I tried to run away. For a while I tried to self-medicate. After all had Paul not encouraged Timothy to take some wine for his stomach *(1 Timothy 5:23)*? I fuelled myself with caffeine during the day and tried to calm myself with herbal remedies at night.

I was fed up with feeling this way and no matter how much I prayed, things didn't seem to be getting any better. I became so bored with feeling this way. In the end, I talked to God less and less. There didn't seem much to say!

The whole role of being a Priest however, was not really compatible with not speaking to God. Leading services and the like, meant outwardly I was praying, but internally there was silence. On a one to one basis, I wanted as little to do with God as possible. And in no uncertain terms, I told Him so.

I realise I am not the first to do this. Weary, despondent and in dark times, many people as they wrestle with God let Him know their struggles. I was thankful at least that I had not yet reached the depths of despair Paul had reached:

'Indeed, we felt we had received the sentence
of death. But this happened that we might not
rely on ourselves but on God, who raises the dead'
(2 Corinthians 1:9).

But nor had I reached Paul's conclusion that whatever I was going through was all part of God's purpose and plan for me.

I will spare you my months, if not years of complaints (they belong to another book) but in a nut shell the following words and phrases paint a picture of life as I knew it. I must warn you, it is intentionally a long paragraph with dodgy punctuation.

I was busy, weary, exhausted, unhappy and disillusioned. I was continually ill from headaches and repeated chest infections. (Blood tests revealed little). I had sores on my legs and a tingling in my hands. I had been losing weight, which for a while I saw as a plus – as I could eat doughnuts galore. I got fed up though when I needed to purchase smaller clothes! I lived in a damp and mouldy vicarage. I was suffering from frequent palpitations. Was it anxiety, stress or something else? Everything seemed meaningless. I was consumed by grief. I had lost six relatives in less than 18 months. I was suffering from compassion fatigue and cumulative stress, with perhaps burn out or a breakdown around the corner. I was bored with conflict, buildings, architects, liturgy, the Church of England and parish working practices. I wondered whether I was under spiritual attack, being tested, or whether I was being led into a wilderness. Was I going through a 'dark night of the soul'? Was I being led to a place of surrender and humility? Was I being encouraged to deal with pride, self-image and identity? Was I in the wrong job/vocation? All I knew was, I was no longer living, but merely existing. I was broken and I had the scars to prove it.

Something had to change, before it was too late..

CHAPTER FIVE:
IT COULD BE WORSE...

So, I thought I had it bad. Not as bad as some, but for the moment, it all seemed bad enough. I guess I even wallowed in self-pity for a while. After all, I was working for God and the church, surely God could give me a 'break' every so often.

A quick skim of the Bible however, shows that I kind of had it easy. In addition God's word revealed how often God allows such times of trial and testing for our own good!

Leaving Jesus aside for the moment as I cannot compete with being crucified, let's consider some of God's people who had it much worse.

What of Jacob? He wrestled with God one night, resulting in his hip being put out of joint *(Genesis 32:22-32)*.

The prophet Elijah had bad days. Speaking out against worshipping Baal, he ended up on the wrong side of Queen Jezebel. In fear of his life, he even asked God to take it from him *(1 Kings 19:4)*.

Moses, the great leader who was to bring God's people out of Egypt could have had a better start to his vocation. The writer of *Exodus* records: *'God was just about to kill him' (4:24)*. It was a good job Moses' wife was handy with a knife and there was a foreskin available, otherwise God's people may have stayed in Egypt even longer *(4:25)*!

What of Jeremiah? A prophet called to speak out, but he too had bad days and he felt able, in no uncertain terms to tell God so:

> *'You deceived me, LORD, and I was deceived; you overpowered*
> *me and prevailed. I am ridiculed all day long; everyone mocks me'*
> *(Jeremiah 20:7)*.

If this complaint wasn't bad enough, being thrown into a cistern (or a pit), must have been a low point. As he sank deeper into the mud (naked), left to starve to death *(Jeremiah 38:6)*, how he must have wished he had kept his mouth shut. You see people didn't dislike him for anything he had done personally. He was despised because of words he had spoken on behalf of God.

Job (someone within the Old Testament, not a form of employment) perhaps had it worse. Animals were killed and stolen. Houses were destroyed. Servants, sons and daughters were killed. Job himself was inflicted with sores all over his body. If this wasn't bad enough he had miserable friends for comforters.

So actually, who was I to complain? I didn't walk with a limp. The authorities were not after me. As far as I could tell, God hadn't tried to kill me. I had never been thrown down a pit, naked or otherwise. I still had a house, albeit a damp one and mercifully I had not lost my son. Perhaps I should just stop moaning and get on with life. And believe me, for several years I tried.

Yet, deep down I reasoned it was surely better to moan to God and to let Him have it, than to not talk to Him at all. It was the Psalmist who gave me a voice to do just this.

We do not always know the background to individual psalms: how or why Psalmists were having a bad day. The song writers clearly knew God intimately. They had both good days and bad days. They always let God know how they were feeling. They are refreshingly honest. For a while this gave me confidence to do likewise.

Initially in my wrestling I used the Psalmists own words. In time however I became more confident to use my own, all be it some of my 'Psalms' would have needed a 'Parental Advisory Explicit Content' logo on them. For a while it seemed healthy and good to let it all out, but after a time, this became a little hollow. After a while, to be honest I even got a bit bored with pouring it all out. I just didn't seem to be moving forward. I wasn't so much in a pit, as in a rut!

So after a busy Christmas period, I spent a week not talking to God. I didn't pray or read the Bible. In fact, I turned my back on Him. I even reminded God every morning, that I was not talking to Him – just in case He had forgotten. After a week of this though, my life had not improved and I also realised that in telling God, *'I am not talking to You'*, I actually had been. Doh! I couldn't even get that right!

9

So, I then tried something different. I turned to the person who had had the worst of days. To someone whose last day no-one would envy. I turned to the Gospels.

If there was a way of understanding how I was feeling and what I was going through, I wanted to hear from the words of Jesus Himself. I still knew He was my Saviour and even my Lord although I had become more reluctant to live the latter.

As I turned to Mark's Gospel, I remember thinking (and half praying) that if Jesus didn't have anything to say directly to me, I was considering, 'moving on'. I never quite clarified, even to myself, just what this 'moving on' would entail. Was I threatening to leave ministry, the church or my faith? Thankfully and most mercifully I never found out.

I would love to say the answer was immediate. I would love to share how as I turned the pages, angels sang loudly and bright lights shone around a text followed by hearing a voice from heaven speaking to me, but no. To be sure, it was good to be reminded of all Jesus had gone through, and of His reaction to those who persecuted Him. It was refreshing to be reminded of His calling, His nature and all He said but nothing specific leapt out. Not for many months anyway.

If I'm honest, whilst I thought many good, hmm, no, great things about Jesus, I couldn't always identify with Him. I knew all He had done for me. I knew He was my Saviour. I knew He had gone to the Cross and died for me. I marvelled that death did not defeat Him and that He came alive again. I knew I was saved, redeemed, washed in His blood and cleansed. I knew I was going to heaven and I was mightily thankful for all of this.

I guess though, I struggled with the whole 'God' part of Jesus. This doesn't mean that I ever doubted He was God. I knew He was fully God and fully human. It was more that I struggled to identify with Him fully, because He was God. Being God surely gives you the edge in life, no matter how human you also are. I mean when it came to paying His taxes, Jesus instructed His disciples to open the mouth of a fish for the payment *(Matthew 17:27)*.

Now whilst a man once, did indeed pay his tax bill on the belly of a fish,[i] on the whole we have to pay our taxes with hard earned cash. I do not fish myself, but I have never heard of coins being regularly found in the mouth of a fish.

Back to Jesus and my struggle to finding inspiration on how to live my daily life, through following someone who was fully God. I know He had testing days, no less so than during forty days in the wilderness when He was tempted by the Devil but He always seemed to know the right thing to say. Deep down I used to think, well up until the last few days of His life, Jesus kind of had it easy! How could I ever truly identify with Him?

Okay, Jesus had 12 Disciples who would have tested anyone. Sir Alan Sugar, pointing his finger, would have yelled to each one in turn; *'You're fired!'* And yes, Jesus was also misunderstood and not liked by religious groups of His day, but on the whole He was involved in a lot of amazing stuff.

Jesus performed miracles galore: exorcisms, healings and He even brought a man back from the grave. His teaching was second to none. There was lots of walking in the fresh air and He could even walk on water. Jesus it seemed had time just to hang out, whether this was at weddings or feasts. He even did a bit of sailing. On the whole, He seemed to have lived a well-paced life.

Also all of this took place 2000 years ago in a very different culture and society. Life just seemed less busy back then. Sure they often had to walk everywhere but at least this provided time for fresh air and some head space. They also saved money on gym membership.

I would ask myself: what would Jesus know about living in the 21st Century? What would Jesus know about living in a frantic, busy, media-overload age? When did Jesus ever commute to work? When did He ever have to get three children to school before work? When did Jesus ever have to go and check on elderly parents, before having the Grand-children round for tea?

Jesus had women looking after Him *(Luke 8:3)*, so He didn't even have to fit in household chores and shopping around His ministry. I was left considering: what can His life on earth honestly have to say to my day to day living? Well, you know, beyond making it possible for me to be with God in the first place, which really is quite a biggie. This I could not deny.

I do not mean to come across as arrogant or heretical in these musings. Rather I so wanted to learn from Jesus for the here and now. I wanted, no I needed in the 21st Century to identify with Him. I wanted to learn from Him how to live life. I no longer wanted to live, feeling so far away from everything. I was tired of considering everything was *'meaningless' (Ecclesiastes 1:2)* and I was bored with being angry at the world.

CHAPTER SIX:
A DAY IN COURT

Again and again I reached for my Bible, each time asking, how could I better identify with Jesus? How can I learn from Him, how to get the best from life on earth?

So I read the Gospels and then I re-read them. I began to note down things He said, as I thought this was where the answer would lie. On my first attempt at doing this, I clearly missed a few things as I overlooked what I have now come to see as the, 'glorious invitation'.

I re-read the Gospels, listing all the things He did; where He went, who He spoke to. Although He didn't travel very far from home, I could not deny Jesus was on the go a lot. The more I read, the more I saw Jesus the person, fully God yes, but also fully human.

I began to see He faced the pressures of crowds; of people wanting something from Him wherever He went. He was hated and hunted down. Even His own family did not always understand Him. I began to see, He too had days when He wanted and needed to get away from it all. Yet even as He tried, He was tracked down.

Jesus, I came to see, faced many things which we too all face. Some of the things I felt in my own life, Jesus too had experienced. Yet unlike me, He seemed to live a more balanced life. I wanted to understand not just how He endured everything, but also how He had lived His life to the full.

As I continued to read, I was grateful, I had never been crucified, whipped, scourged or spat at, but I had ended up in a court. Okay the outcome was never going to be crucifixion, but through no fault of my own, I had faced accusation and lies.

I had ended up having to write witness petitions and the like – all over a loo! In my day in court, (all be it an Ecclesiastical one), I knew I was there because I was serving God. It was not a personal affront. I was there because I was the Parish Priest representing a congregation, who wanted to make their church more usable for the local community. Sadly this did not make the ordeal any easier to bear.

As I was called to the witness stand, I wanted it to go well, but I also knew I had to be true to myself. Above all I could not lie. For me this started even before I was asked the first question. As I took the stand, I was offered a Bible and asked to swear I would tell the truth. The trouble was, I couldn't even do that.

I knew from *James 5:12:*

> *'Above all, my brothers and sisters, do not swear -*
> *not by heaven or by earth or by anything else.*
> *All you need to say is a simple 'Yes' or 'No.'*
> *Otherwise you will be condemned'.*

For me this verse included my not being willing to stand with a Bible in hand, swearing I would tell the truth. I could not swear an oath. My word should be enough. In the depth of my heart I knew this to be right for me. However, at the same time I did not want to appear confrontational before we had even started the proceedings.

Thankfully the Deputy Commissary General that day respected my stand. He even spoke of Sir Thomas Moore who had also refused to swear an oath. Thankfully unlike Sir Thomas in 1534, imprisonment was not on the horizon for me. Although a prison cell with lights out from 10pm to 6am was very appealing.

The court case came out in our favour and the church got their loo, all be it two months before I ended up leaving – hey ho! I passed by the church some months later and even my son, had obviously picked up on things. He commented; *'Look mumma, there's the church where you once worked so hard. You didn't even get to use the loo did you?!'*

Thankfully John remembers that, rather than the holiday (just before the court case), which was ruined as I was plagued with anxiety at the stress of it all. We ended up returning home early as I couldn't rest.

After the court case, I invited a senior colleague back to mine for a cuppa and I all but broke down. It was pretty much during this conversation, when for the first time, I let my mask fall. I could wear it no longer. I was spent. I admitted everything was too much and life could not continue this way. He was surprised, no let's say, 'shocked'. His word for everything I experienced in the Parish was always; *'unprecedented'*. His word to describe me had been, *'omni-competent'*. He had had no idea of what was really going on…

From this point, life (slowly) began once again to make sense. I had admitted to myself and to God enough times previously, that I could not continue the life I was living. It seemed however, before life could get any better, I was required to admit 'it' to another person. I began to tread a path of humility.

From this point, although at times life got even darker, I knew I was on a road to recovery. There was suddenly some light, (all be it a dim one) and even hope that life could change. The Archdeacon suggested two things: counselling and a retreat. He raised an eye brow, when I replied, *'I don't have time!'*

Counselling helped a little. Even going was a big enough step for me. 'Counselling' was something other people did. I only had a few sessions before we both agreed I needed a new Spiritual Director instead. Going on a 'retreat' and guarding a day off also gave me more time to be with God. More time to read His word, eagerly searching for answers.

After over two years of reading and re-reading the Bible, one aspect alone kept repeatedly coming back to me. Time and again I had ignored it, because frankly on a first glance, it looked anything but inviting. To be honest what I had discovered, looked like just yet another thing to do!

With more reflection, study and humility, I began to see the life I was created for. More than this I began to discover how to live this life! To truly live life in all of its abundance. In full, I had found my purpose in life was to…

***

'Love the Lord your God with all your heart and with all your soul and with all your mind and with all your strength.' The second is this: 'Love your neighbour as yourself.' 'There is no commandment greater than these'
(Mark 12:30-31).

***

CHAPTER SEVEN:
THE DISCOVERY

As you can see I have at this point added the second most important command, which is to love others. I had overlooked these verses for many years, but in my brokenness something struck me afresh. At that very point in my life, it was impossible, absolutely impossible for me to do any of this. Here was Jesus asking me to love God with my all and to love others and yet I could hardly live let alone love.

In a nutshell, my heart was filled to the brim, my mind was exhausted. I had no strength and I didn't even really know what my soul was. I spent every day trying to love others and as a consequence I was exhausted.

During counselling, it was suggested that perhaps I had compassion fatigue and cumulative stress. Some people had wondered if I was heading for burnout or a breakdown. I don't actually know as I never made time for the Doctor! All I did know was that I wasn't functioning and there was no way I could do any more loving.

Jesus, as He spoke of this command had summed up life into four facets; heart, soul, mind and strength. None of mine were really living, let alone loving. As I began to take this verse on board I mused and wondered if God was trying to speak to me through it.

As theory turned into practise, if perhaps, if just perhaps I could find a way to live this verse, then life may be able to get back on track. If in some way I could love God with my heart, soul, mind and strength, then perhaps my life could turn around. There were lot of 'ifs', not only just in this paragraph but in my fragile hope...

I was being introduced to loving God in a new way. My way had not been working. I had to give another way a try. My understanding of this verse was going to be refined along the way. Initially all I had to do was to receive and accept it.

Discovering we were created to love God was like, *'phew…so that's why we are here'*. And, *'for a whole moment'*, I rejoiced in having found the answer. I was created and called to love God. End of. The Westminster Shorter Catechism of the mid seventh century was correct after all. It asks; what is the chief end of man? The answer was; *'Man's chief end is to glorify God, and to enjoy Him forever'.*ii

I embraced the verse and I felt peace for the first time in a long while. There was a hope of being able to enjoy life once again. I say, *'for a whole moment'*, because, after a week or so, I saw it as yet another thing to fit in.

This is just how my head works. One day it can be saying, *'Phew thank you God. All I have to do is love you. Praise God'*. The next day, such joyful praise is replaced with, *'Oh great, now I have yet another thing to do, I have to fit in 'loving God'. That sounds more than just ten minutes of quiet time!'*

In the space of a minute, I went from being full of hope to totally downcast. I remained so for quite a while. Somehow (and I guess it must have been through God's Holy Spirit), I found the energy not to give up on it. There had to be a way of loving God without it being just yet another thing to do.

I turned to Jesus again to see how He lived out His own commandments. After all if He didn't manage it, then who was I to even try. It's like people who rave about the latest diet and perhaps even inspire you, only for you then to see them tucking into doughnuts in the local café.

Surely, I thought, Jesus practised what He preached. As I read the Gospels, I was encouraged to see Jesus Himself had had times of deep sorrow and grief. At times His mind, heart, soul and strength were in fact close to breaking. Yet throughout it all, Jesus not only loved God, He lived life to the full.

As I reflected on Jesus and human beings, I came to see God had indeed designed, created, and formed us each with a mind, heart, strength and soul. Created in His image, I just had to believe God knew what He was doing when He did so. God had created us for Himself and had given us four attributes to enable us to come to Him.

I wonder though and let's be honest here, how much attention do we truly give to each of these areas? We may not be so bad at giving attention to our bodies, but Jesus didn't mention our bodies. Sure some people have interpreted the word *'strength'* as our body but the word actually means something more like *'muchness'* (more on this later).

We may give attention to our body or to our strength, especially when it is not functioning as we want it to. Just ask the National Health Service. It is almost at breaking point, as we spend so much time wanting our bodies to perform well. What of exercise regimes and diets galore? On the whole, we do give attention to our body.

Increasingly too, we have become more aware of our minds, particularly if they give us unease. An increase in mental health issues has led many people to become more aware of the fragility of our minds. Depression, anxiety and stress are at an all-time high. Mental health agencies have done some great work in making the subject no longer 'taboo'.

Our hearts though, what of them? When someone is in love (or not), they may give some thought to them. More and more people seem to be wanting to have 'happy hearts'. Daily, people utter the words, *you are just not making me happy any more'*, just before they move on. Actions seem to be more motivated by emotions than by responsibility or even commitment.

One's own happiness must be pursued at whatever cost! Is this an everlasting product of the 'enlightenment'? Perhaps! As 'reason' became the primary source of authority, ideals like freedom of choice, progress and tolerance began to reign. I am not saying these are bad in themselves, but the pursuit of happiness, whilst it may benefit a few, seems in its wake to bring unhappiness to many more. Too many families today are being ripped apart as one person pursues their own goal of happiness.

Finally, whilst in large bookshops under the 'Religion' section, there seem to be more books on our 'Body, mind and soul', few people seem to really know what their soul is. A soul has come to mean whatever someone wants it to mean. As such satisfying one's own soul can lead to unhealthy self-interest.

As I look at the world in which many of us now live: a world where we are bombarded with media, data and busyness, is it any wonder our minds are becoming weary and our hearts over loaded? As we try to fit more and more into our already 'busy lives' should we be surprised that we have little 'strength'. We rarely make time for the physical aspects of our lives, let alone our souls.

If we were to actually stop and seriously look at our lives, how much of it is actually: *'chasing after the wind' (Ecclesiastes 1:14)*. If we do take Solomon's words of wisdom to heart, how much of our life is in fact, *'meaningless' (Ecclesiastes 1:2)*.

God created *'our inmost being' (Psalm 139:13)*; our soul for Himself. As God says, *'For every living soul belongs to me' (Ezekiel 18:4)*. For too long, I had overlooked this. No, that is not honest. I had not overlooked it; I had never known it. And here was me, a Christian for over twenty years and nineteen of these had been working in the church.

In trying to live life, perhaps I had not always been doing so well because I had not been living 'life' as God intends. Discovering how God longs for us to live and love, was about to change my life. As I was being invited to love God with my all, so I was also being invited to be loved by God too. The latter had to happen before the former could even be attempted.

CHAPTER EIGHT:
TWO BECOME ONE

Who would have imagined that a verse, a command given by God, could so powerfully be changing my life? This command, based on two laws, was transforming my life. By the way you did read right, 'two laws'.

Now unless you are a lawyer, you are unlikely to profess to liking the Law, let alone loving it. I have never heard people, in their relationship with God saying: *The Law, oh yeah all of those rules, ordinances, statutes and commands, I just love them. I cannot wait for a sermon series on them. They seriously help me get the best of life. Yeah for Leviticus and Deuteronomy!'*

Yet the Psalmist did:

> *'Oh, how I love your law! I meditate on it all day long'*
> *(Psalm 119:97).*

It's not even as if this was a throw away comment. The whole Psalm is full of references to the Law and the Psalmist's desire to follow it:

> *'Praise be to you, LORD; teach me your decrees. With my lips I recount all the laws that come from your mouth. I rejoice in following your statutes as one rejoices in great riches. I meditate on your precepts and consider your ways. I delight in your decrees; I will not neglect your word'*
> *(Psalm 119:12-16).*

Over time I studied more of God's Law as revealed in the Old Testament. I have to confess however, after a few hours of reading Deuteronomy and Leviticus, I never came away praising God for His laws! For all 613 of them. Yes, you read right, 613!

Now I am aware I may be beginning to lose some of you here, but please give me time to explain. To speak of the Law may seem 'boring' or as though I have lost it but from this I believe comes the key to a better life, to a fulfilling, life-giving life – sourced in God.

However, if it all gets too much, please skip to chapter 12 and maybe come back here later!

So 613 laws given by God to His people...Over time, discussions and interpretations of the Law extended to the Talmud, some 67 volumes! Whilst the Talmud would not be compiled for another five centuries, discussions over the meaning of the Law, took place long before and were certainly on-going during the time of Jesus. For too long the Law had become something to discuss. It had all become a burden.

The law had become something to obey, rather than something to live. God had first given laws to His people as they entered the Promised land. God chose Israel to be His people and He loved them. In turn, He gave them a way to love Him back. As His people formed a relationship with Him, so God longed for them to get the best out of life. The law was a gift to help them.

The Law set apart God's people, reminding them in all things they were the people of the Holy God. The Law marked out a people for His own. The law and structure of Israel incidentally was actually the envy of other nations. Imagine how long it takes to make a law, let alone how many laws it takes to structure a society. Moses however, was given the Law and its associated organisation, in a matter of days.

Sadly over time however, these commands became increasingly divorced from love and even from God Himself. People became more interested in looking as though they were keeping the Law, than actually doing so. The law had become more about the externals. God's people had become accountable to each other, rather than to God.

The Law was always meant to point to the holiness of God and our sinfulness *(Galatians 3:19; 1 Timothy 1:8-11)*. God's people, through the Law, came to know about sin but also about forgiveness. The sacrificial system was after all set up to enable people to become right with God. Through the Law, God's people became conscious of their sin *(Romans 3:20)*; through God accepting offered sacrifices they were able to offer atonement for their sins.

Through sacrificing costly animals, people lost some of their livelihood. God accepted their sacrifices which enabled His people to be restored to Him; to be at one with Him.

The Old Testament repeatedly reveals how God still loved His people and wanted them for His own. The Law for God was His way of keeping His people close. Yes, it involved sacrificing animals and specific rituals, but at the heart of it all was a relationship with the Holy God. God loved His people and wanted them for His own. To the prophet Jeremiah, God said:

'I will put my law in their minds and write it on their hearts.
I will be their God, and they will be my people'
(Jeremiah 31:33, compare also Hebrews 10:16).

Now I have never heard of writing a law on a heart. I have seen laws tattooed on people's skin but never a law on someone's heart. But this is how far God wanted His people to know Him and love Him.

God longed for a living, loving, intimate relationship with His people. And life was always better for God's people, when they were loving God through obeying the Law. God wanted His law to be in the very being of His people. It made Him their God and them His people.

613 laws let's be honest are a lot to read, let alone remember and obey. They covered; marriage and divorce, ceremony, diet, vows, oaths, feasts, agriculture, business practices, first-borns, wars, disease, sacrifices, employment and even clothing.

Through obeying the Law, in particular the Ten Commandments, God's people were able to get the best of life. God gave Moses the Ten Commandments for the good of His people. Few people will deny that if all of the Ten Commandments were kept today, life would be better for everyone.

Let's think about this for a moment...I wonder who in real terms has ever felt better for breaking them? Okay there may be some immediate gratification for adultery, lying, and stealing, but unless you have no conscience at all, longer term who feels better for breaking any one of these Ten Commands. Or, as I prefer to term them: God's better ways of living.

Through making God's Law merely a set of obligations and rules, God's people had lost the love which had instigated them in the first place. It is as if within the 613 laws, amongst the obligations and sub categories, God Himself had been buried. This was starkly opposite to Jesus' take on the Law.

Jesus was always more concerned with being in love with God, with devotion, rather than merely an outward observance of laws. Time and again Jesus spoke of this and He lived it. The law in the words of Jesus had become a *'burden'* *(Matthew 23:4)*. Jesus came as a *'light to the world'* *(John 8:12)*; He revealed God and God's love even in the Law itself. Jesus' very life was to shine as a light, to a new way of living.

By the time Jesus lived, almost in an attempt to reduce the laws, discussions centred on what laws were most important.[iii] Jesus answered this long debated question giving what I term as a 'glorious invitation', as found in *Mark 12:30-31*. In response to being tested, as to what was the most important law, Jesus combined two verses from the Torah, namely *Deuteronomy 6:5* and *Leviticus 19:18*.

Yes you read right, *Leviticus* and *Deuteronomy*. Most people if they even knew where the Ten Commandments could be found, are likely to point to *Exodus 20*. Rather, Jesus was quoting from *Deuteronomy 6:5* whilst the *'Loving your neighbour'* element is actually from *Leviticus 19:18*. If you think what you are reading is heavy going, why not take a light break and look up *Leviticus 19*!

I have to say I am bemused of the origins of such a well-known verse. For centuries people, Christian and non, have encouraged each other to love their neighbour. Yet, in the first instance of it being commanded it is almost lost amongst laws. *Leviticus 19* is full of lots of different laws ranging from not mating different kinds of animals, to not being allowed to eat from newly planted trees until its fifth year of growth.

It is highly probable that the answer Jesus gave had been discussed, but until Jesus, the two verses had never been so inextricably linked.[iv] It seems there was lots of cultural discussion (compare *Luke 10:25-27*) as to whether the two verses should come together.[v]

Schools of thought had spent hours, days if not years discussing what the greatest commandment was and yet Jesus without even a pause of breath knew the answer instinctively. Theologian Nineham goes so far to comment that;

> *'the combination of these two widely separated texts as taking us to the heart of religion is clearly original and creative achievement of the highest order'.*[vi]

Let's face it in life, there are some perfect combinations, which until someone thinks of it, remain unknown. Imagine if 'Salt and Vinegar' had never been introduced. What if 'Cheese' had never given 'Onion' a chance? Imagine Wimbledon without 'Strawberries and Cream'?

Jesus in His answer showed more orthodoxy than the teachers of the day had expected. They could not criticise His answer – it was perfect. As Tom Wright says:

> *'Jesus' answer was so traditional that nobody could challenge him on it, and so deeply searching that everyone else would be challenged by it'.*[vii]

Jesus' answer was perfect.

For all of those who struggled to remember the 10 commandments, let alone all 613 commandments, Jesus gave just two. The incredible aspect of this is rather than limiting the Law, Jesus opened it up. In one instant Jesus both shortened and extended God's Law! 613 into just two and yet if they could be lived, imagine how different our world would be. Jesus revealed both in His words and in His life, the best way to live; God's given way to live is through loving Him and loving others.

CHAPTER NINE:
TWO STILL BECOME ONE...

I hope I haven't lost you. Even now as I am on my numerous edit of these words, I remain astonished how two verses from the Torah, that of *Deuteronomy 6:5* and *Leviticus 19:18,* woven together by Jesus have given me new life. These two commandments known since the time of Moses, took over fourteen centuries to be linked together. In doing so, I believe Jesus reveals the pattern for our lives.

We are created to be loved by God; we are created to be His children. Loving God is not just another thing to do or to fit in. We are asked to love Him, yes, but only from being loved ourselves by Him. After all, how can we come to love Him if we do not already know of His love for us first. From God's love for us, we are invited to love Him. It is only from here that we are then encouraged to love others.

God gives us a flow which throughout this book I am going to unpack. God loves us – we love God – and from this we can love others. Love flows from God to us, to others. From a place of being loved and as we come to love God in return, so we are then called and more able to love others.

For too long you see, I had had the flow all topsy-turvy. My way had been to love others, love God and if there was time, to allow myself to be loved by God. No wonder I had ceased living and was merely existing. I had been living against the intended flow of life for too long.

Loving other people is important. I knew this long before I knew Jesus as my Saviour. I guess on becoming a Christian, out of thanks, I worked all the more to love others. More often than not however, this was in my own strength. I now know God loves us so much that although we are called to love others, He knows we are unable to do this alone. We need God's love in us. We need His love to flow through us.

Loving others is important but it is the second commandment. The first one is to love God. But even before this, we must come to God through His love for us.

In fact if this makes any sense to you and you have had enough of reading, just leave it here. Put the book down and allow yourself to be loved by God, to be truly loved by God. In turn this can flow into loving Him and from this position of peace and strength, you can love others. In God's strength and not merely your own.

If, however, like me, you need a little more unravelling, then please stay with me. Alternatively skip to chapter twelve and I'll meet you there.

Jesus revealed these two commands of loving God and loving others has to come first. Jesus knew by keeping these first, all the other commands could be kept more easily. In fact in keeping just these, we are able to keep all of the others.

To attempt to try and keep 613 laws in one's own strength was always almost impossible. So you have to ask the question, was God not in fact just being cruel giving them to us in the first place? Far from it. Rather these laws were all designed to keep God's people close to Him. To keep the laws of loving God and others is only possible through allowing God's love to flow through first. Jesus knew this and lived this.

It is God who enables us to keep His commands. For too long, the keeping of laws had become trophies to be collected, or levels to be attained. Loving God and loving others were rather the source from which all else can flow. Jesus revealed this.

Jesus not only brought together these two otherwise separated commands, in His words, but also through His life. Jesus *'walked the talk'*. The governing principle of these commands was love. Jesus lived a life of love. He even died for love.

The more I read these commands, the more I saw how much God loved me. The more I read them, the more I had to admit I had been living life the wrong way round. I was so eager, no, 'desperate' to live life right. Jesus' own words seemed to be the key...

'Love the Lord your God with all your heart and with all your
soul and with all your mind and with all your strength'
(Mark 12:30).

Now sure, I had read these words time and again in the Gospels. It is a short verse and perhaps it had become so over familiar that I had over-looked how life giving it could be. To be honest on many readings, as I have said, I had seen it as yet another thing to do. Whenever I had preached on this verse, I had certainly attempted to show we were all being encouraged to 'do'.

As I re-read the Gospels again, I now saw Jesus did not only offer this invitation, He lived it day in and day out. And actually if I got off my high horse, Jesus did have busy days, crazy days. There were days when He had to fight to get through a crowd. Some days, He would be teaching so long that meals were missed.

Jesus had days of people crowding around Him to the extent that He had to push a boat out onto a lake to speak to everyone. Jesus didn't seem to be able to go anywhere for a walk with His disciples, without someone wanting something from Him.

Jesus couldn't even be jostled in a crowd by an ill lady, without feeling the power of God leave Him. He had days of feeling intensely alone, times of being misunderstood. There were times of mental anguish, times of His soul being troubled and of His heart being broken. He had bad days...very bad days.

Yet throughout it all, fully human, God made flesh *(John 1:14)*, Jesus modelled living out this command. In His words, in His actions, in His very being Jesus lived out what it was to love God with His all. As I read the Gospels yet again, I marvelled at how Jesus lived out loving the Lord with His 'all'. I now see loving God is in fact a three-way movement. It involves us and God yes, but also other people.

As we love God in response to all He is and has done, so we interact with each other and hopefully seek to build one another up *(1 Corinthians 14:3-5, 12, 17, 26; Ephesians 4:11-16; 1 Thessalonians 5:11)*. This is how God created us, to be co-dependant beings, to be the body of Christ.

God calls us to love Him with others. We are bigger than something just of ourselves. The linking of these two verses remind us, that God is to be the source of our love. As we seek to love others so we are called to be with others in love.

CHAPTER TEN:
UNRAVELLING THE KNOTS

After many months, of reflecting and praying into being called to love God with my all, I felt it was time for some more study. This couldn't occur immediately as quite frankly my mind was too full to consider anything in any depth. Over time though, through going on a Retreat and taking some holiday, I found my brain did still work.

It was time to look more deeply at this verse. Primarily at how to love God. I knew that before I could consider loving others I needed a lot more of being loved by God and then loving Him. In all honesty with compassion fatigue and cumulative stress I had run out of love for others. With a slightly revived brain, I wanted to look where this verse had been placed, as well as what it meant.

Now, I have to be honest, there will be a little time spent looking at the book of Deuteronomy. There will even be some Greek, but honestly it is just to understand the verse a little more. However, once again if you would prefer not, and you just want to get into the words of the verse itself, please skip onto chapter eleven.

In brief, three of the Gospels have a variation of the verse, which invites us, to love God with our all. You can find it in *Mark 12:30-31, Luke 10:27* and *Matthew 22:37-40*. Initially I was surprised at how John in his Gospel missed out this verse and yet actually he chooses to speak in more depth on the subject of love, in both His gospel and his letter. More on John later.

Mark, Luke and Matthew meanwhile, place the verse in a slightly different setting and even have different people saying it. Mark and Matthew have Jesus saying the words. Meanwhile Luke records the words as being spoken by an expert in the Law. It was indeed an *'expert in the Law'* on each occasion who provokes the conversation about what is the greatest command. As I mentioned previously, at the time of Jesus, a hot topic of conversation was: what was the greatest command?

Each writer placed the verse in the context of controversy. Putting it plainly, Jesus in each instance was being tested. An incredible feature of this is that even after planned attacks from religious authorities, Jesus chose to speak of love.

Jesus was being asked about what is the greatest law. He was being asked about achievement: what should be aimed at above all else. Even as He is questioned, Jesus, in living out a life of love, spoke of love. Jesus spoke not of accomplishment but of relationship. This is remarkable.

Within the gospel writers' accounts there are differences. The verse is placed in different contexts, and different people said slightly different words. I did wrestle with this for some time, however I have reasoned, perhaps Jesus was tested on more than one occasion by different people. In the end I was okay with these discrepancies but I was confused with how the Greatest Command was reported; each writer used slightly different words.

Luke 10:27 records: *'Love the Lord your God with all your heart and with all your soul and with all your strength and with all your mind'*; and, *'Love your neighbour as yourself' Matthew 22:37* meanwhile says: *'Love the Lord your God with all your heart and with all your soul and with all your mind'*.

Mark and Luke at least have the same words, that is, we are to love God with our heart, soul, mind and strength. They don't however, have them in the same order, as Luke chooses to have 'mind' last and 'strength' third. But at least the words were the same.

Matthew meanwhile does not have the word 'strength', which is a little strange because he was writing to Jewish Christians and surely they would have immediately gone; 'What??!!' How has Matthew missed out the word 'strength'? And yet (like Luke and Mark) why has he added the word, 'mind'?

Okay, so now we need to go back to the book of Deuteronomy to where this verse first comes from;

> *'Love the LORD your God with all your heart and with all your soul and with all your strength'*
> *(Deuteronomy 6:5).*

So why on earth did Matthew seemingly miss-quote it and leave out the word 'strength'?[viii] Yet more than this, if you notice, why did all three Gospel writers insert the word, 'mind', because this wasn't in the original text in Deuteronomy.

I nearly became despondent at this point thinking, all of the Gospel writers had had a bad day: they had struggled to concentrate and had just not listened or remembered accurately. Consequently, had they ended up quoting Jesus wrongly? If this had happened on this occasion, then where else had this occurred? This did not sit well with me. Further exploration was required...

CHAPTER ELEVEN:
THE SHEMA

Okay so we need to go back to the time of Moses when Deuteronomy was first written. Deuteronomy was given to God's people as they were entering the Promised Land, a land full of other people and their gods. God did not design His people to share them with other gods. God is the one and only for His people. His commands reflect this. God gave His people Deuteronomy to keep them close to Him.

Deuteronomy can be seen as just a book of laws or it can be seen as revealing what it means to love God. Perhaps barring Leviticus (which has more ceremonial laws with lots of sacrifice and the like), Deuteronomy is perhaps one of the least read books in the Bible. (Actually the book of Numbers, unless you are into genealogies, is often started and yet rarely finished). Many people, even if they start to read Deuteronomy, may not actually finish it. Law after law is listed, with seemingly little relevance to today.

This all said, it is in *Deuteronomy 6:4-5*, where we first come across what I have come to see as one of the most glorious invitations within the whole Bible. To my mind it is second only to coming to know Jesus as Lord and Saviour; these verses have changed my life forever.

God commands Israel to listen and to acknowledge God is God. They are commanded to love Him with their heart, soul and strength. Throughout *Deuteronomy* we see the command of God's people to love God with their all *(10:12; 11:13; 30:6)*. God was available to all who sought Him with their all *(4:29)*. As Wright comments of *Deuteronomy 6:4-5*.[ix]

> *The wholeness, or oneness, of Yahweh (v.4) is to be met with the wholeness of the human person (v.5)'.*

31

were to be no half measures. God is God and He did not want to be
ed with other gods. These verses called for the recognition of who God
and consequently the expectations of His people. In time this became so
important for the Jews that it formed part of the 'Shema', which is a call to
'hear'.

The words of *Deuteronomy 6:4-5* are often the first parts of Scripture that
a child learns, thus fulfilling *Psalm 78:5-6*, which encourages God's people
to teach their children. The Shema (a special prayer containing these words)
is to be said by Jews every morning and last thing at night *(Psalm 4:4)*. Strict
orthodox Jews during morning prayer would have worn 'phylacteries'
around their wrist, that is, little leather boxes containing scriptural passages
including *Deuteronomy 6:4-9*.

The Shema is not only recited twice daily but is placed in a Mezuzah.
Attached to the door posts of a Jewish house, handwritten tightly rolled
parchment scrolls, are enclosed in small containers. The Mezuzah contains
twenty-one lines of the first two paragraphs of the Shema. On the back of
the parchment is one word, 'Shaddai' (Almighty).

The Jews know the Shema, recite it and see it every time they enter and
leave their house. More than this, orthodox Jews as they enter their house
put their fingers to their lips and touch the Mezuzah. In this they are saying,
'I love your Law O Lord'. Every Jew would have known of the call to love
God with all their heart, soul and strength.

As Jews said, and say, the Shema, they were and are to remember and
know that God was and is their God. It is more than an obligation, as they
even say they are 'blessed' to be able to say the prayer. As the oldest fixed
prayer for the Jews, it is perhaps to them, what the Lord's prayer is to many
Christians.

Unfortunately, to be commanded to recite anything can lead to heartless
repetition. I am pained to confess there have been many times when I have
said the Lord's prayer with little heartfelt meaning. Often in services I
would rush through it, just to get onto the next part of the service, not least
because I needed to rush onto another church. Sadly for some, saying the
Shema may be likewise, but it doesn't have to be. More often, I am sure it is
said in and out of love.

Each day at some point I say to my son John, that I love him. Saying, *'I
love you'* to him every day, never ever lessens my love for him. In fact every
day as I say it, I am mindful of my love growing all the more for Him.

The Shema for Jews, which included saying:

'Love the LORD your God with all your heart and
with all your soul and with all your strength'.

was familiar and well known. God longed for it to be inscribed on their hearts and lived out.

Where am I going with all of this? Wasn't I talking about Matthew's apparent slip up of words?

Matthew, as a Jew, would have known of the Shema. He would have known those words of *Deuteronomy 6:5*, as would his readers, who were Jews. This may be why Matthew goes into less detail about them than Mark. Matthew's readers would have instantly known where these words came from.

Mark's readers, however, who were Gentiles, would have known less about the Shema. Mark addressed the Gentile ignorance and included more of the Shema as Jesus answered the question of what is the most important command, Mark states: *'The most important one,' answered Jesus, 'is this: 'Hear, O Israel: The Lord our God, the Lord is one' (Mark 12:29).*

Jesus too knew of the Shema, and not just because He was fully God, as well as being fully human. Jesus would have grown up saying the Shema. It would have been the first thing He ever had cause to remember and recite.

Jesus would have seen it visually at His home. He would have known of its origin from the book of Deuteronomy. We can see in His temptations and testing just how well Jesus knew of Deuteronomy. He quotes from it three times to the Devil *(Matthew 4:1-11)*.

So, how on earth did Matthew drop the word, 'strength'? Meanwhile how did the word 'mind' get inserted? Let's start with the word 'mind'. I mean it's a good insertion. Perhaps the question should really be, why didn't it get included in the first place in Deuteronomy? Well it did, actually, just not as the specific word, 'mind'. You may now feel like you're losing yours...we're nearly there, I promise!

During the time of Moses, the heart and the mind were so closely intertwined that they shared a meaning. The Hebraic word was *'le•va•ve•cha'*. The *'heart'* did not merely refer to an emotional entity or a place where feelings dwelt. Rather the *'heart'* in Hebrew referred to the place where your *'intellect'* and *'will'* lay. It referred more to your mind and motivation than to an emotion.

33

Take *Deuteronomy 4:9* as an example of this:

> *'Only be careful, and watch yourselves closely so that you do not forget the things your eyes have seen or let them fade from your heart as long as you live. Teach them to your children and to their children after them'.*

In encouraging Israel to remember what God has done and in exhorting them to commit this to their memory, rather than using the word mind or even brain, the word *'heart'* is used. A person's heart shaped their thinking, their choices and who they were. In Hebrew the heart and mind were one. It was their inner being.

Now for those of you who remember me quoting *Jeremiah 31:33* earlier, you may try and come back at me, saying, *'That quote has the words mind and heart in it, so you must be wrong'*. I queried myself on that one for a while until I found the Hebrew was; *'lib•bam'* which once again means the mind, the heart, the will.

Some translators insert the words mind and heart so we can more fully understand God's meaning. Originally however the word *'lib•bam'* was just one word encompassing both the heart and will. *'lib•bam'* and *'le•va•ve•cha'* are one and the same, just as in Hebrew, the heart and mind are one.

Yet, some 1500 years after Moses first received the command of *Deuteronomy 6:5*, Jesus chose to insert the actual word *'mind'*. It was a Greek word; *'διάνοια', 'dianoia',* meaning, *'mind'*. It means, intelligence, understanding, as used by Plato. Over the 400 years since Plato, it seems the word *'mind'* had become more widely used.

The Hebrew word for heart (*lev or levav*) meanwhile, by itself came to mean less to the hearers of Jesus. Words widely known in the time of Moses, in time became less so. Jesus Himself is likely to have spoken Hebrew, Aramaic and Greek. Words and terms change.

Thus Jesus uses His licence of being the Son of God to upgrade the meaning of *Deuteronomy 6:5*. Jesus enabled His hearers to understand it more fully. As I came to appreciate this, my own mind let out a sigh of relief. To be fair it had taken quite a battering, but here was my mind, along with my heart and soul being encouraged to love God. Even though it was the worse for wear, God still wanted my mind.

Meanwhile your very own mind may have become more confused rather than heartened by all of that. If so, a little light relief in the next chapter.

CHAPTER TWELVE:
THE GODBIT

Without mentioning the actual gadget, (as I am not into product placement), it has become popular to wear something on your wrist to measure your heart rate and the amount of steps you have trodden. I have to say, I find people's relationship with it bemusing. Some, especially on first attaining one, do as many steps as they can, competitively building them up each day.

Few it seems on having this gadget, seem able to live their life as they once did. They are now mindful that their activity is being observed, all be it mostly for their own good. After all its concept is to encourage people to adopt a more healthy lifestyle.

I know of others, who try to cheat, for example, a pianist I know, tries to hit out as many steps as possible as they play. One lady goes even further and gets her children to take it in turns to wear it for her. Others after a while leave it on the side by the bed before it ends up in a drawer somewhere.

I have to wonder, whether or not this can sometimes reflect our relationship with God? I know when I first became a Christian (at University) I was 'obsessed' by it all. I couldn't help but tell everyone about God. I used shameless ways such as manipulating conversations, playing loud Christian music and leaving tracts everywhere.

After a while though, (actually it was in working for the church), my Christian life resembled someone who sometimes tried to do 'just enough'. Some time here and there with God, until I felt my requirement was fulfilled. I never gave my relationship with God completely over to my child, but at times my son, John certainly seemed to know more about Him than I did.

A little like on one occasion when he asked me what a Christian was. In between meetings, trying to cook tea and entertain him, I gave a rambling answer of how a Christian, *'reads the Bible, prays and goes to church'*.

John looked at me and said: *'Oh, I thought a Christian was someone who loved God'*. I often think the Psalmist must have also had a switched on child, as he too recognised; *'From the lips of children and infants you have ordained praise'* *(Psalm 8:2)*. The challenge for adults, is to listen...

I also never quite got round to putting my faith in a drawer but at times I certainly put my relationship on hold. I have however, heard of some people who say, they will save loving God for when they're in heaven. After all, there won't be much else to do!

Perhaps I had ended up having faith in faith and belief in belief but along the way I had just forgotten what I had faith and belief in.

Coming to this verse of loving God with my all and acknowledging how loved I am as His child, has however, totally re-energised my relationship with Him.

On my arrival at a Retreat (I was forced to take), there was a verse written out and placed on my pillow. It was from *1 John 3:1*:

> *'See what great love the Father has lavished on us, that we should be called children of God! And that is what we are!'*.

It was so what I needed at the time and I am forever thankful that God still longs to be my Father. God loving me. Me loving God. Me loving others, in the strength of God's love continues to be the only way ahead for me.

In this verse I also came to see the nature of my relationship with God. I knew I was not God. I knew I was not equal to God, but I did not always remember that I was a child – God's child.

Babies and young children look to those who are older to provide for their needs: for food, comfort, clothes and the like. I had been too independent for too long. I once asked my mum when I began to become independent. She replied; *'As you came out of the womb!'*.

Being a Priest, being in the Army is quite grown up. I guess I had got so used to being a grown up, that I had been forgetting to come to God as a child. In a way because I felt life was crumbling around me, I was having to acknowledge my place in the grand order of life. God longed for me to come to Him in trust, humility, faith and surrender. With little strength left feeling depleted and weak I wanted to give God my all and I knew this had to start from a place of surrender. For too long I had tried to come to God from a position of strength...

CHAPTER THIRTEEN:
A PRETZEL

The only way I could truly make sense of this glorious invitation of loving Him with my all, was to break down the verse bit by bit. Healing and gaining understanding seemed to run in parallel for me.

*'God loves us with His all and invites us
to love Him with our all'.*

All too often however, rather than living this, I had ended up trying to get round it somehow. On occasions I have tried to cheat and just do the minimum, whilst at other times I have seen it as yet another thing to work for – to strive for.

God has invited me and everyone to do something quite simple, 'to love Him'. He has even shown us how to do this: through His Son coming to earth and through His Son dying for us, we have been shown just how much He does indeed love us.

God's very nature is love. God is love. All about Him and everything of Him is love. He is always looking at how we can get the best of life. We may not always recognise this, nor agree, but there at our core, is God's love.

Let me try and explain by using the image of a Pretzel. It's a simple food, made plainly from flour, salt and water. Pretzels were first made by monks, and were originally called, *'bracellae'*, which is Latin for *'little arms'*. If that makes little sense, consider its shape.

At the centre of a pretzel is an image of praying arms. Surrounding these arms are yet bigger arms. Monks created the picture of our praying arms within a larger one, namely that of God. Here we have the beautiful image of us being drawn closer to God. The three holes incidentally serve to remind us of the Trinity: of God the Father, God the Son and God the Holy Spirit.

As we come to God in prayer, so He is there for us, surrounding us by His love. We are only able to love God, when surrounded by His love. For this to happen, we have to come to God first. We are asked to 'be' in the middle – to 'be' in God's love.

God knows us so well that He knows we cannot even love Him, without Him being there for us. The shape of a pretzel is also loosely a large 'heart' shape surrounding a smaller 'heart' shape. Our love in effect is surrounded by God's love. The Cretan philosopher Epimenides quoted by Luke seemed to know of this great love; *For in him we live and move and have our being' (Acts 17:28)*. Essentially we are at our best when we are in God.

At times of uncertainty my son comes to me and says; *'Mumma, I'm your little chick'*. This is often when he is fearful of something, tired or more often than not when he has done something wrong. Rather, than running away from me, when I have had to speak to him, he draws closer. After saying sorry for what ever has happened, he then wants the biggest hug possible. He curls up and I have to somehow try and cover his body with my own. This I have to say was easier when he was smaller.

In dubiety, John needs to be completely surrounded by my love, by my physical presence. He needs to know He is loved and forgiven. He needs to know that whatever he has done is not bad enough to be cast away from my presence.

God, I believe, as we come to Him in love, longs to be like this with us. The key is our coming to Him first. It is impossible for me to hug and comfort John if he is not there. If my son does not make himself available to be loved, it is hard to show him my love. Likewise with God, He longs to love us and to be there for us but we are required first to come to Him.

Without knowing of God's love I cannot in fact really know what love is. In being loved by God I am able to love Him. I cannot however, truly love God without allowing Him to intervene in my life.

One day John spoke to me of his Grandma, whom he calls 'Meme'. John said; *'Meme is never cross or sad with me'*. In response I said; *'I am glad my darling and nor do I like being so with you'*. *'Then why do you tell me off sometimes, Mumma?'* he asked.

Taking a deep breath, I answered; *'As your Mumma, it is my responsibility to help you to become the best person you can. As part of this I encourage you, hopefully guide you and sadly on occasions I have to discipline you. I do so out of love and it often hurts me more than it hurts you. To hear you cry or grumble hurts me deep inside, but if it makes you a nicer, kinder, better person long term then that is for good'.* 'Oh' said John, *'that's okay then'.*

Mercifully John is a well behaved child and I very rarely have to pick him up on his behaviour. In fact we did employ a 'time out step', but he only went on it twice. The second time he put himself on it, claiming he had remembered from the day before he had done something naughty! Meanwhile I have spent many a minute on there.

Few people like discipline. Myself included, but if God does for me as I seek to do for my own son, then I welcome it and I am grateful for it. As Solomon says;

> *'My son, do not despise the LORD's discipline, and do not resent*
> *his rebuke, because the LORD disciplines those he loves, as a*
> *father the son he delights in'*
> *(Proverbs 3:11-12).*

None of us are perfect and as such there are always things which we could do better. 'To love', I have come to see, is not loving in spite of someone's imperfections. 'To love' is knowing someone's imperfections and loving them anyway.

Back to the image of the pretzel. If you remove the part which is our praying arms, the pretzel loses its centre. There is still the shape of loving hands, of a heart, but it is now empty. God longs to love, and longs for us to be with Him. It's not so much that we invite God into our life, rather it is God who invites us into His. Out of love, in love and through love.

This love is shown first in God's great love for us, most notably in His own son – Jesus. Through acknowledging all Jesus has done for us, through entering a relationship with Him, we begin to live our lives as God intends. Through salvation in Jesus, through acknowledging God's holiness and our sinfulness, we begin to get the best of life.

I say begin, because as we enter a relationship with God so it is the start of something new. Who ever knew of anyone who said they had fallen in love and got married on the same day, only to divorce the next? Drunkenness in Las Vegas excluded!

I had entered this relationship of love with God long ago, but somewhere down the line I had made it more about me. My focus was on doing things to please God and others, rather than basking in God's love.

Busyness had filled the space which was designed to dwell in thankfulness declaring God is my God.

For too long I guess I had overlooked the small print of being invited to eternal life. I spoke of it to be sure, but I think deep down I had reserved this part of life purely for heaven. Salvation however, is not merely a golden ticket for entry into heaven.

Rather, on acknowledging and accepting all Jesus has done, we are invited to a new way of living. For too long I had acknowledged Jesus merely as my Saviour. Now don't get me wrong – coming to Jesus as your Saviour is a good thing. To have come to know Jesus as my Saviour has changed my life radically and I am so thankful for this.

I had misunderstood however, that eternal life is not just something that began on my death. In thinking this for too long, I had over looked life on earth first. At times it almost felt as though life was something to plod through, before the good stuff. The trailer if you like before the main event. Eternal life was reserved for heaven.

This resulted in my missing out for so long on the invitation to live life, to truly live life, with God on earth first; to live life as God had intended. Yes, life for our soul will be perfect in heaven, but before this, there is a life to be lived with God, our God, my God, maybe your God - on earth before heaven. I was coming to this afresh, some twenty years after having first become a Christian.

Before we move on, a final thought on a pretzel. As we are invited into God's life, so we are invited to come with our everything, with our burdens, our sin, our cares, our baggage. As we seek to live our life, so we are invited to do so wrapped in God's love. With God's Holy Spirit, as we live in this world, so it is God who enables us to live and to love. We have responsibilities yes, and we have free will, but if we choose we can live from God's love, in God's love and through His love.

***

*'**Love the Lord your God** with all your heart and with all your soul and with all your mind and with all your strength'*

***

CHAPTER FOURTEEN:
AGAINST THE ODDS

Maybe part of the challenge of this verse, is that we do not really understand what we are being invited to. I had read it frequently and I had even sung songs based on these words. But it wasn't until I broke the verse down, I truly began to be led to love God with my all. So here goes, a little break down of the verse, looking at just the first five words.

Rather than starting with the word *'Love'* though, I want to begin with the word *'your'*. In this simple word, in this pronoun, Jesus reveals how God longs to be our God. God longs to be your God.

We in turn are able to be intimately connected with God; Yahweh; the Lord Almighty; the Creator; Father; Ancient of Days. We are able to be His people, His children, His sons, His daughters. This is amazing, incredible, awesome and at times renders me speechless...

How often have you dropped into conversation some celebrity who you may have met or just seen in passing? I had a friend who didn't even wash her t-shirt just because Robbie Williams once spilt a drink over it! Yet we know God. We can say we know God, the Creator and Sustainer of all. Even more so, God invites us to call Him 'ours'.

We are God's and God is ours: not in a possessive sense, but in a loving intimate relationship. From the time of Jesus, anyone who calls upon His name can call God their God. It's almost too much to comprehend. Words can hardly convey such a relationship.

Now I realise I am far from the first person to discover this. In fact there are many others who have come to know God more against the odds than me. For centuries God was most closely identified with a people, first called Israel, then they were known as Hebrews and in Jesus' day, Jews. Yet, in addition, against the odds, Gentiles (non-Jews) also came to know Him as their God.

Israel was called to be God's people and God was their God first. Yet any skim of the Old Testament shows a number of Gentile-people who came to know God as their God. Even more it was often at the invitation of God Himself. Gentiles were healed, spoken to and saved.

Take Ruth for example. Ruth was a Moabite. Moabites first originated from Lot, Abraham's nephew, after his daughter encouraged her father to commit incest *(Genesis 19:31–38)*. Their off spring was called Moab. This non too great a start, only worsened as the Moabites began to worship, 'Chemosh', which is a posh name for 'fish-god'!

Okay, so everyone has relatives they would rather not remember, so perhaps it was okay some years later that Boaz (a Hebrew) marries Ruth (a Moabite). Except no! The people of Israel were only meant to marry their own people *(Genesis 24:3)*. More than this, Moabite's were expressly prohibited from participating in Israel's worship for at least ten generations *(Deuteronomy 23:3)*, no sorry, make that forever *(Nehemiah 13:1)*.

Ruth (the Moabite) also doesn't even just marry one Hebrew. Before Boaz, Ruth married a Hebrew who died before they could have children. Long story short, Ruth ends up staying with her mother-in-law Naomi, even though she tried to send Ruth away. They return to Bethlehem and in time Ruth marries Boaz.

Not only did God save Ruth, bless her and have a book of the Bible named after her, she ends up being the Great-Grandmother of King David. The very line to which Jesus was to be born into. All from a night of incest and a nation who had a high opinion of fish!

Why is this important? Well, when Ruth's mother-in-law is trying to get her to return to her own family, Ruth says the following:

> *'Don't urge me to leave you or to turn back from you. Where you go I will go, and where you stay I will stay. Your people will be my people and your God my God'*
> *(Ruth 1:16)*.

Ruth (a Moabite), turned to God as her God. She came to love the Lord. God became her God and she became God's child.

There were other Gentiles that God looked favourably upon, and who like Ruth played a significant role in Jewish history. Rahab and her family were the only ones to survive as their town Jericho was destroyed. Having sheltered the spies of Joshua, this Canaanite family were saved when all others were killed *(Joshua 2 and 6:23)*.

What of Namaan? He was a commander of the King of Aram. Amongst his spoils was one of God's own people, a young girl, and yet God blessed him. Namaan was healed of leprosy *(2 Kings 5)*.

It is remarkable that these three Gentiles were seen and blessed by God.

God on occasions even sought to save whole towns. If He hadn't, Jonah wouldn't have ended up in a big fish. Jonah was called to preach to Nineveh which was the flourishing capital of the Assyrian Empire. Not only were they wicked *(Jonah 1:2)*; they were not even of Israel. Yet they came to believe in God, repented of their wickedness *(Jonah 3:5)* and as such they were saved.

I find it fascinating just how many Gentiles, in fact how many foreign Kings came to know of God through the faithfulness of God's people. Several people who knew God to be their God lived this life of love and adoration, even under the rule of their foreign captors.

Consider Daniel, Shadrach, Meshach and Abednego. Through their faithfulness and willingness of even going to a fiery furnace or a den of lions, their Kings came to know of their God. During the time of exile, far from their homeland these faithful Jews impressed King Nebuchadnezzar, King Belshazzar, and King Darius.

King Xerxes too (in the book of Esther), rather than killing all of the Jews as the evil Haman had hoped, ended up saving and protecting them.

We may not read of an actual conversion of the Kings from their own beliefs, but they witnessed God's power and strength. How? Quite simply through God's people knowing God was their God. They knew they were in a relationship with God who at any cost, should be loved, worshipped and served. Time and again even Gentiles could not help but notice God was a God of relationship.

By Jesus' day, Gentiles were even allowed in the Jewish Temple complex. Okay they had to stay in their restricted area (the outer court), but they were getting ever closer.

Jesus Himself, time and again broke with convention and social niceties. He ate with Gentiles, outcasts, tax-collectors and prostitutes. He spoke to women. He healed on the Sabbath. He was accused of blasphemy. Much of what He did unsettled those around Him. Some of what He did incensed others so much they wanted to kill Him.

Luke records one such incident *(Luke 4:28-30)* where some furious people tried to throw Jesus off a cliff. I find it interesting just how their anger was generated. In *v.22* of that same chapter, Luke draws attention to how, *'All spoke well of Him'*. Yet these same people turned on Jesus and wanted Him dead just moments later. Why? Because Jesus reminded them of how Gentiles at times had had more faith in God. In a nutshell Jews of Jesus' day were being told, God was a God of the whole world, of everybody.

Throughout His life, in His words and actions, Jesus began to reveal God was indeed available to all who turned to Him. God wanted to be known as your God, as my God, as our God. With great statements, God revealed how His Son had come for the whole world *(John 3:16)*, even to the Samaritans *(John 4:23-24)*. Jesus invited people to come to love God with their all and as they did so they were able to acknowledge God as their God.

I do not think it is any accident that Luke places the verse:

> *'Love the Lord your God with all your heart and with all your*
> *soul and with all your strength and with all your mind'*,

just before the parable of the Good Samaritan *(Luke 10:25-37)*. The Samaritan, (a Gentile), in this parable is shown to know more about loving his neighbour than any of the Jewish officials. Rather than trying to limit who to love, God widens this to reveal that we should love everyone.

The response of Gentiles, of people who had not always known God, was impressive. In Mark's Gospel we come across a lady who has so much faith that Jesus can drive a demon out of her daughter: she is willing to accept any crumbs, Jesus can offer. Knowing the value of those crumbs she is not afraid to ask for them, to in actual fact push for Jesus' help *(Mark 7:24-30)*.

Furthermore, who does Jesus applaud as having the greatest of faith? A Centurion, a Gentile whose very job was to keep the Jews under control in their homeland. Jesus said to the crowd, recorded in *Luke*:

> *'I tell you, I have not found such great faith even in Israel'*
> *(7:9)*.

High praise indeed! Gentiles were coming to know of Jesus; they were beginning to recognise God as their God. Time and again Jesus spoke with Gentiles. Today also, God is in communication with people who are not Christians. How else would I have ever come to know Him some twenty or so years ago?

However, whilst God may be in communication with people who do not yet belong to Him, He is not in communion with them. This is in Christ alone, through acknowledging all Jesus has done for us and coming to Him in thanks and repentance. As we come to be in a relationship with Jesus, so we are then in union with Him.

Please do not accept my words, but those of Jesus, who stated as we become His people so we are able to be one with Him and the Father *(John 17:22-23)*. Christ is able to be in us, testifies Paul *(Colossians 1:27)*. Through the Holy Spirit we are able to be one with God. The Lord becomes our God.

In Jesus' death, not only did He show He had the power to defeat sin and overcome death, a side show in the temple gave a foretaste for the future. Matthew records, something which perhaps seems of little significance. I mean after all, all eyes are on the Son of God being killed. Yet as Jesus died, something else was going on in the temple. The interior design was due for a makeover.

Matthew says: *'the curtain of the temple was torn in two from top to bottom.' (27:51)*. Big deal! Well, perhaps, if it wasn't for the fact that this curtain was more than likely 14 metres high (compare *1 Kings 6:2*) and perhaps 10 centimetres thick. This was no flimsy curtain in a cheap hotel room!

This curtain separated the Jews from the Holy of Holies; the place where the Presence of God dwelt. Only the High Priest was allowed to enter and even then it was once a year and only then to atone for the sins of Israel *(Exodus 30:10; Hebrews 9:7)*.

On the day of the crucifixion of Jesus, the curtain of the temple was torn in two, from top to bottom. This signified how on that day Jesus was the ultimate sacrifice for our sins. He was and is, superlative love. No longer was a High Priest required to atone for sin. No longer were Jews or Gentiles separated from the Presence of the Lord. Through Jesus Christ access to all areas was being revealed.

I always think if the Bible records something, no matter how seemingly insignificant, that there is a purpose in it. After all scrolls were precious; you wouldn't want to waste writing. So, why mention the curtain was torn from top to bottom? Quite simply a curtain is harder to tear from this direction.

It made the event all the more miraculous. Although to be fair, either way, a curtain of 14 metres high and 10 centimetres thick being torn into two was pretty miraculous.

With the death of Jesus and the tearing of this curtain, access to the Holy of Holies was no longer restricted for one nation. From that day and forever more, Yahweh, God, the Lord Almighty, was inviting ALL people to become His people. You and I likewise some two thousand years later are also called to love the Lord our God and to be loved by Him. I can say to another Christian, you can love the Lord YOUR God. God longs for us to belong to Him and for Himself to belong to us.

CHAPTER FIFTEEN:
MADE FOR KEEPS

I find reflecting on these words; *'Love the Lord YOUR GOD...'* quite breath-taking. Breathing them in, stopping to acknowledge that God is my God, and as such, He invites us to love Him which is just incredible. 'Incredible' doesn't really do that sentence justice, but I am at a loss for a word really.

The Creator of the world: God Himself, wants us to identify ourselves in Him. God is mine, God is yours...no words seem to fit just how awesome this truly is. God designed and created us, and He wants us to live the best of life. I love the words of A.W Tozer on this who says;

> *'God formed us for His pleasure...*
> *He meant us to see Him and live with Him...'* [x]

As I write these words I am mindful that some of you reading this, will not be able to believe God loves you. Nor will you be able to believe God formed you for His pleasure or so that YOU could glorify God, let alone enjoy Him forever. There are likely to be many reasons for this, and it is unlikely you will be able to take my word for it, that God indeed does love YOU – but He does.

Now, I am many things but one thing I try so hard not to be is a liar. This is hard, especially if people accuse you of lying when you have tried so hard not to. I vowed on John being born that I wouldn't lie to him. I didn't want him not to be able to trust me. It is very hard never to lie to a child, hence him knowing the facts of life from the age of 3 years old!

Sorry, I digress. If however, you are willing to at least consider that God does love you, please do not take my word for it, but take God's. If you haven't come across the 'fathers love letter', an amalgamation of verses from the Bible, please either look it up[xi] or flick to the back of this book, where there is a copy. I hope and pray as you read it, you will begin to know God's true love for you.

Even if you do know and accept God's love for you, there is still so much of our life which is not of God. As we come to acknowledge God is 'our' God, one challenge we all face in seeking to do this, is, as Tozer recognises:

> *'We have broken with God. We have ceased to obey Him or love Him and in guilt and fear have fled as far as possible from His Presence'.*[xii]

As I consider these words, I am grateful for becoming a Christian, but also I am so thankful for this second chance of being with God in a deeper relationship. Through loving God with my all, I have come to see we are made to be with God, to love God and to dwell in His Presence.

Our goal is to please God *(2 Corinthians 5:9)*. For too long I had equated pleasing God with 'doing' and 'busyness'. I have come to see instead, the way to please God is to live as He intends.

Jesus makes it clear that this is to love God with all our heart, mind, body and strength. I now believe we were created, 'to love God', so on a level of reason, it makes sense that when we put other things first our life will feel out of sync.

We were created by God for God. Created in His image *(Genesis 1:27)*, we exist so the LORD may rejoice in His works *(Psalm 104:31)*. Any designer or creator surely wants what is best for their product. Every inventor designs and refines, so their invention works as best as it can. Just ask James Dyson.

Dyson is now a household name. His vacuum cleaner may now have contributed to a net worth of several billion pounds but in the late 1970's and early 1980's, he was supported by his wife's income. Dyson worked on over 5000 prototypes and it took over five years before his idea of cyclonic separation was developed to a standard which he could sell.

Thankfully God did not have 5000 Adams to modify. One was more than enough! Remarkably though God has not given up on us. Even when His first people (Adam and Eve) rebelled and sinned, and even when we too continue to live against Him, God continues to be there for us. He wants us to come to Him as our God.

Some creators/inventors meanwhile have regretted what they have made. Mikhail Kalashnikov, who designed the original Kalashnikov rifle, on seeing Bin Laden with one, is reported to have wished he had invented a washing machine instead!

Remarkably God has stuck with us and more than this He continues to love us. Thankfully He has never wished He had made 'bodlins' rather than us! God created 'human beings', and did not trade us in for 'bodlins' (this is a made up word!).

As God created us, it stands to reason He knows the very best way in which we can love our lives. As our Creator I long to trust Him, so I can become the person He has originally intended me to be. It stands to reason that if He made us, He should know best.

Take a simple flower pot – it is designed to hold soil and a plant and it comes with a drainage hole for water. If we use the flower pot as it was designed to be used, we can use it well. We can also try of course to use such a pot as a hat or even as a bucket, but it wouldn't work as well. Objects which are made for one purpose but used for another, may last for a while, but they will not be fulfilling their original intention.

Recently I broke my husband's circular saw (he was actually incredibly forgiving about it). I had been using a circular saw, (which was designed for carpentry), to saw logs. Initially it did pretty well and for a few hours it sawed through wood fairly happily, but after a while it gave up. It was a circular saw after all, not a chain saw. He eventually got me the latter for Valentine's day. I was so excited – who needs flowers when you can have a chain saw?

I have also found hedge cutters do not like being used for cutting through wood either! Likewise nor do lawn mowers like cutting through dense undergrowth. I know I should have used a strimmer, but at the time I did not have one. The mower seemed happy enough for a while but then it quit. Moving swiftly on...

God created us for Himself and yet, how often do we strain in our own strength, trying to live life by ourselves? We were not created to be independent. God created us for Himself and created us for each other. God wants to be known as, *'The Lord your God'*.

The first words of the Lord's prayer, indicate this; 'Our Father'. We are created to be inter-dependant beings: on God and on others. John Donne (clergy man and poet), summed it up well: *'No man is an island, entire of itself'*.[xiii]

As I first began to write and people asked what I was writing, my tag line was, *'looking at a way to seek the best of life'*. I have now seen however, to talk of this suggests this was something I could do by myself. Seeking the best of life could almost become yet another thing to work towards, to strive for.

Rather I have come to see this discovery goes deeper than this. I consider God has given me an opportunity to reflect on how He has created me, or rather what He has created me for. To my great surprise it was not just to do yet another thing! Primarily I am to be loved by God, which is me receiving rather than giving. God loves me. God also loves you.

CHAPTER SIXTEEN:
IS GOD NEEDY?

So, wow, Praise God indeed, I had been given an invitation, a command, a new way of living: to be loved by Him and to love Him. But there were still a few niggles...not least the shortest question...Why?

Why was I designed to love God? Can't we just get on with life as best we can? Will I be punished if I do not love God? Why do we really need to love God? Is God 'needy'? Does God require my love?

Surely it would be better if I just cracked on with loving others. Surely, 'loving God', well, if it needed to be done at all, presumably it could be covered in heaven.

At some points in my life the very thought of loving God with my strength, with my all, was quite frankly asking too much. At times I could hardly function, living was a struggle, let alone loving God with my heart, mind, soul and strength. The mere hint of doing yet something else, was just too much.

My apprehension in being called to love God was that it was yet another thing to do, on what was already a pretty full schedule. At this point I could not imagine having energy to do yet another thing, even if it was something as awesome and incredible as to be loving God.

I would cry out no and also why? Why does God need this? Why does God need my love? Eventually I came to see God does not 'need' my love, God is not 'needy', far from it. God exists independent of us. God is the creator of everything, the sustainer of all. God does not need us, as such.

More than anything in the world, God wants us to know we are loved by Him, unbelievably and absolutely loved by Him. But, when God commands us to love Him, He is not screaming out, 'love me, because I need it'. God is not a co-dependant deity. Rather God is self-sufficient. God in seeking us to love Him, is actually saying: 'I am love'.

God's invitation, or command if you like, for us to love Him, is God saying, 'you can become part of me'. We can enter into an extraordinary love that defines God's relationship with all that He has created. We can love God because we have experienced His love first. We can love ourselves and come to love others, because we have experienced His love first. In fact we can only truly love God because of His great love for us.

In being called to love God with our all, so we can receive God's love, but also we are fulfilling our purpose of being. I come alongside many others who have reached this conclusion. Julian of Norwich put it like this:

'God has made things to be loved by men or women who have been sinners; but always he loves and longs to have our love, and when we have a strong and wise love for Jesus, we are at peace'.[xiv]

Some people claim that to be commanded to love God is inhibiting. It is almost making us into robots. Rather I have come to see the more I love God, the more I allow myself to be loved by God. Instead of this being restrictive, it has given me freedom to live, truly live; freedom to love, truly love.

Being loved by God is by far the best thing in the world. It is more than a feeling, more than a sensation and it goes deeper than words can say. Yes it brings peace, yes it brings a completeness but also it brings the deepest sense of belonging. I have come to know who I am. God's love, makes life make sense.

I am not saying that everything in life makes sense – far from it. I wrestle with why there is suffering, illness and so much bad stuff around. I wrestle with why marriages break down, with why people abuse others and misuse their power.

I am a caffeine-free, vegetarian – I wrestle with most things! I struggle with poverty, social justice and so much more. Many criticisms I realise should be less levied at God and more at humanity, but still I wrestle with so much in life.

Through loving God however, I am making myself more available to be the person God has created me to be. Life itself is making more sense. I have come to see God does not need us, but rather He loves us and longs for us to be with Him. We are created for His pleasure, for His glory *(Isaiah 43:7).*

It's like in one very real sense, I do not need my son to live in this world. I lived perfectly well for 37 years without him in my life. But my goodness, how I love him and how I want to be with him. How I long to spend time with him. How I enjoy being with him, providing: food, shelter, clothing, education, love and hopefully even fun.

I hope always to be in a relationship with my son, but that actually is down to him. I am here for him but it is up to him (longer term), whether he wants anything to do with me. On a day to day basis, I try to help John to live the best of life.

Of course John may not always agree, especially at times when I have refused to buy him a train or when I make him tidy up his Lego. He would then argue that I am not helping him to get the best of life. He of course in this instance, is looking short term, whilst I am trying to invest in the long haul.

Loving another is often made easier if you know they will love you in return. From a place of being loved, of love presenting itself in word and action, two people can love each other.

One day John was trying to 'show off' and in front of a friend he told me, he did not love me. I knew he didn't mean it and it was the wrong time to make a big issue. Thus my initial response was: *'Well, that makes me sad. But I want you to know, I will love you all the days of my life, even if you do not love me'.*

Later at bed time, he took my face into his small hands and said; *'Mumma I love you all the time, even when I say I don't'*. I smiled at him and as we hugged, I said quietly, *'I know babe. I love you too – always, unconditionally'.*

I hope to do all I can to love and provide for my son, but I am mindful all of this is only life on earth centred. I am after all only human. I have limitations. God however, is God. God created us and longs for us to be with Him, so He can love us. How many times do our actions and even our words say to God, I don't love you? Yet, God remains there for us...waiting.

It was only at my point of surrender, when I realised life wasn't working out so well my way, that I was introduced to something which perhaps I had overlooked for too long - Jesus has done all of the hard work.

Jesus has come to this earth. Jesus has died for me. Jesus has risen again. Jesus has ascended to heaven. Jesus is now at the right hand of God interceding for me. But even here on earth I am not left alone, as He has left the Holy Spirit on earth for me, to dwell within me.

In being asked to love God, it was not yet another thing to do, to strive towards. In loving God, I was being invited to love, to live and it was less about doing and more about being.

'The past informs the future but we live in the present'

I really like this quote and it may even be from me! I found it in a scribbling of mine, but it sounds too good to be me. I have tried to look it up but I have failed, so apologies if it is from someone else. I repeat:

'The past informs the future but we live in the present'

I have come to see that whatever I have been going through, has all been for my good. The why's and how's matter less than the what. The what for me, is becoming more aware of God's invitation to love Him and of how to do this.

I am grateful for this ever growing desire in my being, and I am fully aware I do not have all the answers. In fact every answer I seem to gain throws up yet another question, but I am beginning to be okay with this. I have discovered my soul and I am learning to listen to it. Every day my soul reminds me to 'Love God'. He is my God. He is able to be your God and He can be our God.

Okay less waffle, perhaps it's time to consider what this really means...

CHAPTER SEVENTEEN:
IT TAKES TWO TO TANGO

In a nutshell, we can love because God first loves us *(1 John 4:19)*.

I hope there are people who make you feel better about yourself: a friend, a family member, a work colleague perhaps. I have been very blessed in my life to have a supportive family and good friends who have always encouraged me in whatever I have been doing.

Recently I have realised that some of these wonderful people help me to love, because of the love they have for me. Some people simply bring out the best in me, because of their love for me. From this I love them and trust them. I know I could turn to them for anything at any time.

The more I am loved by them, the more I am able to love them in return. Such love can be life-giving. It is as if in life-giving love, a two way channel is opened up. It is always sad to see when one person loves another and the love is not reciprocated. But when two people are open to love, it is a beautiful thing.

There is a lady who I bump into just twice a year, and even then it is only fleetingly. However, whenever I see her, she makes me feel good about myself. Her name is Mrs Smith (yes, that is her real name, I have not gone for anonymity here).

Mrs Smith lives up the road from my mum and if I see her it is usually when I am jogging around the country lanes. We have a quick chat and whenever I come away from her, I have a deep glow within me. She usually takes me back to my days of childhood remembering something which is encouraging.

I literally leave her feeling lighter. The last time this happened, it prompted the thought of how much more I can be like this, if only I spend more time in the Presence of God. After all God is God. He created me. He loved me first and longs for me to live life as I was designed to live. The more time I spend loving Him, the more I am in His Presence. The more I am in His Presence, the more open I am to receiving His love for me.

I am fortunate as I grew up that I knew what it was to live in a loving family. However, I am aware not everyone has experienced love on a human level, but this does not mean you cannot come to know God's love.

God's love far outweighs any human love, and God can heal past hurts like no other. I am not denying how hard it can be to trust God with your love. It takes faith to trust and this involves risk. This said, I have seen, as people open themselves to receive God's love, so they can be filled with love and immeasurable joy.

There are however at least two aspects which can get in the way of us loving and being loved by God. The first is 'sin', the second is 'time'. Frankly 'sin', gets in the way of being loved by God. God is Holy and by His very nature can have nothing to do with sin and for some this poses a difficulty. For one, in society people increasingly do not like to even acknowledge they are ever wrong.

If someone believes they are always right, then they would not consider they do in fact sin. Such a person would not believe the things they do are wrong – against God or against other people. If this is the case, such people are unlikely to see the need to confess anything wrong or have a desire to be forgiven. Even if they wonder if God exists, they may never see a need to come to God to be saved, to be loved and to be sorry.

To such people, I say, *'bless you'*. I just wish I was someone who always put others first and never did anything wrong ever. Let's be honest no-one is ever perfect, no matter how much we may think we are.

I was walking down some steps recently and a father inadvertently stepped on their child's foot. The child squealed, but the father did not turn around. The child then informed his father what had happened. The father said nothing. The child asked his father to say, sorry. Rather than doing so, he just grabbed the child's arm and told him to *'stop messing and hurry up'*.

Whilst the father had not meant to hurt the child, in ignoring the incident and refusing to apologise, what was this teaching the child longer term? Meanwhile I know of others who have raised their children to not only say sorry, but to forgive. To receive forgiveness however, the parent first has to admit wrong and apologise. It can be mighty hard to say sorry to a little child and yet longer term hopefully it is worth it. To hear the words,

'I forgive you', are precious words indeed. How much more are we able to receive God's forgiveness and love, when we ask.

I was so impressed with the Bishop of Dover, who on one occasion publically asked me to *'forgive him'* and to *'forgive the church'*. On a Palm Sunday service, at the event of 'the blessing of the new loo', he thanked me for my endeavours. As I was due to leave shortly, he also took the opportunity to thank me for my ministry in that church.

I have to admit the service was all a bit too much for me and I had taken to looking after a toddler who was bored and wandering around. Bishop Trevor as he was talking in front of everyone, walked up the aisle, looked straight at me and asked me for my forgiveness! Such an act was incredible in itself but for me it also gave rise to deeper healing.

For some time (perhaps immaturely) I had been crying out to God in angst over the 'Church of England' - for what I had felt 'it' had done to me. To have spent so much time on building projects, management, conflict and liturgy, rather than on God and discipleship…well it had taken its toll. As Bishop Trevor spoke those words of forgiveness, I felt I had been heard by God and I was being asked to forgive, not a Bishop, who had more than enough on his plate, but the 'Church of England'! Rightly or wrongly, as I was invited to forgive and I chose to do so, I experienced great healing and God's peace. Bishop Trevor – thank you.

Not everyone, however is able to acknowledge they do wrong as their independence is so strong they do not want to admit it. Such people may have been so hurt or had life modelled so bleakly they never feel the need to say sorry. To acknowledge there is a deity or something greater than them, can be too much to handle.

God however is God and in His very nature is Holy. He longs to be with us, yes, but He cannot have anything to do with sin. He has given us the way to Him, it is through His son. Sadly for too many people this remains a stumbling block. Many people either do not acknowledge they sin or they do not want to consider their sins, lest they become 'depressed' about their wrong doing.

We all sin. We are all sinners because we sin, and we all sin because we are sinners. The Bible with its account of God's people gives us a window into the imperfections of others. God in His holiness cannot have anything to do with sin; it is against His nature. Yet through Jesus, He longs to be in a relationship with us. He longs for us to be His child.

For our part we are invited to come to Him through the means He has chosen. Through His love and invitation of confession and repentance in the name of Jesus; God makes it possible for us to come to Him. In coming to God, through acknowledging our wrong, we are able to be cleansed, restored and brought back to God. To not do so, is to be like a person drowning who refuses to accept the outstretched hand.

A second aspect I see as preventing us from coming to God in love, is 'time'. It has been said the greatest lie the Devil gets us to believe is that he does not exist. I have come to see the greatest way of him ensuring he gets his own way, is for us to believe we just do not have 'the time'.

Rather than time working for us, we are increasingly allowing 'time' to run our lives. There never seems to be time for our family or time for ourselves. And yet remarkably, at no time in history have we actually spent more time on leisure, social media, or watching television. Increasingly people seek jobs not to put food on the table but to fund a better lifestyle, to buy more things - often to compensate for the time they do not have to spend together.

We are allowing time to run away with itself rather than taking control of it, and taking back our lives. I only mention 'time' because so often we do not allow ourselves time to come to God. How often do we allow God to love us? How often do we allow ourselves to be overwhelmed by God's goodness, peace and love?

Actually, perhaps, just put this book down and allow yourself to stop...to be...to be loved by God. This could be through sitting quietly, going for a walk, listening to some music, looking at art.

Simply stop and allow yourself to be loved by God - for no other reason than that He loves you. It is only in God we can truly find peace and rest. And if you never pick this book back up, but choose to dwell in God's love and peace forever more, Praise God.

***

So, if you did have some time out, good for you. It may prepare you for my next rant. If you didn't put the book down, you may well want to shortly.

So much in society tells us, in order to rest and relax, we have to spend, spend, spend, doing this or that. We are bombarded through advertising to watch more television, to surf the net or to be on social media.

Never before has there been so much 'fantasy' fiction; all to take us to another place, away from our troubles and stresses. Increasingly however, I am discovering such 'time out' does not bring the rest and relaxation it says it will. We may feel rested for a while, but whatever we are seeking to escape from still remains. When the television is switched off or the social media account closed, we are still having to live our same life.

Increasingly, on occasions when I may settle down to watch something, I become restless, bored even and far from relaxed. Finding rest and peace I have come to see, can only truly come from God Himself. At times if I have become absorbed in something other than God, I soon feel hollow and empty. I have wrestled with this, as after all surely it's just a little odd.

A.W. Tozer, has however given words and a voice to this feeling:

'Our break with the world will be the direct outcome of
our changed relation to God'.[xv]

My soul it seems would rather I rest with God, in God, through being quiet, through being still, through reading His word or a book by people who know and love Him. This to me at times, if I am honest, still seems, quite frankly a little odd. It is I guess counter culture. To willingly abstain from such entertainment is rarely spoken of, and less modelled in life, or in our churches. At times I then begin to think I am becoming a fundamentalist crazy person, who is becoming more and more detached from the world.

Yet curiously in a world of media overload, I have found this easier to do than perhaps even ten years ago. There is now so much going on that it is impossible to keep in touch with everything. This makes it easier for me to have nothing to do with any of it.

Too often in the past I have used the 'media' to clutter my mind with nonsense. Rather than praying about something which was troubling me, I tried to drown out my thoughts. I rarely allowed myself time or space to actually listen to what God may be saying.

Today, I praise God, for I have come to embrace silence: in the car, in the house and outside. I no longer need to be plugged in, or to fill my life with noise.

I cannot deny the peace, this new way of life gives me. This way of loving God and being loved by Him brings peace. Things which I had once enjoyed have become almost a distraction. They do not hold the appeal they once did.

Now some of these things are necessary of course, such as household chores, work and caring for others, but I have come to try and do even all of these things in God's Presence. I tend to fail on this more often than not, but I am just starting out. More on this way of living later, for now, let's return to what 'love' really means.

CHAPTER EIGHTEEN:
LOVE BY ANY OTHER DEFINITION...

Okay, I am aware that I keep talking about 'love' without really defining what is meant by 'love...' One of the challenges for me is quite frankly the English Language is pretty lazy in this department. We have and use the word 'love' frequently. Love is seen as a deep feeling or affection or emotion.

To speak of loving God though, of course is not the same as the love for a lover, a friend or a child. Our love after all can be fickle; dependent on feelings. God's love meanwhile is constant and will never let us down. No matter what, He is able to be there for us.

The challenge with love is we can often only identify with the Western idea of it. And let's face it, this kind of love is a love which we can fall in and out of. At times people believe they are in love, when actually it is so changeable and short lived, it is more like lust.

Even when we come to the Bible and see God is love, and that we are created to love and that it is good to do so, our language puts us at a disadvantage. Sanskrit has ninety-six words for love. We have one word – just one and I believe we are all the poorer for it.

We have only one word to describe our affection for: a lover, a pet, a child, a car, a meal or our favourite sport. It is bonkers that we use the same words, *'I love'*, for a plate of food and also a life partner. Perhaps this is why we throw the word around so casually – we just don't know what it truly means!

Please bear with me for the next couple of paragraphs – there will be some Hebrew and Greek coming out, but if it means we come to understand what love is a little more, hopefully you will bear with me. Alternatively skip to the next chapter.

Love in Hebrew, in the main, has the word, *'Ahava'* which is *'to give'*. As one gives, one loves. In this action there is a connection. *'Ahava'* is not a feeling and as such is not dependent on a mood or even circumstances. *'Ahava'* is both a noun and a verb – it is an act of doing. To love God is not just based on words or feelings, but on action.

With the word *'Ahava'* there is no understanding of waking up one day and no longer loving your life partner, as this is limiting love to merely a feeling. Love meant action; it meant doing; it even meant forbearing, rather than just up and leaving because you no longer felt 'in love'.

As Israel first became God's people so they were called to love Him: this love was born not from feelings but out of obedience with action. Israel was called out of Egypt to the Promised land and called to love God through obeying His commands. None of this was based on feelings, but in an act of doing.

By the time of Jesus, society's understanding of love had developed, influenced by Greek thought. There were now four types of love within the New Testament: eros, storge, philia, and agape.

The Greek language understood differences between romantic and sensual love (eros); human affection, family love (storge); brotherly love, that is, care and compassion for fellow humans, friendship (philia); and unconditional love, this is God's divine love – perfect and sacrificial (agape).

The word used by Jesus in; *'Love the Lord...'* was ἀγαπήσεις *(agapēseis)'*. Such love was based not on feelings and extends beyond emotions. In being commanded, to love the Lord with *'agapēseis'* love, so we are to love in an active form of love. As we see God's love for His Son and His people, likewise we too are to have this active love for God and for others. The word involves the idea of affectionate reverence, prompting obedience and grateful recognition of benefits received.

So for all of those who love 'to do', never fear, the love we are called to love God and others with, is a love of action...not, I hasten to add, at the expense of 'being'. It's a both/and.

Agapēseis love, agape love, is altruistic, unconditional and is demonstrated through actions. It is the love of the will, the love of sacrifice and the love of obedience. Perhaps this type of love is best understood in the context of Jesus' own life and death:

'For God so loved the world that he gave his one and only Son,
that whoever believes in him shall not perish but have eternal life'
(John 3:16).

It was love that led God the Father to send His Son to earth for us all. It was love, an action which resulted in Jesus dying on the cross, defeating sin. As the apostle Paul says:

'God demonstrates his own love for us in this: While we were still
sinners, Christ died for us'
(Romans 5:8).

CHAPTER NINETEEN:
LOVE IS MORE THAN 4 LETTERS LONG

I once had the great privilege of being part of a team who set up 'Active Church'. Think Messy Church but take out the craft and insert games and action. There were already two Messy Churches in the town and we didn't want to duplicate. Equally however, our format was created to try and keep some more 'energetic' children involved and interested.

As we met one Sunday afternoon I tried to visually represent just how much God loved everyone. As I spoke about love, I read the words of how God loves us so much that He even knows how many hairs are on our head *(Matthew 10:30)*. I asked if anyone could guess how many hairs there were on my head. Guesses of 100, 500 and 2000 were bandied around. I said, *'Let's see then!'*.

With this, a friend of mine shaved my head! The children were astonished. My hair had grown quite long, so there was a lot of visual impact that day. As my hairdresser shaved, I spoke of God's great love for them and how He longed for them to know of His love. I spoke of how He loves us so much and knows us so intimately that He knows everything about us, including how many hairs are on our head. My shaved head for the next few weeks was certainly a talking point in the parish.

This does not mean of course we all have to shave our heads. Nor does it mean we have to have visual reminders of all passages of the Bible. I once asked my husband if he was willing to offer to volunteer to do a visual reminder as we looked at *1 Samuel 18:27*. He declined. If you are not familiar – David attacks 200 Philistines and circumcises them all!

Moving swiftly on...

By only having one word for love, not only do we limit our understanding of love, but we rarely acknowledge that *'God is love'* *(1 John 4:8)*. God loves us quite simply because He is love. The love God has for us, is not merely an attribute, it is His very essence. God is love. We're back to the pretzel; God is love and longs for us to live within His love.

God doesn't love us because we please Him. Love is His very nature. God exhibits all the characteristics of love; God is the perfection of love. God is love and loves with an everlasting love *(Jeremiah 31:3)*. If we allow all of this to dwell within us; it can have a radical effect on what we mean by love.

Was the love Jesus spoke of merely a feeling? Hardly! He died for us. Even before this, Jesus' love for us was so strong He left being with His heavenly Father to be with us on earth. Jesus set aside His divinity and His home in a throne room with God. Instead He dwelt in the womb of a peasant girl for nine months before being born and laid in a food trough.

Did Jesus feel warm and fuzzy as He hung on the cross? Hardly! Jesus' love was agape. To love is an action. To love is sacrificial. To love is to keep God's commands as these ensure we live life how God intended. But as we love, as we keep God's commands, so we are also told we will remain in God's love *(John 15:10)*.

The kind of love God calls for, is for us to remain in God. Quite simply we cannot 'love' by ourselves. Jesus' command, to love God with our all, was a new kind of love. In addition to us loving God because we are created to do so; this form of love is a witness; it is mission.

Just consider how different this world would be if we loved this type of love, if we lived this form of love. A sacrificial, unconditional love, dependent not on feelings but on action. Love-forming behaviour formed through choice and strengthened through the very nature of love itself. This is God. This is love.

Paul understood this and said simply to the Church at Corinth: *'Do everything in love'* *(1 Corinthians 16:14)*. Being loved by God, being born of God, enables us to love. God's greatest desire for every one of us and for the whole world is to know how much we are loved by Him. The commandment to love God comes from His love. We cannot help but love Him because He loves us first.

In loving God, we open ourselves more to being loved by God. The more we understand 'love' and the more we love God, the less open we are to sin. Yes of course we are human and we do sin, but the closer we come to God and His love for us, the closer we are to living His life of love. The closer we are to living the life God created us for.

If the greatest command is to love, then perhaps the greatest sin is not to obey. To not put God first is to sin. It is the first of the Ten Commandments after all. We are created to put God first and from this flows the best of life.

By loving God with our mind, soul, heart and strength, we are more open to love and less open to sin. This does not mean we will never sin, we are but human. However, the more we love God and allow God's love to flow through us, it stands to reason the more we will be living the life God intends which has to be more good than bad.

CHAPTER TWENTY:
FIFTEEN VERBS

Love is not merely an emotion or a feeling. Love is a choice. I repeat, love is a choice. Perhaps the most famous passage in the Bible on love is *1 Corinthians 13*. It is certainly the most popular text to be read at weddings. I find Paul's writing about love interesting, when he speaks of love, he doesn't use words to describe feelings but he uses fifteen verbs. Paul uses fifteen words to describe an action. Paul describes agape love.

Paul describes what love is as well as what it is not. Love is not ENVY, therefore it is not being jealous. It is not BOASTING, or bragging. It is not being PROUD, it is not being arrogant. Love is not RUDE, that is, it is not being careless or insensitive. It's not being SELF-SEEKING, which means trying to put others first.

Love is not EASILY ANGERED, thus it is not being touchy and bringing up old hurts in discussions. Finally love DOES NOT DELIGHT IN EVIL: essentially love looks for the good in others and not the bad!

Paul does get round to say what love is, but even as he does it's far from easy to live it...Love is PATIENT, Love is KIND, Love always TRUSTS, Love always HOPES, Love always PERSEVERES, Love rejoices with the TRUTH, Love always PROTECTS. All of these words, which Paul uses to describe love, are things we must do.

Let's take the first verb, *'Love is patient'*. Patience in old versions of the Bible was translated as 'long suffering'. Paul is not referring here to marriage, but rather we are to accept the weaknesses of others as well as their strengths.

I find it no accident that Paul listed patience first. Yes I do suffer from impatience but more than this, it is incredible just how patient God is with us.

My son, John recently acknowledged that I tend to speak more slowly with him, than other people may. As he said this, I thought I was about to be criticised for doing so. Imagine the surprise of a Mumma who is usually in the wrong, when I discovered that this was a good thing! Through speaking more slowly, John reasoned it allowed him to process thoughts and he was able to remember more of what I said.

As I consider God's patience with me and His people, I marvel at the measure of His patience. The Psalmist grasped it, saying:

> 'The LORD is gracious and compassionate, slow to anger and
> rich in love'
> (Psalm 145:8).

I am eternally grateful for God's patience and forbearance with me. God is indeed rich in His love.

Another description, Paul uses for love, is *'love is kind'*. 'Kindness' too is an active word; it means thinking of practical things to do to help others and then actually doing them! Love is kind. It is far from sentimental, it is an action.

Reflecting on all of this, namely that love is an action sat well with me for a while. Right up until, that is, I panicked, lest it was yet another thing I had to do. I reasoned surely if love is an action, it is something else I need to be doing.

I had certainly spoken of this at a number of weddings. Love was to be worked at. I often used the image of a cake, speaking of the ingredients you do and don't need. Likewise for love in a marriage. You need patience and kindness. You do not need anger or boasting.

For too long you see I had looked at this verse and thought Paul was telling us to be patient and to be kind. When I tried to love and be all of these things, imagine my frustration when time and again, I would fail. Where did this leave me?

It took a while to realise Paul is not telling us to do these things, rather we are being encouraged to see this is what love is. We are encouraged, yes to choose to love, but we are not to love in our own strength or by ourselves. We can try but it is impossible.

There is hope, but it is found in the next chapter of *1 Corinthians*, and let's be honest if we read the Bible we often stop at the end of a chapter. This is one down side of the Bible having been put into chapters and verses. When Paul first wrote this letter to the church in Corinth, it would have been one seamless manuscript which would have been read out as a oner.

Paul in *1 Corinthians 14:1* talks of *'following love'*, or *'pursuing love'*. It is love that is patient, not us being patient. It is love which is kind, not us making ourselves to be more kind.

As we come alongside God's love, so we can find ourselves living this love. As we dwell in God's love, in His abundantly over-flowing love, so behaviours such as being kind and patient flow. It's less about doing and more about living God's love.

For too long, I had been running towards love, rather than dwelling in love. I had succumbed to 'doing', to 'achieving' by myself rather than allowing my life to flow from God. Being loved by God and loving Him is less about keeping my head bowed low: trudging along, working with all my might. Even though agape love requires action; the love called for is less about doing love, than to be loved. It is more about being in love; falling in love with God.

The more we dwell in God's love, the more we find ourselves living this life of love. In turn we become a person of love. We end up living love, rather than trying to 'do' love.

Love is not being happy all of the time. Love is not having full 'love tanks'. Love is not looking at someone and thinking they are still stunning. Love is not dependant on someone's salary. Love is not dependant on great sex every day.

Love is not based on being fulfilled all of the time. This isn't love. Love is not just a feeling or something based on circumstances. Love in its truest form is so much bigger than we can perhaps ever appreciate.

To be commanded to love God, is not to falsely generate affection. We cannot be commanded to feel, but we can be commanded to act. We cannot produce a feeling, but we can form a behaviour. We can act and love only as we allow the source of true love, to flow through us. In no way am I saying this is easy. Far from it.

As I consider love on a human level, at some of my lowest times, I have remained married, because I have chosen to. During times when I felt Jack had more freedom whilst I was chained to a job, I chose to love. At times when I have not had any energy to love anyone, I chose to stay with Jack. There have been 'times' however when I have come close to quitting...mostly up a mountain!

During many a walk up a mountain with Jack I have prayed for a divorce lawyer to come round the corner. I do not like mountain climbing – Jack does. I have rarely seen the view promised from the summit; it is always foggy. Also as I have reached a peak; I am then told there is another one just some 600 feet further on!

Jack however, has chosen to love me, more than I have of him. There have been many times in our marriage when I have been so grumpy and bad-tempered that I didn't like being around me, let alone Jack having to do so. I am grateful for the many occasions, when Jack has chosen to love, chosen to stay, chosen to forgive.

Actually in all honesty Jack and I at times have stayed married, because I am useless at paper work and Jack doesn't agree with divorce. But hey, we are still together - choosing to love. Dependant not on feelings but on actions and behaviour.

Prior to meeting Jack, if a relationship I was in was going through a rough patch, I would go to my dad and ask him what love was. My dad was not a theologian or a scholar, but his advice was perfect. He always responded: *'Love is wanting to be with a person for the rest of your life'*. On the third time I asked him, he warned my mum that I was heading for another break up!

Thankfully by the time I met Jack, not only had I accepted my dad's understanding of love but also Paul's, because wow, to love someone is hard. Yes it can be fun and lovely and all that good stuff, but to truly love someone is really hard. Paul himself wasn't even married so he didn't even know the half of it - sharing; a bed with a 'wriggler', a sink, cupboards, and the television remote!

I think to Paul's list I would add: Love is compromise, but I guess Paul wrote love is not self-seeking! In all honesty as I look at Paul's characteristics of love, I know I do not keep them all of the time. Equally I do not know of anyone who does - it just doesn't happen.

On coming to know of God's love I am so thankful that God and God alone exhibits all of these facets of love. However, from being loved by Him in these ways, I too am able to love – truly love. The love of God is like no other. Prior to becoming a Christian I guess in relationships I had looked for His kind of love in people. I went out with some lovely people, with whom for a time we shared special moments, but I always wanted more…

I guess I was always influenced by the love of Sydney Carton in Dickens', '*A Tale of Two Cities*'. Carton's love for Lucie Manette was so sacrificial that he gave up his life, so her husband Charles Darnay could go free. Carton died at the guillotine for his love for Lucie. This was the kind of love I looked for in a man. Was it any wonder that only Jesus would do?

Jesus' love is sacrificial and life-giving. Through Jesus' life and death, I am able to become a child of God. Paul says:

> *The Spirit himself testifies with our spirit that we are*
> *God's children'*
> *(Romans 8:16).*

Even more Paul tells us we can call God, 'Abba'. In effect, 'Daddy'. We can call God, 'Daddy'. Jesus Himself called God 'Daddy' and He invites us to do so. God longs for this relationship and intimacy with me and you. Surely this is a reason to love God.

God created us to love Him and to be with Him. God made us for Himself. In coming to love God, I have come to see it is letting our spirit commune with His Spirit. I do not want to limit God's love for us or ours for Him, to a purely 'spiritual' realm…but there is a spiritual element.

The spiritual hunger we feel deep inside can only be satisfied in God. As Augustine of the 5th Century aptly penned in his book, *Confessions*:

> *You made us for yourself, and our heart is restless until*
> *it finds rest in you'*. [xvi]

Other things may satisfy for a moment, but they are fleeting compared to the permanence of God's love for us forever.

We have a part to play yes, it is after all up to us to become available to be loved. God will never force us to be loved by Him. It is up to us to allow our spirit to be with God's Spirit. As we allow ourselves to be loved, so we will truly experience what 'love' is.

As I come to love God with my all, so I have come to see that it is in this love that we are fulfilling the very reason for which we were created; we fulfil our purpose of being. To love God helps us to fulfil our destiny. It stands to reason if God created us with the purpose of loving, it is only in doing just this, that we will ever be able to get the best out of life. Loving God is just as much for us, as it is for God. God knows what is best for us.

72

This past weekend I went swimming with a friend and their child. The toddler loves swimming and I had chosen a pool which had large inflatables and lots of activity. Sadly he was overwhelmed and kept screaming: *'I don't like it'*. We could have taken him out but I knew once he got over his initial fear he was going to love it. I hugged him tightly and encouraged him to look into my eyes. Calmly, I kept repeating; *'I know you say you don't like it, but let's just try.'* After five minutes of bobbing up and down the pool, (with his anxious mum looking on), his grip lessened and he stopped crying.

As he began not only to trust me, but to experience that it wasn't as scary as he had initially thought, he began to enjoy himself. By the end of our time there, he was enjoying himself so much, jumping around with glee, that he was actually beginning to scare me half to death.

I truly believe God wants us to love Him, because He knows this is best for us. Sure it will take faith on our part and perhaps even experience but thankfully God is patient and promises to be there for us – always.

But is this easier said than done? Humanity, let's face it, has never been too good with accepting that God knows best. From as early as in the garden of Eden, human beings have thought, they know better than God. A cursory glance through the Bible shows again and again how God says; 'Do this' and so humanity 'does that'! Human beings repeatedly seem to get into a muddle when they think they know best and go their own way.

CHAPTER TWENTY-ONE:
NO SECOND BEST

The Bible reveals God is the author and source of creation *(Genesis 1 and 2)*. God is our Creator God. Humanity is called to respond and praise the Creator God. Not necessarily because we have to or should do, but because we cannot help but do so. Please do not just take my word for it, let's dip into the Bible for a bit.

Praising the Creator Lord should occur as humanity becomes aware of creation in all its goodness *(Genesis 1)*. The Lord is worthy and deserves thanksgiving, praise, worship and love of all people *(Psalm 148; Revelation 4:6-11)*. King David understood this and as he looked back to the time in the womb, he marvelled at being created by God:

> *'For you created my inmost being; you knit me together in my*
> *mother's womb. I praise you because I am fearfully and*
> *wonderfully made; your works are wonderful, I know that*
> *full well'*
> *(Psalm 139:13-14).*

As human beings we are special indeed. We can either just go about our daily business, like animals and plants, or we can lift our heads towards God and choose to worship Him. God has given us this option, this choice, this gift. Other aspects of creation, through their very existence glorify God and pour forth His praise. Only human beings however, have the ability to make a conscious decision of whether they do or not.

As human beings, the only created being to bear the image of God *(Genesis 1:27)* we are created to be in communion with our creator God. Tom Wright puts it better than me:

'The task of humans is to bring to conscious thought and expression the worship of the rest of creation. Heaven and earth are full of God's glory, but God's image-bearing creatures, we humans, are called to know that it is so and put it into words of praise'. [xvii]

God is the creator of the universe, the all-powerful incomparable Lord. God in His very nature is love and in creating us, formed us to be in a relationship with Him. There is none other like Him. As Solomon said: *'LORD, the God of Israel, there is no God like you in heaven above or on earth below' (1 Kings 8:23-24)*. Just take a look at other passages such as *Exodus 15:11; Psalm 86:8; Deuteronomy 4:39*, which all confirm this.

God is faithful and true and He keeps His promises. He listens and answers the prayers of creatures created in His image. God forgives and through God's acts of salvation, God has made it possible for us to respond to God: to love Him. Anyone who calls upon His name is able to become His child.

As I have come to love God more, so I have seen that He deserves this love more than any other. In fact the love humanity has for God has to become something more, it has to become worship.

The word *'worship'* itself, is an English word deriving from the Anglo-Saxon word, *'weorthscipe'*, *'worthship'* suggesting honour and rendering homage to the Lord. This is seen repeatedly throughout the Bible, where the response of a human being is to love God yes, but even more, it is to worship: for example, *Exodus 20:1-6; Revelation 5:9, 12*.

Few in God's presence have found they can refuse to bow and acknowledge He is the Lord *(1 Kings 18:39; Psalm 96:4, 8; 99:9; 138:12,13; Malachi 1:1; 1 Timothy 2:8)*. God is Creator, Sustainer, Saviour, Holy and Sovereign. My love for God finds expression through adoration, praise, remembrance, thanksgiving, service, obedience and actions.

Throughout the Old Testament we see God's people were able to engage and interact with Him primarily through prayer and sacrifice. As a vegetarian, I am very grateful that as children of God today, we are no longer expected to come to God through the sacrifice of animals. The only sacrifice now acceptable is of God's own Son. Through the sacrifice of Jesus only, we are able to come to God, to be in His Presence.

The Lord is Holy and Sovereign. As human beings I believe we should worship in response to the recognition of who the Lord is (just take a peek at: *Psalm 24:1-2; 89:11; 95:3-5; 100:3; Isaiah 46:4; 48:12-13*). The Lord has saved us and redeemed us. I repeat: why should we love God with our all? In a nutshell, because we are created to do so. At the invitation of our life giving, life-saving God we are called to love Him because this enables us to live life.

For those who recognise Jesus as Lord, loving God with our all, directs our love. We are able to give thanks not only to our Creator God but to Jesus Himself. After all Jesus has become the sole mediator of salvation for humanity (check out, *John 14:6; Acts 4:12; Colossians 1:19; 2:13-15; 1 Timothy 2:5-6; Hebrews 7:25*). We are now able to come to God through Jesus His Son. Nothing offered to God, unless it goes through Jesus Christ is acceptable *(1 Peter 2:5)*.

A danger, I fear of looking at; 'Loving God with our all' is the temptation to believe any acceptance of this invitation is all about us. It is not. It has to start from a place of acknowledging all Jesus has done for us and continues to do for us.

To try too hard, purely in our own strength bears upon, *'pelagianism'*, that is to try and earn merit with God. Sometimes called, *'works righteousness'*, this teaching is named after a fourth-century monk, Pelagius. The focus was more on what we can achieve rather than seek to receive.[xviii] We cannot love God and others merely by our own will-power or strength. We are not designed to. We are created to love and to be sourced in God.

Our salvation is founded on God's love for us. From being loved first by God, we are able to let God's love flow through us. In turn this enables us to love God. From this we are able to love others and this includes loving ourselves. Even after twenty years of being a Christian, I had in a sense been accepting second best for too long.

Last summer, some friends and I, with our children, were heading towards the beach. Along the path, the toddler with us, finding small mounds of sand to play in, would stop every few paces. No matter how much we encouraged him that there was a whole beach just below us, he wouldn't move any faster. He was perfectly happy with wind-blown sand mounds. In the end we picked him up to show him the beach below, yet still he wanted to play in the small mound at our feet. Only when we were down on the beach itself, did he believe us. He was happy to accept second best because he did not know any better. Even seeing this was so, was not enough, he had to experience it for himself.

Having been given a second chance in life, I hope and pray never to return to just existing, to just surviving. I long to live, to thrive, to love and to flourish. Through God and in God and of God.

CHAPTER TWENTY-TWO:
KEEPING YOUR EYE ON THE BALL

I have often wondered why God loves us. I have reasoned, argued and wrestled at length, but thanks to my son, I have now come to accept God loves me because He does. During a wrestling fight between John and I, in a crafty move, he managed to sit on my head and do a bottom burp. It was pretty smelly.

I looked at him and said: *'Why do I love you?'.* He replied: *'Because you do'.* Whenever he does anything which would make me question my love for him, I just say: *'Why do I love you?'.* He always replies: *'Because you do'.* This fits for me with God as well...

Why does God love me? Because He does!

From this position of love I am able to live and love.

God loves us. If you are still uncertain, what is the only unforgivable sin? *(Mark 3:28-30).* It is, *'whoever blasphemes against the Holy Spirit will never be forgiven'.* To blaspheme against the Holy Spirit in my book, is when we do not invite God to live with us. It is to not love God as He loves us. It is to live our own way without God.

The unforgivable sin is not to invite God's Holy Spirit to dwell within us. To deny God in our lives, is not allowing God to love us. It is not to acknowledge His love. It is not to return His love.

As I have said, to love God is an action. At times loving God, leads to praise and adoration. There can be times in worship, in song, in meditation, in quiet when people cannot help but pour out praise onto God.

Out of thankfulness at times, we may even be lost for words as we come to God and are loved by Him. God doesn't mind – He just longs for us to dwell with Him. But here is a top tip – as you come to worship God, there are times when you should keep your eyes open and your hands down!

Two lovely people shared with me how in a time of adoring God in song, they had been so overwhelmed by love that they did those two very things: they shut their eyes and raised their hands.

This is fine just so long as, one, you are not on a treadmill in the gym or two, in a car! The latter ended up crashing in a hedge! The former, as she fell to the ground, was laughed at by fellow gym users! Whilst I admired their passion and fervency I do not believe God wants us to injure ourselves in times of worship.

Such times of heightened passion can however, be good for us; they can strengthen us, heal us and transform us. To love God however, is more than even this. To love God is a choice, a behaviour, it is action, flowing from His love.

I am grateful for the lengths God went to, to get my attention. I now see this was an act of love. Thankfully He didn't have to use a talking donkey, as for Balaam or a fish, as for Jonah, or the Maji as for Mary and Joseph.

It seems my attention was gained through becoming 'gracefully broken'.xix At the time I sought healing from ill health, without realising that my ailing state was actually leading me closer to God. If He chooses, God can use troubles in a marriage, illness, the loss of a job, a near death experience or the loss of a loved one.

Now, please do not read me wrong, I am not saying all bad things which happen are because God is trying to get our attention – sadly some bad things, some terrible things just happen! However, when bad things do happen, we have a choice whether to turn to God or not.

I wonder, generally in life, what has got your attention? Falling in love? A red traffic light? The beauty of a sunset? Far from your thoughts is probably the dark: several hundred feet under-ground 'darkness'!

I had never wanted to go caving. A previous boy-friend had wanted to take me but a dream had put me off. I will spare you the gory details but in brief, everyone I went caving with was poisoned by gas and I was left wandering until I died of starvation. It kind of put me off pot-holing and going underground.

For some reason unknown to me, when Jack asked me to go caving with him, I said yes! We had only been going out for a few weeks, I guess I was giddy in love and I wanted to prove myself to Him! We went caving once!

Deep underground, for me to experience the dark, Jack asked me to turn off my caving light...Well, he was right, I did experience darkness in all its fullness. The dark got my attention.

At that very moment I also realised I never wanted to be in the dark ever again. Instead I always wanted to be in the light. At that point of being in the dark, I also had the thought that I had never taken out a safeguarding check on this guy. He may just be about to murder me!

After I realised he wasn't going to kill me, the trip however didn't get any better, as Jack later uttered the words; *we are lost*. A tip to anyone leading a caving expedition – never (EVER) say you are lost! Even if you are, no-one else needs to know. It is a thought which NEVER EVER needs to be shared.

The dark sure got my attention that day, all be it for all the wrong reasons. I remember coming out from underground, seeing the light of the sun and vowing never to return. I was created for the sun, not the dark. I am created for the Son, not darkness.

I was reminded of this a few years ago, away in Canada with my son. Walking with John on a dull day in a river, as far as we could see, it contained little life. Much to the amusement of John I stumbled and fell over quite a bit. He meanwhile, was quite safe in a dinghy, which I was pulling along.

The following day the sun shone brightly and we re-traced our steps along the same river. Imagine my surprise to now see a whole new world under the surface of the water. There were fish galore, toads, crustaceans and even terrapins. I had a bit of a fright when what I thought was a stone moved! It was in fact a snapping turtle. The river was far from dead, it was brimming with life. It was only the light which revealed these wonders and life.

I am eternally thankful to Jesus for calling me out of the darkness. As the light of the sun revealed a better path for me, so the light of the Son shows the best and only way to truly live. Some twenty years ago I was called out from eternal darkness and I was saved. More recently I have been called out from another darkness, from one of frenetic busyness, of focusing on things other than God.

In an attempt to 'slow down', I have recently started to play golf with John. In trying to get him to hit the ball, (like my father before me), I find myself saying, *'keep your eye on the ball'*. I do not understand golf enough to know why, but somehow in keeping your eye on the ball, (rather than on the green or the club), the ball travels better.

I am also being called to keep my eye on the ball in life; to keep my eye on God. I know ultimately where I am going – to heaven – but along the way I am not so sure which paths I will travel down. With God as my guide however, with His commands for my good, with His love enabling me to love, my part is to keep my eye on Him.

I praise God for the *Gospel of John* and his collection of Jesus' 'I am' sayings. Jesus said:

> *'I am the light of the world. Whoever follows me will never walk*
> *in darkness, but will have the light of life'*
> *(8:12)*

> &

> *'I am the way and the truth and the life. No one comes to the*
> *Father except through me'*
> *(14:6).*

Jesus helps us to live our life, not only in giving us salvation but through guiding us. Jesus, on earth was the perfect model of how to live and love. With Jesus as my guide, He is able to keep me out of the darkness and in the light. Each day is one step at a time.

Consider a baby's first steps: those defining moments when a baby begins to become a toddler. In those first steps they are not wearing running spikes. Nor do they really know where their feet will lead them through life.

Toddlers, by their very nature, are just happy enough to be able to walk – often to the great praise and pride of all of those watching. Within time this of course changes. As they grow into a child, they will walk without great applause – they just get on with it. This, I have come to see, is not unlike our Christian walk.

As a new Christian, I tangibly sensed God's love a lot, if you like, I even felt it. Crazy prayers were answered, parking spaces were found. God was close. I felt it. I knew it. Over the years however, I began to feel God was less close. At times I even felt deserted or abandoned. I wasn't – but this was my perception.

I now recognise what was happening was not God abandoning me, rather He was allowing me to grow up. God knew I no longer needed those fuzzy feelings of praise and congratulations. I may have wanted them but I didn't need them. I didn't need brushing down and a kiss every time I fell over.

God had not created me to control or even monitor my every moment. There was a time to grow, a time to develop, and a time to trust in Him in a different way - in a deeper way. Yet somehow along the way I had gone off track. I was stepping on turtles, imagining they were merely stones!

Jesus came to live life and had given me the greatest command and yet along the way – I had come to ignore it. God eventually got my attention through ill health and a change of circumstances, and through this I have found life. *'Living, no longer existing'.*

In being called to love God with my all, I see God is seeking a total commitment of life to Himself. As I am beginning to love God with my all, I am noticing positive changes are occurring in my character and personality. I am beginning to become a (genuinely) nicer person, a kinder person, even a person with more patience. If you know me, then you will totally attribute this to God and God alone.

As I strive less in myself and became more content in God, I think I am also becoming easier to love. Perhaps it is as Barclay said; *'It is only when we love God that man becomes lovable'.* xx

My love, indeed the love of a human being, is sourced in God's love *(1 John 4:9-11)*. In recognising this, I am able to love all the more and in turn be loved all the more. It seems even my being able to be loved, is less about me working at it. Rather it is about something more beautiful, it is about God's love flowing within me and through me. But this is now and it has not always been this way.

***

*'Love the Lord your God **with all your** heart and with all your soul and with all your mind and with all your strength'*

***

CHAPTER TWENTY-THREE:
THE LORD IS MY SHEPHERD

I am able to multi-task. In my frenetic days, I could listen to music, eat lunch, be on the phone and answer an email, all whilst being on the loo! I never managed to answer the door at the same time but I was working on it. The trouble was, if I am honest, I was never giving my full attention to any one thing.

Seeking to love God with my all has been a challenge. To do anything with my all, is to give myself completely. But how is this possible when there are so many other things which need to be done each day?

For a while I comforted myself with the idea that God longs for us to love Him with what we have, rather than with what we do not have.

The miracle of Jesus at the feeding of the 5000, began with a young boy and his meagre lunch. As the disciple Andrew looked to see what food he could scavenge from this great crowd, he must have hoped for a little more than a few fish and some small loaves.

What amazes me in the story, (nearly as much as the miracle itself), is that Andrew even took this lunch to Jesus. It was hardly worth it. What on earth could even Jesus do with so little? Yet, Andrew took what the boy offered and in the end there was even more than they had started with – 12 baskets of left-overs *(John 6:1-13)*.

I wonder how many people in the Bible looked at themselves and at how little they had to offer and as a consequence nearly said no!

What of another young boy, this time with a slingshot and a smooth stone?

What of a lady whose only offering was being a Jewish glamour model?

What of a lady who had only enough flour and oil to make one last loaf of bread?

What of someone born left handed?

And yet, David, Esther, the Widow at Zarephath and Ehud all took what they had and loved God with it. With each of these people, it turned out in the end, with God, what little they had, was enough.

Coming to God with what I had, rather than with what I did not, worked for quite a while. During my months of sleep deprivation, (no make that years), when the only prayer I had was: *'thy will be done'* - well it was enough. God asks us to love Him with our 'all', but when my 'all' really wasn't very much, I reflected it was 'all' I had, and He was welcome to it.

The offering of a widow, one day in the Temple, was a meagre few pennies. It was hardly going to repair the Temple and yet she gave her all, and Jesus praised her for it *(Luke 21:1-4)*. In the giving of her all (quite literally her all), she knew in the future she was going to have to depend on God for everything.

For a long time, I felt I had little to offer, but I tried to give even this to God. And there for a long while, lay the problem. I was seeking to give from what I had, rather than giving from what God had.

It took many more months of becoming close to breaking point, before I acknowledged my strength was not sufficient. From being loved by God, I could love God yes, and actually that was all He wanted. The Lord was my shepherd, longing to look after me and wanting to lead me to quiet waters *(Psalm 23)*, where I could be with Him. It was to take even longer before I painfully acknowledged God meets more people in the valley's than in green pastures.

God didn't want new initiatives and more work; He wanted me. Just me. *'He loves me just as I am'*. Okay I know that wasn't God but Bridget Jones of Mark Darcy, but it kind of fits. God does love me just as I am, but He knows there is always more for me to receive from Him. As I do so, I am able to love Him all the more in return. We are designed for God's love to flow through us. I am just beginning to understand this. As I come to love God with my all, it is less about how much I have to offer, and more about whom I love and the actual ability He gives me to love Him and others.

CHAPTER TWENTY-FOUR:
FOUR IN ONE

In being commanded to love God with my all, I was particularly drawn to the fact that Jesus spoke of our being as four different parts. My own mind, heart, soul and strength were all weary. Each in their own way had been crying out. I was attracted to consider what it meant to love God with each different part of me. Yet even as I did this, I was mindful that some people would be uncomfortable with me doing so. Looking at each part of us in an individual way for some could be seen as taking things too literally and for others it perhaps went beyond Jesus' original intent.

In the Hebraic religion, human beings were thought of less as a collection of parts and more as a whole being. Looking at human beings as less integrated wholes, developed amongst Greek philosophers. Such thought however, continues to influence our own understanding of ourselves and therefore I believe we should look at each individual part of us.

Some theologians such as France however, consider we should not look at the four aspects of loving God as separate entities. France says; *'Heart, soul and mind are not different 'parts' of man but different ways of thinking of the whole man in his relation to God; no clear distinction can be drawn between them'.* [xxi]

I concur: the three nouns of mind, heart and soul are the essential parts of a person. Yet, I cannot believe God would have allowed these words, with their different significances to have continued down the centuries if somehow, their individuality was not important.

Jesus after all, rather than minimising the three words of, *Deuteronomy 6:5*, adds another, the word *'mind'*. I cannot ignore the significance each facet of mind, heart, soul and strength has, as I come to love God, and become the person God created me to be.

I believe it is important to look at each aspect individually, not least to become more aware of how God created them to function. From this, with the Holy Spirit I am subsequently able to offer them for healing and renewal. As I do this I am becoming more aware of God at work in my life.

This said, I realise as I come to love God, I cannot do so with only one part. My heart, mind, soul and strength form my very being and cannot literally be divided up. For example, my mind inevitably influences my heart, (my actions).

How can I truly say I love God with all of my soul if I bad mouth people, steal from work and commit adultery? If I was to say I love God with my mind and with my thoughts, but then murder someone, once again, am I truly loving God with my all? NO, of course not! In attempting to love God with my all, I cannot just try and love God with only one part. I either love God with all of my being or I don't. All parts of me are interconnected and bound in myself.

The more I seek to do any of this, the more I am aware that actually to love God with my all, is... impossible! Yep, impossible. Perhaps it's time to throw this book away! Here I am hardly a quarter of the way through, and I seem to be suggesting we cannot love God with our all, after all.

Well it's kind of true isn't it? We are human, we do sin. We cannot ever love God with our all, all of the time. So, where does this leave us?

As I look to Jesus, I know that He knew what it was to love God with His all perfectly, but then He was without sin. We can aim to love God truly, but it will always be imperfectly. So, should we perhaps stop trying? By no means!

Recognising that it is impossible to love God with our all, should bring us to Jesus even more. Jesus promises forgiveness and as we come to Him, so we can be forgiven, healed and restored. Forgiveness is an incredible gift to us. Yet more than this as Isaiah reveals, it is not just for our sake but for God as well:

> *'I, even I, am he who blots out your transgressions, for my own sake, and remembers your sins no more'*
> *(Isaiah 43:25).*

God loves us so much and wants to be with us, that He wants to blot out our sins. This is love indeed.

With the Holy Spirit, God enables us to love Him with our all, albeit imperfectly. God is delighted in the love of His people. Through His Holy Spirit, God longs for us to be the best we can on earth, in an imperfect world, before heaven. Through Jesus, God accepts us.

Now on the lines of forgiveness, please forgive me...We are nearly at the stage of unpacking what it is to love God with our mind, heart, soul and strength, as well as with our whole being...except there are a few things I have neglected to mention. If however, you can wait no more, skip a few chapters to 29! To do so though, you will miss out on understanding more fully what it means to love the Lord, so you may want to hang around...

***

*'Love **the Lord** your God with all your heart and with all your soul and with all your mind and with all your strength'*

***

CHAPTER TWENTY-FIVE:
VEHICLE REVERSING, PLEASE STAND CLEAR

In my haste to unwrap this glorious invitation of God, of loving the Lord with our all, I realise I have managed to skip over the words, *'the Lord'*. So let's back up a little.

In these words; *'the Lord'*, Jesus invites us to know God by name. A name to the early Israelites was everything.

It was their identity, it was who they were: their name often related to what was going on in the world around them. Let's consider a few names...

Moses – 'to draw out'. Moses was never going to forget the day he was pulled out from the Nile.

Isaac – 'laughs'. Isaac would remember his parents both laughing at being told they were going to have a baby – fair enough though, they were in their eighties!

Some names stated the obvious such as Esau, who was 'hairy'.

Personally, I always feel for Hosea's children as they had a rough deal when named. Okay their mother was a prostitute and Israel was being rebellious, but imagine being called: Lo-Ruhamah, which means *'not loved'*, or Lo-Ammi which means *'not my people'*. Every time they were called in for a meal, they heard the words; *'not loved'*, *'not my people'*! If there was ever a case for changing your name by deed poll, this had to be it!

On occasions people did change their name, often to reflect a change in their circumstance. Naomi, in the book of Ruth, having lost her husband and two sons, changed her name to Mara – 'bitter'.

At times people's names were changed by a conquering power.

The King of Babylon changed some Israelite names to Babylonian ones. However, if I had been changing the names Daniel, Hanniah, Mishael and Azariah, I think I would have gone for Dan, Bob, Tom and Ben, and not Belteshazzar, Shadrach, Meshach and Abednego. The latter hardly run off the tongue, do they?

Having your name changed was a massive deal for Daniel and Co. Their Israelite names were part of who they were, it was their identity. It was one thing for their land to be conquered and for them to lose their homes, but then they had to lose their names too. Your name was your identity; it was who you were.

Within Israel a name and a person's soul were almost indistinguishable. A person's whole personality was present in their name. Every time your name was called, so you, your very being was being called. Within Israel, to know of someone's name was to gain an insight into their nature. It was to acquire a relationship with them.

If you think about it, it took a long time for God's people to get their name, 'Israel'. For centuries God had been known by His actions or as the God of Abraham, Isaac and Jacob. It wasn't until after a wrestling match, that God's people became known as Israel *(Genesis 32:22-32 & 35:10)*. It's interesting to note, Israel means, *'May God prevail: He struggles with God'*. Israel and God have always wrestled and struggled together. In my own wrestling's, I feel I am in good company.

It took even longer in Israel's history for God to reveal His own name. Up until their escape from Egypt and the burning bush incident, God was known by His characteristics and by the names of the patriarchs.

Throughout the book of Genesis and Israel's earliest beginnings, God was known as the God of Abraham, Isaac and Jacob. This was still used even in the early church *(Acts 3:13)*.

It was not until Moses heard a voice from the bush that God revealed Himself as: *'I am who I am' (Exodus 3:14)* which means: *'I will be what I will be'*. Summed up, God was saying: *'who always was, who is and who is to come'*. God was letting Moses and everyone know, He is a being of His own. Jesus later confirmed this revealing God has life in Himself and in no other *(John 5:26)*.

Who did God reveal His name to? To a man whose own name was *'to draw out'*. To a man who had lived a privileged life in a palace. To a man who threw this privilege away as he murdered another. God revealed Himself to a fugitive, to a shepherd.

When the time came for God to reveal Himself by name, a bush burned and a voice said, *'I am who I am' (Exodus 3:14)*. To call upon God's name was and is to call upon His Presence. It is to call upon His will. God's name was not just a title. The name itself had mystery, power and substance. Consequently the Jews developed the highest regard for the name YAHWEH (LORD) – spelled YHWH.

YAHWEH was a name not to be used lightly. The name itself pre-supposed reverence and awe. The name had the highest regard, the greatest awe and respect! Orthodox Jews wouldn't even use the divine name in any context. They developed an alternative title, so cautious were they not to use it in an abusive way! So great is the use of God's name that it forms the third commandment, *(Exodus 20:7)*.

The LORD's name became of importance in both its utterance and in its written form. Scribes copying a manuscript, on coming across the word YHWH, had to adhere to strict regulations. Scribes had to wash, put on new clothes and use a new quill. There were to be no interruptions. If he had started writing YHWH, then he could not be interrupted, he had to finish it!

To be able to love the LORD, to be able to talk to the LORD, to be able to call upon the LORD was never to be taken lightly. How sad today, the LORD's name is not only taken in vain, but it has also become condensed to OMG? I am always amused if people apologise to me for blaspheming. It is after all God who takes offence. To apologise to me implies they know it is not right or that it may cause offence – yet they rarely think of whom they are actually offending.

There are in fact, two meanings in the Bible for the word LORD/Lord. It depends on how it is written. It will either read as Lord or LORD. The latter refers to Yahweh, the proper name for the God of Israel. The former refers to Lord: *'κύριον', (kurion)* as in supremacy and authority, but it also became the Greek form of LORD, that is Yahweh.

Am I just being geeky again? How does this help us? Well, Jesus could have after all just said; 'Love God...' but He didn't, He said; *'Love the Lord your God'*. He included the words; *'the Lord Your'*. In one respect you could say, why is Jesus saying God your God?

I believe such an emphasis reminds us that God is to be our Lord. Just as we have limited words to describe love, so we do of God. To hear of God being our Lord encourages us to come to Him and to give Him our all. Created in the image of God I find my purpose for being in loving Him and others.

***

'Love the Lord your God with all your heart and with
all your soul and with all your mind and with all your strength'

***

CHAPTER TWENTY-SIX: EGYPTIAN TAT

I'll be honest, when I first came to Jesus, it was easier to acknowledge Him as a friend and saviour. He was someone I could turn to: He was there for me. Jesus was someone who had gone to great lengths to let me know just how much He loved me. He had died for me and saved me. He truly loved me. This approach even seemed to work for a while.

I guess I just glossed over the word: *'Lord'*. I was ready to accept all Jesus had done for me and all He was willing to do for me. Looking back, I was on the take! I wanted all I could get without necessarily being willing to allow much change in my own life. I guess I just wasn't really ready to let Him have Lordship over all of my life. Jesus had warned of this, when He spoke of people who called Him Lord but they did not do what He said *(Luke 6:46)*. To be Lord of me, was for me to come to Him as Master, as Authority, as GOD.

At the time however, I would have said God was the Lord of my life, but actually there were areas which I had kept for myself. The 'Do not enter' signs were small but there nevertheless. Partly this was because I considered some areas too insignificant for Jesus to be interested in. More honestly though, I wanted to remain in control of some aspects of my life.

I confess I am a person who often needs to be in control. I think this is one reason why the English weather drives me mad. There is just no control over it. In this past week we have gone from beautiful sunshine of 25 degrees, to today which is splashing down with rain and is a cool 7 degrees.

Such is my need to often be in control, that recently when it was raining I moaned to my son, *'I wish it would stop raining. I need to go and water the garden'*. As he rolled his eyes, even I realised how ridiculous this sounded.

Even though I knew God wanted what was best for me, in too many areas of my life, I thought I knew best. After some twenty years of patiently waiting for me to surrender some issues, God gave me the nudge I needed. I am just grateful that at last I had ears to hear.

Some people describe the Bible as God's love letter to His people. Others see it as books of patience as God's people time and again got it wrong. The book of Judges sums up the whole Bible really. In this short book, we see God's people being led by various 'Judges' - leaders.

Each new period of an appointed judge usually starts with Israel having got into a mess. They have fallen away from God, usually because they have started following other gods. Over time they remember to cry out to God who (patiently and lovingly) sends them a judge.

Each judge with the Holy Spirit upon them, in different ways brought God's people back to God, and all is good for a little while. Right up until they forget God again and the spiral starts all over. The book of Judges describes the history of Israel from the time of Joshua's death, to the time when Samuel gives way for Israel to have a king.

God knows to worship many gods is to lead a divided life. It makes for a wishy-washy existence. It's like the difference between a maze and a labyrinth. The latter is designed so there is one route to follow to get to the centre. A maze meanwhile does have a centre, but to reach it there are a number of paths, some with dead ends.

God longs for us to be with Him and gives us one path to follow. Too often however, we like to chop and change, living more towards, *'variety is the spice of life!'*. Often relying on our feelings or depending on our circumstances, we may take a little of this way of life and a little of that. Anything which makes you happy, right!

Some people who live in such a way, profess to live in a much more free existence, as they live with fewer rules, more choice and more options. However, it can be very disjointed and it can lead to conflict, after all, how do you choose which god to serve at what time?

It's also a very 'me' way of looking at things. To live such a life is to follow a 'god' for your own purpose and desires rather than following the actual truth. Life becomes what we can get out of it rather than living how we are intended.

In the days of Israel entering the Promised land, when the Ten Commandments were first given, God's people perhaps understood more of what it meant not to follow other gods and idols. In the land which lay ahead of them, they were to encounter the gods of Chemosh, Baal, El, Asherah and Astarte. These were often made into graven images. Models of stone and wood were visible and if desired worshipped.

Nowadays other 'gods' may be more difficult to identify, but they exist all the same. We may not have carved stone and wood with names like Chemosh and Baal, but there are plenty of things which are put before the Lord our God. Often these other 'gods' whom we worship, are so subtle that we often overlook them.

Jesus knew this and sought to reveal this in the hearts of people of His day. For example as Jesus one day looked at a rich man, He loved him. But He also asked the man to sell all of his possessions, at which the man's face fell, and he went away sad *(Mark 10:17-31)*. Money you see, had become this man's number one god.

For many people today, our accumulated wealth is in fact a 'god'. With mortgages, credit cards and cars taking years to pay for, the amount in the bank may be little, and so we do not consider ourselves rich. Sadly however, more often this results in us living beyond our means.

We may not consider ourselves to be rich, and yet if you are reading this book, it is highly likely you are. To be educated and to be able to afford this book, let alone perhaps having a loose change bowl means you are in the top 7% of the richest people in the world.

Other gods today can include: ambition, fame, success, addictions, social-media, relationships and the like. It is impossible to mention all of the rebellious activities, sinful habits and wrong desires that we can fall foul to.

Don't misunderstand me though. I am not saying ambition, relationship and success etc. are bad in themselves or even 'gods'. It's more that they can become so. Anything really which can be put ahead of God, anything which has God coming second, no matter how close, is to live a divided life. This is worshipping other 'gods'.

Paul spoke of it as us not living merely for *'the cravings of our flesh'* *(Ephesians 2:1-3)*, that is our sinful nature. Paul calls for us to put to death bad things in our lives *(Colossians 3:5)* not because he was a kill-joy, but because God has a better life in store for us.

God longs to allow His love to flow through us: His patience, His kindness, His once and for all overflowing love for good – for our good. Through putting God first, through accepting God as our Lord, we are freed to love God and to be loved by God first and foremost.

To not worship other gods however does not come without its challenges. Whilst I may be tempted to the 'gods' of busyness and identity, at least they were unlikely to lead to a fiery furnace. Obedience to the command to love the Lord our God with our all, throughout history has landed God's people into trouble.

Just think of Daniel and his three friends. Remember we are calling them Bob, Tom and Ben *(Daniel 3)*. As Shadrach, Meshach and Abednego still hardly run off the tongue? During the exile they were taken to Babylon, but they still had good jobs working for King Nebuchadnezer. There was always food on the table, and compared to many from Israel and Judah, life was pretty good.

Until one day King Nebuchadnezer gets carried away and wants them to bow down to his statue. He wasn't banning them from worshipping their own God, but they also had to bow down to him.

Now surely this wasn't a biggie. Just bow down physically, whilst internally, with your heart, soul and strength you are doing no such thing. Surely this was a key to survival - keep quiet and crack on with life. But Bob, Tom and Ben would not do so, even when threatened with imprisonment and being thrown into a fire. As the King threatened them they answered:

> *'If we are thrown into the blazing furnace, the God we serve is able to deliver us from it, and he will deliver us from Your Majesty's hand. But even if he does not, we want you to know, Your Majesty, that we will not serve your gods or worship the image of gold you have set up'*
> *(Daniel 3:17-18).*

Now I can go along with their faith in God being able to save them. God can! But what of their second sentence? It is one thing to totally 100% believe God will save you, but here they were saying, well even if God doesn't save us we are still not going to bow down to your statue. Wow! God was so truly number one in their life that under no circumstances, (not even if God chose not to save them), would they bow down to any other god. Their obedience and faith was rewarded that day - God saved them.

At the time of Jesus, the Roman authorities were equally bewildered with the Jews. The Romans had many gods - you could almost liken it to a blanket insurance policy. As they conquered lands, they encompassed other religions into their own. The more the merrier hey!

The Romans allowed people to serve their own gods, but they also called upon those conquered to follow the Roman gods as well. The Romans thought such an openness would be appreciated. The Greeks before them had also had many gods. Paul even comments on the openness to many gods. On a trip to Athens he saw an altar *'to an unknown god' (Acts 17:22-23).*

The Jews however, could not and would not bow down to any god other than their God and it caused them trouble. Many Romans and other conquering nations, just couldn't see what the big deal was. Just do it! Bow down, do what we say and then serve your own deity as well. Job's a good 'un' – surely!

To the Jews however, this was a biggie. It was a huge deal! God, Yahweh, *'I am that I am'*, was God of the Jews. He had brought them out of slavery. God had rescued them and enabled them to escape across the Red Sea.

God guarded them in the wilderness against the enemy of starvation: He kept predators at bay. He was their God and He did not want to be shared with anyone. He did not want to share His people with other gods. He is the Lord Almighty, the supreme God, the only God. God is self-existent, self-sufficient, He is the Living God. God was theirs and they were His.

A bit of an aside here, but I have often wondered why God didn't just wipe all the other gods from the earth – surely it would have been easier. I mean time and time again God's people got it wrong and started worshipping other gods. Baal was a particular favourite.

There was a great allure to follow other gods, such as promised prosperity and sexual experiences. Through the making of idols, you could also have a graven image, something to physically see, something to bow down to.

Yahweh however, did not want to be followed in a visual form. He wanted to be known for His actions, for saving His people from Egypt, for loving His people. Israel however, on seeing how other nations worshipped, often lusted over graven images. Following other gods repeatedly got Israel into trouble. Eventually they would come back to God and be forgiven and all was well, but it only lasted until the next time.

God proved again and again that He was the LORD God, He was all powerful. Take *1 Kings 18:16-46* as an example. Elijah ended up on a mountain with 450 prophets of Baal and for good measure, 400 prophets of Asherah. As just one prophet, Elijah put 850 prophets and their gods to the test. He challenged Baal to light a fire to burn a sacrifice. Easy enough! Well, except human intervention was not allowed.

The prophets end up shouting to Baal to come and light the fire. They even danced. Take That and Lulu would have been impressed! But no go, no relighting the fire, on that day. So, they slashed themselves with swords and spears but still no go.

God however, proved His Sovereignty and power that day. The prophets of Baal had slashed, danced and shouted. Elijah meanwhile poured water all over his sacrifice and the Lord sent His fire down *(v.38-39)*. All the people on Mount Carmel on that day, recognised God was God!

So, back to my first question: why did God just not eliminate all other gods once and for all? I guess it comes down to where would God stop rather than where would He start? If you get rid of other gods and other worshippers, there wouldn't be many people left.

Until Jesus returns to judge the world once and for all, we all have a choice as to whether we follow God or not. God longs for us to turn to Him out of love, out of free will. Other gods remain today *(1 Corinthians 8:5)* but we are called to undivided loyalty to God. For one it is because of His nature: God is God, the only God. To follow God alone is more than enough; it is all we need.

Today perhaps the allure to stones, clay and wood is less but of course there is nevertheless an allure to other gods. 85% of the English population say they believe in God. However, if you ask people to describe who God is, you are likely to have as many different answers as the people you ask.

Even Christians believing in God may make Him into something He is not. God longs for us to be loved by Him and to love Him. Yet rarely it seems, is God enough.

Worshipping something other than God, following or allowing ourselves to be influenced by something other than God, has been around nearly as long as people themselves.

Adam and Eve put eating fruit from the only forbidden tree ahead of God. In the family of Jacob, (the third patriarch), other gods make an appearance. In *Genesis 31:19*, we read of Jacobs wife Rachel, stealing her father's household gods. Strangely there is no editorial comment on this! Instead we read she hid them, by sitting on them, telling her father, she was having her period, so she couldn't stand up.

Sometime later, Moses goes up a mountain to get the Ten Commandments. It promises to be an amazing day. God's people have been led out of Egypt – they are free. Their leader goes up Mount Sinai to be with God – this promises to be a day to remember.

The Israelites wait in anticipation...and they wait. They wait, until in fact, the waiting becomes too much. Moses is gone for too long, and it doesn't take long before Israel want their own god in a physical form.

Made out of Egyptian tat (gold ear rings), God's own people end up with a golden calf *(Exodus 32)*. At the very time Moses is up the mountain being told by God, He wants His people for His own, they are down below melting 'tat'. At the very time God is saying, He does not want to share His people *(Exodus 20:22)*, they are at base camp making a calf statue out of gold – from Egypt.

I have to ask, Why? Why did they do it? As I ask this, I turn it back onto ourselves and ask, why do any of us do it?

I know God is Lord of all. I know God sent His Son to earth and yet time and again I depend on things other than God. Perhaps I had even made 'ministry' an idol. I wouldn't have said I was worshipping work, but actually at times it was certainly number one in my life.

CHAPTER TWENTY-SEVEN:
'MUMMA, GOD IS NUMBER ONE, I'M NUMBER TWO'

At times, (like many of us), I put all the things I had to do, before worshipping God. I had made many an idol. An idol is what elicits our primary focus, our affections and our interests.

At times, I am sorry to say, I had also put my son before God. I wanted to be with John so much, that with work taking so much of my time, I tried to give any spare moment to him. I reasoned (wrongly), as God had called me to serve Him in the church, any other time should be devoted to John rather than to God. God's time, if you like was my work! Some days as I shut the study door, it was almost as if I was leaving God in there too!

One day however, John brought me up sharp. Whilst playing and spinning him through the air, he landed and gave me a massive hug. I kissed him and said; *'Baba, you are my number one'*. With a look that only he can give, he replied; *'Mumma, God is number one. I am second'*.

I was stunned! Not only at John's understanding, but at how through him, God very clearly was speaking to me. John understood even at four years old, that God should come first. Equally he was not threatened by being second. Up against God, second was more than enough.

I wonder...what is first in your life?

Did you think about that question? Or have you just read on? Let's be honest we all try and ignore such questions in a book. Either because we don't want to be too searching or because we want the book to give us all the answers. Equally if I said please read *Matthew 1*, well, you may look it up but on seeing it is the genealogy of Jesus, I have a feeling you may skim at best, or just jump to the end.

So, why not get a cuppa and I repeat, what is first in your own life? What do you think about the most? What do you focus your life on?

Whatever is first in your life is likely to either enslave you or release you. Which is it?

Some people put wealth (their possessions) before God, some would say their family, others put their goals and ambitions, or the way they look. We are created to love and worship. We are filled with a desire to love and at times it is easier to love things other than God.

Partly we may love things other than God because we have never really thought about it. Equally we may allow ourselves to put things in front of God, because they are more concrete and even socially acceptable. After all to put in long hours at work is often commendable. To pursue good things for your family is seen as good and necessary and up to a point, yes they are.

At the time of Moses, Israel wanted to see an actual image to worship - they chose a calf. We choose not a graven image, but often life itself. At times we may opt to love and worship things other than God, quite simply because they seem less demanding and frankly more enjoyable. Overlooking that this world is not all there is, too often our sole focus is on life in the here and now. But does it really matter? Does God still need to be number one?

If God did not love us so much, perhaps it wouldn't matter, but God's nature is to love and it is to love us. God's love for us is so great, He wants us for Himself. God created us for Himself.

God does not want to share us with other things. Many of these 'things' of course in themselves, are not bad for us. Right up until they become our primary focus and we forget God. Worshipping things other than God becomes bad for us, when we pursue them, rather than loving God first.

The Devil knows this, and he knows our weak spots. Did the Devil not tempt Jesus with 'things'? The Devil showed Jesus the kingdoms of the world, and offered them all to Him. All Jesus had to do was worship the Devil.

To have everyone looking at you as their ruler, must have been tempting. Surely such power could have influenced the world for good? Yet, Jesus knew to do so, would have been putting something before God. Jesus' reply from Deuteronomy, *'Worship the Lord your God and serve him only'* *(6:13),* shows that even He, the Son of God had to put God first. God was to be Lord of all – of everything.

Loving things first over God quite simply puts our life out of balance. It denies God the love He deserves. We end up not living the life we are created for *(Psalm 115:3-8)*. Worshipping God alone leads to contentment, real contentment and everlasting peace.

Everything else will inevitably lead to division or conflict. To be sure for a short time, a new partner, a new job, a new car, a new hobby may seem fulfilling, but such satisfaction is often fleeting.

I have come to see, all other gods will disappoint. False idols cannot fill the 'God-shaped hole' within our lives. We are encouraged to keep away from idols *(1 John 5:20-21)*. To worship things other than God, tempts us to accept second best. They cheat us, enslave us and are ultimately as satisfying as drinking salt water.

We can never be truly satisfied with anything other than God: it is impossible. Compared to eternal living, being loved by God, nothing compares. You see, God loves us so much. He loves us passionately, compassionately, altruistically and sacrificially. Why else would He go to such lengths to be in a relationship with us? God wants us to stop hurting ourselves with things which are not right for us.

So, what about the invitation to love God? Does it release or enslave?

I have been brought up sharp on this. How can I possibly call Jesus, *'Lord'* and not allow Him access to all areas of my life? How can I call Him Lord and not follow what He says is good for us? Dallas Willard, an amazing philosopher and theologian (and former spiritual director of Jon Ortberg) has really helped me in this.

I have come to see in calling God, 'LORD', it has as much to do with discipleship as anything else. After all, Jesus in the Great Commission did not ask His followers to make converts or even Christians. Dallas Willard calls this the 'great omission'.[xxii]

Being a disciple is to be a learner of Jesus and this means sitting at His feet, following His way of living and life, in everything we do. Willard speaks of us trying to live our lives as though Jesus was us. Coming to God as LORD, is hearing His word and then living His word - putting it into practise. Hence my devotion to writing a whole book on just one verse of the Bible.

I acknowledge as we seek to imitate Christ *(1 Peter 2:21)*, we have to translate and interpret the ways of a 1st Century Palestinian Jew for our lives today. We have to try and make the cultural adjustments. This is the daily challenge for every disciple of Jesus.

Jesus commands us to love the Lord your God with our all. In this book I am wrestling with what this means theologically. My spiritual and practical wrestling's of how I live this day to day are reserved for another day. Suffice to say, a lot more 'being' and a lot less 'striving' is changing my life.

Putting God first and allowing God's love to flow through me are the first stumbling steps on an eternal journey. But back for a moment on the love for my son. Embracing God as number one and acknowledging John as number two, has been so much better for our mum and son relationship.

No longer am I seeking from my son that which can only be received from God. I am in fact able to love John all the more as the flow is now right. No longer am I loving John to fill a gap. I am loving John in and through God's love. This love is less obsessive, less destructive and more 'pure'. From loving God first I am able to love others better too.

CHAPTER TWENTY-EIGHT:
FOR BETTER, FOR WORSE

Before we come to look at loving God specifically with our mind, soul, heart and strength, a few words on discipleship. By this I mean, how to follow Jesus, how to live in *'The Way'*.

I became a Christian through the 'evangelical wing' of Christianity. In the main I consider this has served me well. One of the major downsides however, is my evangelical faith has often spurred me to 'do', rather than 'be'. In following Jesus' great commission of, 'Go' - I have often done exactly that.

I have 'gone', quite literally around the world, talking about Jesus, hoping and praying others would come to know Him. I have run many evangelistic courses, and I have preached God's word wherever possible. I have tried to make the truths of God relevant to both toddlers and the infirm, and everyone in between. I have talked, walked, gone and sadly I got tired!

Do not hear me wrong, I am eternally grateful for my evangelical inheritance. It encouraged me to fall in love with God's word, with the Bible. Sure there are hard passages, and yes, there are bits that do not seem to make much sense. There are even aspects many Christians would rather were not even in the Bible. Furthermore there are elements which quite frankly seem utterly bonkers, I mean, when did donkeys ever learn to talk? *(Numbers 22:21-39)*.

And yet here we have it, the Bible, containing 66 books, 1189 chapters, 31 102 verses. Written by over forty authors, over a period of 1500 years. It still remains the most popular book ever sold – selling over 5 billion copies.

In the Bible, there is a word for every occasion. We may not always realise it, as we may not have read it all or even if we have, we are unlikely to understand it all. The Bible continues to be God's word to us, if only we knew of it.

In seeking to love God with my all and to follow Him as Lord, I am convinced knowing God's word is of such importance. The life of Jesus confirms this. Earlier I mentioned Jesus in the wilderness. Having been led there by the Holy Spirit, Jesus was tempted by the Devil.

On at least three occasions the Devil tried to catch Jesus out. The Devil's arguments were even quite convincing. Jesus is likely after all, to have been able to make an incredible impact on the world, if He had done what the Devil said. Turning stones into bread could have ended poverty for good. Jumping from great heights only not to die, would have gained many followers.

Jesus knew, however, that He had not come into this world merely to provide food for people's stomachs or to gain personal popularity. Jesus came to speak and live the Kingdom of God; Jesus was interested in eternal living and not just our life on earth. Jesus knew the word of God. Now of course, He was God so He had an edge for memorising scripture. However, as fully God He could have used His own words to outwit the Devil, but no, He chose to use the words of Moses.

Three times Jesus quotes God's word (from the book of Deuteronomy no least), in order to combat the Devil's lies. The Devil knew of the Old Testament and he tried to turn it against Jesus, but Jesus knew it better. Jesus knew the heart of God's word, not merely the words themselves.

Jesus knew God's word and He lived by God's word. Likewise He encouraged others to know God's word. He knew within God's word, lie eternal truths. As Jesus says in *Luke 11:28; 'Blessed...are those who hear the word of God and obey it'.*

Hearing the word of God was a start but it was not enough: Jesus looked for people to obey it also. Only in obeying what was written, could people live the life God wanted for them. It is only in discovering God's plan for us, that we can begin to live it. I see the Bible as revealing our purpose on earth.

Time and again in Jesus' ministry He encouraged others to know God's word and to obey it. Within Judaism it was the role of Pharisees and experts in the Law to help with this. Sadly as recorded in *Luke 11*, Jesus criticised the very people whose role in life was to understand God's word. Jesus went so far as to say to them: *'Woe to you...'*

Interestingly Jesus uses the word *'woe'* more than anyone else in the Bible. Each time He used it, He was offering judgement from God. On this occasion Jesus condemned those, whose very job it was to enlighten others. Not only had the Pharisees misguided themselves, they were leading others into sin, hence Jesus' anger. Their focus was on the action of the Law, rather than the heart of it.

In loving God, we are encouraged to come to know God's word more. In doing so, in understanding it and becoming immersed in it, like Jesus, we are able to respond to the lies of the Devil. Even more though, we are able to see how God longs for us to live our life.

To be able to *'Love the Lord your God with all your...'*, enables us to live the life we are created for. As I seek to live this, so I am aware of how God longs for me to know Him through His word all the more. The Psalmist praised God on one occasion saying; *'Your word is a lamp for my feet, a light on my path' (Psalm 119:105)*.

God's word not only gives us an account of the history of Israel, the life of Jesus and the early church, it leads to life...to eternal life...in heaven and on earth. Jesus *'the word' (John 1:1)*, came to live amongst us and in His own words became, *'the light of the world' (John 8:12)*. Not even a light for the world, but a light of the world. This light shines and points to His Father; to the Creator and Sustainer of the world. To the Heavenly Father of you and I.

The Bible reveals God's deep abiding love for humanity. In spite of humanity constantly turning away from Him, God keeps loving and forgiving. He has given us a way to live the life we are created for.

Now, I have tried to write as much of this book outside as possible – I love the light, fresh air and the sun. On one occasion as I was reading from my laptop, I could see not only these words of the Bible, but my own reflection on the screen as well.

For a moment I was distracted and I began to look at myself. As I did so, I began to lose sight of some of the words on the screen. Equally as I concentrated on the text, gradually I lost sight of my own reflection. Both the text and my image were on the screen, however depending on my focus, one or the other became more dominant.

As I live life, my strong desire is that I may lead it immersed in God's word. I hope to allow God's words to inform my life. It has not always been this way though. Prior to becoming a Christian I studied theology at University – mostly to argue a case against it. As I sought to undermine the beliefs of others, I was probably the bane of every Christian on that course.

In the end I lost the battle but ultimately I won. In realising Christianity was right and I had been wrong for so long, it took a giant leap of faith to begin to believe the Bible was true.

In coming to the Bible as God's word rather than a book to be pulled apart, I found the relationship I am grateful for. The more I allow God to speak to me through His word, the more I am able to love God, my neighbour and even myself.

It seems ironic at a time when we have more opportunities than ever before to read and hear God's word, that we seem to be taking it less and less seriously. Never before have there been more translations or more access to the Bible.

If you are someone new to the Bible, it's important to find one that works for you. For some people this will include, the translation, the size of it and even the colour. I know someone who loves her 'pink cover Bible', whilst others prefer to read online. My favourite Bible is dog-eared and falling apart.

The Bible comes over the internet, it can be listened to, downloaded and even watched. Never before have there been more places where we can have God's word. The advent of technology means for many they are able to listen to God's word in the gym and in the car, just as much as in a comfy chair at home. God longs for us to get to know Him and ourselves better, and I believe this happens through talking to Him (prayer) and through reading His word (the Bible).

It stands to reason that as we are called to love God with our all, so we are called to come to know Him more. Not in a striving way, but in a longing way. However, it is important to point out that whilst we are called to love God, we will never 'totally' know God.

God has revealed Himself throughout history, in the Bible and through Jesus, but to know God completely is beyond our comprehension. We are however, able to know God as fully as we can cope with.

Too often though, we try to bring God down to our level. Perhaps this is as we seek to understand Him. God however, is God.

Even the great and learned apostle Paul realised this. Any quick look at Paul's writings show just how clever he was and how much he knew of God, but even he admitted there was a limit to his knowledge. To the church in Rome he disclosed:

'Oh, the depth of the riches of the wisdom and knowledge of God!
'Who has known the mind of the Lord? Or who has been his
counsellor?', 'Who has ever given to God, that God should repay
them?' For from him and through him and for him are all things.
To him be the glory forever!'
(Romans 11:33-36).

Paul marvels at God and how God can never be completely understood. He does this by referencing writers of the Old Testament *(Isaiah 40:13 and Job 41:11)*. Human beings, no matter how hard we try, are incapable of knowing God completely.

I'll be honest though as I read the Bible, I continue to have so many more questions than answers. So much so that the title of this book, 'FOREVER WrestLING', was originally going to be a compilation, of all of my questions and wrestling's.

But just as Jude (writer of a small letter, tucked towards the end of the New Testament), felt compelled to write of something different, so have I! In place of my many wrestling's, I have been given a peace from God that He is God. He is Sovereign Lord, and some things pale into insignificance when I am now with Him. I still wrestle, believe me, but nowadays my wrestling is from a place of rest.

Believe me, I still question, but I am now striving less to find an answer. I am more at peace with myself and with God. Throughout life, perhaps particularly through the darker times, I wanted to know of God's plan. I asked Him repeatedly what His Will for my life was. I needed to know.

More recently however, I have come to see, this was less about wanting to know of God's plans and more about my wanting to be in control. God, mercifully, has released me from this pressure. Knowing just enough is now more than enough.

Loving God and following God is enough. I know where I have come from and where I am going. Everything in between is to be lived and loved. Travellers have an old saying; *'a car's headlights only shine for 15 feet...but that 15 feet will get you all the way home'*.

God knows how much we need to know and how much is good for us. If I had known on the day I became a Christian that I would get a collar and join the army...well the conversation with God would have been a bit longer.

If I had known what little sleep I would get for the first four years of John's life – Jack would have been banished to the spare room, forever more! Sometimes God lets us know just enough.

But neither does God ever lie. He never says it will be easy. Too often today, companies, products and gyms, lie! We are sold a lie that a product will change our life. We are told a product is easy to assemble. We are even led to believe joining the gym will make us a toned size 10.

I realise, I cannot always blame false advertising for this...I had a friend who once belonged to a gym who often moaned she was over-weight. I asked how often she went to the gym, to which she replied, *'oh, never, I don't have time for that'*.

God never says following Him will be easy. We are asked to be a *'living sacrifice' (Romans 12:1)*, *'to carry our cross' (Luke 14:27)* and even to *'give up everything' (Luke 14:33)*. This does not mean however, that we will necessarily have to, rather it means we live our lives putting Jesus first. If push came to shove it is being able to put Jesus before anything or anyone. It's a life choice.

Jesus (as revealed in *Luke 14:25-35*), states how hard following God is. Jesus asks 'potential disciples' to weigh up whether they can commit or not. Jesus by His own life and death did not live a half-hearted life. We too are called to live wholeheartedly at the feet of Jesus.

Being a Christian isn't always easy. But then again living life without Him doesn't seem a whole lot easier either. Life is hard. Too often we want life on the cheap or life to be as easy as possible. Jesus didn't do anything on the cheap. He lived and even died so we can come to His Father in heaven – our Father in heaven. Jesus' life was worth more than the thirty pieces of silver which Judas betrayed Him for. Jesus' life was worth every living soul.

And so now, we are coming to the flight above the clouds. It feels on this journey together, we have taken a long time to get off the ground. We have gone through some clouds and have even encountered some turbulence. However, we have now looked specifically at the first seven words; *'Love the Lord your God with all...'*, so perhaps we are ready to have a go at exploring our heart, soul, mind and strength.

Even in this though, I have wrestled, as I haven't been sure what order to approach them. The evangelical side of me needed me to look at them in order. However, I sense I need to be honest. I need to share with you as they were first revealed to me.

Thus let's look at our mind first as this was the part of me that was most battered. As my mind came to rest a little, so my soul was given a voice. My heart could then focus as it no longer felt the need to lead all of the time. All of which has had an everlasting impact on my strength.

Perhaps it's time for a cuppa.

***

*'**Love the Lord your God** with all your heart and with all your soul and **with all your mind** and with all your strength'*

***

CHAPTER TWENTY-NINE:
24/7

The reason I have to start with 'our mind', is quite simply because I thought I was losing mine. On this note, aren't some non-literal sayings quite bonkers. Consider what a state we would find ourselves in if we really held our tongue, allowed ourselves to crack up, had an actual broken heart or stretched ourselves fully before going for a run! We would be a mound of bandages. This all said, at loss for a better phrase - at one point I thought I was losing my mind!

The busyness and frenetic pace of life had taken a toll on my mind. I am not sure if I was at burn out or close to a breakdown, as sadly I never made time to go to the Doctor's. There was no denying though my mind was weary, full to the top and not always thinking straight.

I felt as though I was literally going out of my mind — but hey I guess this puts me in good company. Was it not Jesus' own family who thought He was going out of His mind? *(Mark 3:21)*. And all because He wouldn't go to the door to see them! I hid a lot of what I was going through from my family, right up until I couldn't any longer. God's healing for me started in my mind, so as I explore loving God with four aspects of my being, this is the one I am starting with.

Sadly in today's society people having a mind which is weary or overwhelmed, is all too common. Finding someone whose mind isn't, is perhaps all the more surprising. It is estimated that 1 in 6 people over the past week would have experienced a mental health problem.

Depression, anxiety and other mental health issues are only on the increase. Mental and emotional dysfunctions are epidemic. [xxiii]

Pharmaceutical companies have never done so well. Diazepam is now even available for pets!

Depression, anxiety, rates of self-harm and eating disorders amongst teenagers have increased as much as 70% over the last 25 years. Family breakdown, increasingly complex lives, developments in education, (not least increased testing), all are contributing to the lowering state of our mental health.

I am heartened though that mental health issues are now being highlighted and discussed a lot more. At least the workings of our mind are less of a taboo subject than it once was.

But let's be honest, illness, hard work and responsibilities have always been with us, so, just what has changed over the past century?

Several studies have begun to attribute the increasing fragility of our minds to – 'change'. [xxiv] Such change, includes the pace of life, the speed of travel, our instant availability and new threats transmitted to our devices through the rapid advances of technology.[xxv] Our 'always on' culture is seen as widely contributing to a decline in mental health.

Neuroscience studies are now revealing how the neural pathways of our brains are actually being rewired according to the different pace of our lives. So much so that our capacity for continuous concentration is decreasing. We watch programs on fast forward. We are increasingly distracted...our minds are noisy, they are distracted and ever wandering.

Our minds in a nutshell, are being pushed full to bursting. I know of one person whose job it is to watch up to five tennis matches at the same time. Thankfully they like the tennis! With five screens, they are looking at each game, trying to predict who is going to win. How can our brains compute so much information at once?

Our minds are becoming more full and having to work at a much faster pace. The very things which were designed originally to make our lives easier, seem in many cases to be having the opposite effect.

Social media, the pace of work and life in general now has many people on call 24/7. People are available at a bleep, even whilst on holiday. One of the top things people look for when booking accommodation for their holiday is no longer an 'en-suite', but internet coverage and the speed of it!

Many people as soon as they wake up, (that is if they haven't been woken by a message already), are checking social media accounts to see what they may have missed. FOMO has become a word.

The *'fear of missing out'*, is anxiety caused when someone believes an exciting event is happening and they themselves are not a part of it. Posts on social media are massively contributing to this. Many people are becoming obsessed and even addicted to what other people are doing.

As I write this however, there has been a recent backlash against some social media sites. Some large companies are withdrawing from using some sites. Some saying the sites are becoming too addictive, others realising we are all suffering information over load.

Whilst I would like to hope this is the beginning of the end of social media, it seems it is here to stay. Just as I have always known of the existence of the telephone; we now have a generation that doesn't know anything other than 'instant' information.

An interest in others and a fear of missing out however, is far from new. Some 600 years ago, Thomas a Kempis warned his own generation of such a growing trend. He encouraged them rather to listen to God instead:

> *'my son do not be curious, nor trouble thyself with idle matters.*
> *What is this or that to thee? Follow thou me...'* xxvi

I guess the difference between Thomas, his friends and us, is the amount of people they had access to. Villages were often less than a hundred people, thus there were fewer people to watch and quite simply there was less going on.

With no electric light and little entertainment beyond the local tavern, there was less to miss out on anyway. They possibly had the potential for hundred 'likes', which really (in our modern world) is not to be 'liked' very much at all!

Some six centuries on, rather than learning from Thomas a Kempis, sadly our record high levels of stress seem only to be increasing. More and more health conditions are being attributed to stress.

A friend recently was stuck on a train for several hours. Two people in front of her, who were previously strangers, dealt with this delay, by forming a 'relationship'! Another lady meanwhile, as they waited for the train to move again, became more and more stressed. Clearly suffering from Alopecia areata, she literally had hair coming out in handfuls.

Rather than, 'love is all around', it seems in the 21st Century, 'stress is all around'. Is there any good news? Let's go for a quick re-cap...

First and foremost I have come to see humanity exists to love God. We are created to love God and others. As we do this, in being loved by God, so we can live the best of life. We can live the life we're intended to.

As I consider my own life and that of those around me, I just wonder whether we need to acknowledge, we are not in fact designed for the fast paced world in which we now live. Perhaps we were not created for such an avalanche of information.

This does not mean that we are out-dated, nor that God belongs to a pre-technological age. Rather we need to take control of our lives. And by this I mean, we need to let God take the lead in the life we are living. We need to allow God to slow down our pace of life to a pace worth living.

Some people within the world seem to be recognising this and practises such as 'mindfulness' (Christian or otherwise) have become increasingly popular. So much so in fact, on a recent visit to a national high street book shop, there were more books on this subject than on the Bible or even C.S Lewis.

During my darker moments, (when I think my counsellor was grasping for anything which might have worked for me), mindfulness was suggested. I explored the origins of Christian mindfulness, but I felt greatly unsettled. To me, it didn't fit right.

This may be because I was born near Glastonbury, and thus I am extra vigilant to anything which may not be good for me. More than this though, it also felt like second best. I knew something else was out there, but at that point I wasn't quite sure, so I kept on searching. I later found this 'something', was simply being quiet with God. More of this another time.

CHAPTER THIRTY:
'DIANOIA'

As I explored briefly earlier, the actual word *'mind'* was not included in the command to love God with your all. Using the verse *Deuteronomy 6:5*, Jesus some 1500 years later added it. I say add, but actually Jesus was not adding some new dimension of how we are to love God. Rather, Jesus was using additional vocabulary to help His hearers understand what was meant by the Hebrew word, *'heart'*.

Within the Hebraic world there was little distinction between heart and mind. The word referred less to an emotional entity or the intellect. Rather its meaning encompassed the essence of who we are: to our *'will'*, to our *'inner being'*. Whether you use one word (heart), or two words (heart and mind) essentially they mean the same; we are to love the Lord with our absolute all, with our very being, with our everything.

Heart and mind were in a sense, one and the same. By the 1st century AD however, a differentiation between the two words was more commonplace. For example, to the church in Philippi Paul says:

> *'And the peace of God, which transcends all understanding, will*
> *guard your hearts and your minds in Christ Jesus'*
> *(Philippians 4:7).*

The Greek word, *'dianoia'* – *'mind'*, meaning understanding and intelligence had come into being. The mind became more located in our head rather than in the heart of our inner being. The mind enables us to be aware of the world. It is the thinking part of us, it is our consciousness. Our mind can concentrate on aspects of our past, present or future.

Personally for me, Jesus' inclusion of the word *'mind'* in His invitation to love God, was pivotal. I wanted to love God with my mind, I really did, I just couldn't see a way of doing so.

As I have disclosed, I did go to counselling to help ease my mind.

At one point it was suggested to me, I should take anti-depressants but this didn't feel right for me. It wasn't that I felt ashamed of a possible need for medication, it was more that although there were indeed 'dark times', I never felt I was actually 'depressed'. Perhaps subconsciously I was saving them, in case at some later stage I began to feel even worse.

For many people medication and science can be part of a healing process. I knew of someone who thought they were failing as a Christian because they had been prescribed anti-depressants. Eventually someone wisely counselled them, saying maybe medication was part of God's healing process. My friend was encouraged to take them, but as he did so, to thank God for them and to ask God for continued healing.

Frequently I asked God for healing but even as I did, I also felt guilty for being this way. After all I had food on the table, I had a loving and supportive family. I had a home, a job and enough money to go on holiday. What else did I expect from life?

At times I battled with such thoughts, I also felt that perhaps God didn't love me after all. Surely if He wanted to, He could heal me. After all, I only wanted to feel better so I could give more of my all as a parish priest.

Now I realise God does not always heal everyone on earth. I know that God is more interested in eternal healing, but this didn't stop me from shouting out for healing. Not least because I only wanted to get better, so I could serve Him better in ministry. Me being ill and having at times to withdraw from ministry made little sense to me.

At other times I felt that I was not a very good Christian. Jesus Himself encourages us not to worry, so why did I feel like this? Was I not saying the right prayers? Why did I feel 'stressed' all the time? Was I sinning in some way? Was it a sin to be stressed? Was I not relying on God as I should?

I even wrestled with why we would have been created with the potential to produce cortisol in the first place. After all, if it was a sin to be stressed, why would we have something within us which aided us when we were stressed? None of this wrestling really helped my already fit to bursting mind!

CHAPTER THIRSTY-ONE:
IS ANXIETY A SIN?

Eventually, I took wisdom from King David who had the confidence to approach God saying:

> *'Search me, God, and know my heart; test me and know my*
> *anxious thoughts. See if there is any offensive way in me, and*
> *lead me in the way everlasting'*
> *(Psalm 139:23-24).*

David came to God with his all, including his anxious thoughts.

Perhaps being anxious was not a sin, rather it is what we do with our anxieties. The Psalmist asked God to know his anxious thoughts. The Psalmist was not hiding his thoughts from God and I didn't want to either.

Maybe the key was to look at eternity and not to just fixate on my life in the here and now. David after all, asked God to lead him in the *'way everlasting'*. This was all well and good but I still had to live in this world in the here and now.

Thankfully (in a way) at a particularly low point one Easter, I read (afresh) that even Jesus had thoughts which could be considered as 'anxious ones'. It was in wrestling with passages of Jesus' last days that I began to feel a little better about life. Now I do see the irony...there was Jesus having the worst week of His life and yet that seemed to be making me feel a little better...!

I guess as I looked at Jesus as a human being, I felt some comfort that He was indeed fully human. It seemed to me He too suffered from an anguish of the mind. Jesus in His very humanness had bouts of intense suffering. I wrestle with whether to say Jesus suffered with anxiety, as this may imply a worry or unease about an uncertain outcome. Jesus knew the outcome – He knew He was going to die. This brought on suffering and certainly unease. Was it anxiety? I am not really sure.

Now, please do not take this as heresy. I can see that Jesus trusted in God at all times and He was without sin, even in His worst of days. In the Garden of Gethsemane, on the day of His arrest, trial and execution, He trusted in His Father.

Jesus was willing to go along with God's plan, even if this was to lead to His death. But as He acknowledged to His Father, He was also very willing for this not to be the way ahead. If it were possible, He would rather not die such an agonising death. Jesus' actual words were:

> *'Father, if you are willing, take this cup from me; yet not my will,*
> *but yours be done'*
> *(Luke 22:42).*

If this is where Luke had left it, perhaps we could interpret these words as just being an off the cuff remark. However, the following verses reveal just how much stress Jesus was under:

> *'An angel from heaven appeared to him and strengthened him.*
> *And being in anguish, he prayed more earnestly, and his sweat*
> *was like drops of blood falling to the ground'*
> *(Luke 22:43-44).*

An angel from heaven strengthened Him – Phew! Things are going to be okay. Jesus is surely going to be supernaturally able to sustain whatever comes His way. We can rest easy. Well, except for the physical manifestation of His anguish – as it seems He sweated blood. Through the pores of His skin, blood fell.

Luke glossed over the term 'hematidrosis', but he did describe the condition: *'His sweat was like drops of blood...'*. This most often occurs when capillary blood vessels that feed the sweat glands rupture, resulting in blood seeping through the skin. The causes of hematidrosis are severe mental anxiety, extreme stress, and acute fear. Was Jesus suffering anxiety? The word still doesn't sit right with me, but He was certainly experiencing stress, fear, angst and unease – He was after all fully human as well as fully God.

As He cried out to His Father, as He began to sweat blood, Jesus knew He was soon to be arrested; He knew the pain ahead of Him. Jesus was in severe mental, physical and emotional anguish. Yet even in this, Jesus modelled a way for us; He gave everything to God – several times in fact. Jesus repeatedly asked for the, *'cup'* to be taken from Him and yet on each occasion, He also said: *'yet not my will, but yours be done'* (Mark 14:34-41). Jesus trusted in His heavenly Father. This encouraged me to lament to my heavenly Father as well as to trust Him.

But is anxiety a sin? We know Jesus was without sin (Peter and Paul both write of this: *1 Peter 2:22 and 1 Corinthians 5:21*), so if anxiety is a sin, Jesus did not experience it. Perhaps to suffer 'anxiety' is to not be trusting in God wholeheartedly. Yet nor could I escape how at times Jesus suffered in His mind.

In reflecting on Jesus' humanity, I began to allow myself to recognise that yes we can fear and be stressed. In themselves, they are not a sin; they a product of circumstance. We can suffer from an over full mind. Even Jesus did, and not only when He faced His own death. In *John 13:21*, it states; *'he was deeply troubled'*. Jesus also knows of the doubts which can exist in our minds *(Luke 24:38)*.

Thus at times when I felt anxious or stressed, I reasoned this was no longer something I had to feel guilty about. It was part of being a human being living in a fallen world. To be sure there were things I could do to minimise stress and perhaps even anxiety, but for now when I experienced it, I didn't need to feel I was also committing a sin. Praise God. I felt a tiny bit better. Well, all for a moment…

After wrestling some more, I realised it is what we do with our anxiety, stress and fear. It is this which can lead us into sin. Turning away from God, self-medicating in an unhelpful way, becoming angry and the like can all lead us into sinful behaviour. But the actual feeling of 'stress' was perhaps to be human. So, okay…to have such afflictions of the mind, was to be human. Got it. But then, what was I to do with such occurrences? It didn't seem any angels were coming any time soon to strengthen me, so I needed another path.

Mindful of an occasion when Jesus had said to Peter, that he *'did not have in mind the concerns of God but of humans'* (Mark 8:33), I wanted God's best for me. This was surely to have a mind more of God. I wanted Jesus to open my mind just as He had the minds of the two disciples on the road to Emmaus *(Luke 24:45)*.

I came across *Romans 12:2, 'Be transformed by the renewing of your mind…'* and I sought to claim it. Paul it seemed, knew of what it was to have a mind renewed and I longed for this too. Paul calls for a new way of thinking and for a new heart – that of Jesus'. Healing however, didn't seem to be occurring through a one off healing miracle. It seemed I was being called to a longer process.

CHAPTER THIRTY-TWO:
CASTING

As I prayed into my mind, praying it would be healed, I was directed to some words of Peter, who spoke eloquently of God:

> *'Cast all your cares and worries unto me*
> *because I care for you'*
> *(1 Peter 5:7).*

Unlike Peter, I am no fisherman, but I am familiar with the idea of casting, which is to throw the line as far as possible.

Anxiety and worry love to dwell – they almost feed on it. It is interesting to note that both of these words have reference to being strangled or choked. For anyone who has suffered from anxiety or worry, I am sure this resonates. Not being able to breathe is a classic symptom.

God wants us to throw all of our anxiety, worry and cares onto Him. Not some of them but all of them. Now, I do not know about you, but my mind loves to obsess. Even at times when I think I have given everything over to God, my mind loves to revisit them – particularly at night!

To cast all of my cares onto God, seemed to be offering me a choice of what to do with them whenever such thoughts would revisit. I could entertain them or I could cast them on to God. I was being invited to throw them as far as I could, onto God. God doesn't want anyone, other than Himself to take them. Why does He want us to do this? Because He cares for us. He cares for me. He cares for you.

I have come to see that just as to love God is a behaviour and a choice, so it is a choice how I deal with cares and anxiety. I have a choice whether I continue to dwell, or whether I give everything over to God. Recently a friend heard someone say: *'If you have trouble sleeping, don't count sheep, talk to the Shepherd'*.

In being commanded to love God with my mind, I seek to give Him all things of my mind. This includes sleeplessness, stress, anxiety, weariness and anything else which inhibits me from living a life of love. God asks for all of my cares and He gets them - I have come to see the battle belongs to the Lord. What God chooses to do with them, really is up to Him. I am invited to cast, and I am called to love Him with my mind – in whatever state it may be.

CHAPTER THIRTY-THREE:
NO PLASTERS THANK-YOU!

At times my mind has been nothing more than a crumpled mess, but if this was all I could offer to God, then so be it. To offer all of a weary and confused mind is better than not to offer Him anything at all.

In an ideal world, I would have rather offered God a sharp, intelligent, fully functioning mind, but as it is, for a long time, I did not have one to offer. I have come to see God asks for all of my mind; He doesn't ask for a perfect mind, just my mind and all of it.

I knew from the New Testament Jesus was able to heal minds, that He was able to restore people back to their *'right mind' (Luke 8:35)*. I did not think I had the demons which had plagued Legion, but for a long time I had longed to be back in my 'right mind'.

For too many years I had expected a miracle – I had wanted to be healed in a day. I had looked for a sticking plaster when actually there was a lot of surgery to do. Not actual surgery you understand, although at times a lobotomy may not have been out of order.

Too often we do look for a quick fix. God can of course perform an instant miracle, but more often than not, God is into the long haul. This can be seen throughout the Bible.

After their escape from Egypt, Israel wandered for forty years before they entered the Promised land. Before this Moses had spent forty years being a shepherd, living humbly off of the land. Prior to this Moses had been pulled from a river and later pulled from a position of privilege. God spent time forming Moses to be the person God wanted Him to be and He refused to rush!

What of Jacob's son, Joseph? The dreams he had aged 17 years *(Genesis 37)* took 23 years to be fulfilled. Who would have thought aged 17, that before his dreams could come true, he would end up down a well, a slave and in prison?

God takes apprenticeship training seriously and He will use any length of time He sees as necessary.

What of Jesus? He lived on this earth for thirty years, the son of a carpenter, working with wood daily, living with His family, before He took on an active ministry.

A challenge we face is we are living in an ever increasing 'instant' world . As a consequence, we tend to focus on this world alone, squeezing as much as we can into it. Meanwhile God is more interested in eternity – which let's face it is a very long time! God is also interested in us as people and our spiritual formation. Every so often God may 'fast-track' someone but on the whole God's training is slower than ours.

We would do well to remember the words of Psalmist who declared;

> *'A thousand years in your sight are like a day that has just gone*
> *by, or like a watch in the night'*
> *(Psalm 90:4).*

God's timing is perfect. We just often want to speed it up.

Over the last year, as I have come to love God with all of my mind, so I am seeing healing take place. Partly this is in a miraculous sense and for this I am grateful. In a very real sense though, healing is also coming from learning to live with my mind and seeking to love God with it.

The more aware I am of my mind as a separate entity, of my mind being designed to love God, the more I am taking care of it. The purpose of this, is not just for my own sanity, but so that my mind, fragile though it is, can actually love God.

My mind exists and functions, yes to help me through each day, but it also exists to love God. It therefore deserves being looked after better. It is part of our being and needs to be considered within the whole, alongside our heart and soul, but it is also a separate entity.

I realise our minds are all different and as such our capacity to receive and process information differs. I am not threatened by this. In fact I love to marvel at some incredible minds, at how they think and inform others.

Each of our minds are individual, formed by God, for God. Yes, we have a responsibility to look after them and develop them, but we can do this in partnership with God.

Now, I admit, I am not great at working at anything at less than 100%. Call it a high work ethic, call it coming from an agricultural background, but I am useless at working at anything less than full on. I have currently stepped back from my full time employment and yet I can still see this work-ethic within myself even now.

I have a friend who owns a vineyard where there is always something to do. On occasions people offer to go along to help out. Partly I think, in a beautiful part of the countryside, it is because it's a lovely occasion to get together in the fresh air. Partly I think it is also because she is so lovely and makes everyone so welcome. The lunches are incredible and the wine flows generously. Everyone enjoys a natter and a break from time to time. But me, not always.

For some reason, unknown to me I find it really hard to stop. If I can see work to do, I just want to get on and do it. It's not my vineyard, I'm not even being paid to it, yet still there is a drive to push myself! It must be quite annoying for other people who have a better balance of work and rest. There they are sipping a cuppa and enjoying a chat and I'm encouraging them to keep on working – sorry guys, my bad!

Equally my mind does not like to procrastinate. My husband is the king of procrastinators, and my son, it seems, is seeing it as a worthy pursuit. Recently though I have been trying to weigh up the pros and cons of procrastination. In the past I have only seen it as time wasting.

My philosophy is: *'Do what needs to be done and then rest...'.* But perhaps I am wrong. Those who procrastinate do seem to work at a slower pace of life, and often seem to be less stressed – well right up until the deadline! As I reflected (perhaps unkindly) to my husband last week, *'there was no danger of either of my boys ever suffering burnout!'.* Perhaps every so often however, not working at 100% and delaying some things wouldn't be the worst thing in the world.

I have come to see our mind can be our best friend, but also our greatest enemy. Consider for a moment how you feel about yourself. How is your self-esteem, self-image or ego?

Our mind affects how we feel about ourselves. Our mind may dwell on lies we have heard. We may begin to believe we are ugly or stupid or that we deserve being treated badly by others. If we allow them, as they bring up old hurts, our minds can be cruel.

Our minds can try and control us in a way which is not good for us. I now see my mind's limitations for what they are, as well as being more aware of what my mind is capable of. In being invited to love God with my mind, I have come to rejoice, that someone other than me and my mind, is in charge. We were designed to be dependent on God and in loving Him I have come to value and appreciate the workings of my mind all the more.

On one level this has resulted in my having a choice what to do with thoughts. I can let them fester, grow and take charge, or I can give them to God. I can wallow in self-pity and listen and succumb to some lies of my mind or I can lift up my mind, along with my eyes to God *(Psalm 121:1-2)*.

I have realised that as I lift my mind to God, as I lift my eyes to God, it is not possible to also look down. The more I look to God, the more I love God with my mind, so in turn the closer I am becoming to knowing what is right for me. For example, if my thoughts are in opposition to what is taught in the Bible, then increasingly I am trying not to believe them, or act upon them.

Thoughts which are not good for me, may enter my mind, but I do not need to listen to them. I can cast these along with any cares and anxieties onto God. Part of giving attention to my mind, so I may love God with it, has been to evaluate my strengths and weaknesses.

Sadly I am aware one trait of my mind is remembering people's words and faults. Just ask my husband! In the past I have been able to store these up and lash out. This is unkind and this behaviour is not honouring to God. I use the words of the Psalmist to protect me in this:

> 'Set a guard over my mouth, LORD; keep watch over the
> door of my lips'
> (Psalm 141:3).

In asking God's help, by asking God to set a guard over my mouth, I am less likely to say unkind words. In time, I hope to have fewer of these thoughts in the first place. In coming to God in love, I have sensed God's love is making me a nicer person, but also a stronger one.

Through loving God and through becoming more aware of how cruel my mind can be, I now have a choice whether to go my way or God's way. As I love God, the more I am realising, God does not just do this automatically for me.

God wants what is best for us, is loving and full of compassion and forgiveness, but He does not want to make us into robots. The choice of what to fill my mind with and how to use my mind lies with me. God, in His love for us, gives us this responsibility. As I come to God in love, so I am loved more by Him and so I am no longer wanting to be what I once was.

Through God's love and being shown a better way, I am becoming more aware of what I am capable of. In turn I have come to protect myself more. Through prayer, through embracing God's invitation to love Him and through allowing His Holy Spirit to work within me, I am able to become a more likeable person. Certain thoughts may enter my mind but with God's love I have a choice whether I act on them.

CHAPTER THIRTY-FOUR:
SOAPS DON'T ALWAYS CLEAN

In becoming more aware of the influence of things which I allow to enter my mind, I have become more aware of what is good for me or not. I have long stopped watching horror films and psychological thrillers, but I am discovering there is more which is not good for my mind and being.

I have a very active and creative imagination and I do not need to fuel my mind with scary things. I am not saying these are necessarily wrong and I even know of Christians who write in such a genre. For me however, I do not need horror and violence in my mind. What we watch, read and absorb is likely to affect us…

There was an occasion, whilst I was in the Army, when a number of mums came to fight on the playground. Having dropped their children off for school, some-one said something to another and before we knew it, things had kicked off big time. The Military police were called, mums were separated and eventually things calmed down.

There seemed to be two widely contributing factors to this incident. The first of which was that many husbands were on an operational tour. Life is always more fraught and strained if a partner is away, let alone in a conflict zone. Of more interest though, was it seemed all of them had watched an episode of a popular soap opera the evening before. One of the scenes was so dramatic and fuelled with emotion, that it seems the next day some of these women were literally living out the fictional plot.

There is a road close to Brands hatch race circuit, where police after a race, station themselves. More often than not, having watched a race, fuelled with adrenalin and excitement, ordinary car drivers put their foot down too fast. Are not video games often blamed for violent episodes? What we see, do and allow into our minds inevitably has an effect on us.

Dallas Willard says: *'What simply occupies our mind very largely governs what we do'.* xxvi Our mind influences our thoughts and actions, so it makes sense we need to be careful what we put into them. There is so much distraction and confusion in the world, if I can limit this, surely this is a good thing.

The more I come to God, the more I see how much my mind needs renewing, changing, cleaning if you like, so I can see things as I am intended to see them. In coming to love God with my mind, I have become more wary over what I fill it with, lest I too could be led into doing something which is not good for me.

Certain 'sitcoms' and the like have also been losing their appeal for me. Watching people drinking endless cups of coffee or beers, advocating promiscuous sex, no longer holds the interest it once did. Not having a television of course helps in this, but nor would I want one.

It stands to reason the more our mind is filled with God, with His love and His goodness, the more our mind is able to be what it was originally intended to be. With fewer hindrances in our mind, hopefully we will want to be the people God longs for us to be.

In filling my mind with more of God's love and the ways of Jesus, so it is easier to free myself from former habitual patterns of thought. Some people may see this is almost making me into a robot. On the contrary, I see this is liberating me from things which have enslaved me for too long, (*John 8:34* and *Romans 6:6* confirm this for me).

I am not advocating to be a Christian, or in loving God we have to get rid of our television or other forms of technology. Jesus Himself after all relaxed with friends over meals, went for walks and socialised. Coming to God with our all and our mind does not mean stopping doing ordinary things.

For me personally however, coming to love God with my mind has been a journey of coming to know myself. I am becoming more aware of what is good for me and what is not. I am becoming more responsible over what can clutter my mind. Paul himself in speaking to the church at Corinth warned of how our minds can be influenced:

> *'your minds may somehow be led astray from your sincere and*
> *pure devotion to Christ'*
> *(2 Corinthians 11:3).*

I have come to embrace my mind for what it is, with its strengths and limitations. I am called to love God with my mind, not anyone else's. Each of us are created differently, but we all have different imaginations, pressures, responsibilities and circumstances. God longs for my mind to love Him and to be loved by Him.

CHAPTER THIRTY-FIVE:
I WANT TO SEE THE NAIL MARKS!

God seeks us to come with what we have, rather than with what we do not. As I have wrestled with God, I have also become less afraid of questioning and doubt. The latter can frequently seek to occupy our mind.

Some people fear doubt as if to doubt will result in losing their faith. I have come to embrace it. As I doubt and question, so I seek answers. This may result in my being downcast for a while but on every occasion, after a period of doubt and wrestling, I have come back stronger.

I know many people in the Bible were warned not to doubt, not least because nothing is too hard for God, but on some occasions a little doubting has made me stronger.

Thomas, bless him, from his doubts has become forever known as 'doubting Thomas'. Let's consider Thomas, because yes he did doubt. After the disciples spoke of Jesus being resurrected from the dead, Thomas said;

> *'Unless I see the nail marks in his hands and put my finger*
> *where the nails were, and put my hand into his side, I will*
> *not believe'*
> *(John 20:25).*

Let's also consider Jesus' reaction to this. Did Jesus show anger towards Thomas or leave him to his doubts? No! Jesus showed Himself to Thomas and even encouraged him to put his fingers into His wounds. I think a danger with saying 100% we should not doubt, is that when we may do so, we do not think we can bring them to God. Not least because we shouldn't be doubting in the first place. This can often draw us further from God.

I believe God is able to take whatever we throw at Him, warts and all; doubts and all. I believe He would much rather we came to Him with

131

everything. If you do struggle with doubt, Jon Ortberg's book; *'Know doubt'* could be a good place to turn.

On another note, for a while, with an overloaded mind, I could not even listen to the news – everything was just too much for me to process. I wrestled with this (of course), but in the end I had to let it go and just cope with what I could.

In a positive attempt to fill my mind with God and good things, I also now listen to more Christian music than the radio. Alternatively I prefer silence. Once again I am not saying there is anything wrong per-Se with popular music, but for me I came to hear some of the lyrics in a new way. Many songs would be singing of lust rather than love; of affairs rather than life lasting relationships. As I came to love God with all my mind, I felt I had to take more responsibility about what I was putting into it.

If you haven't already put this book down, you may be thinking; 'Oh my, no social media, hardly any television and now not even the radio. Is this girl for real?' I guess you would have to meet me to answer that question. Though perish the thought - for your sake rather than mine!

If you think I wrestle on paper, meet me in person. And this is me writing a year after being as messed up as I once was. I made even less sense then and I was grumpy with it. Mercifully though, God is good. At my husband's ordination, I met up this past weekend with some people from my former parishes. I apologised to a few of them for being so grumpy! A number said they hadn't noticed, yet they all said how much better I now seemed in myself.

All I know is that as I come to lay more things at the cross, I do so not with regret but with relief. There is now more time for other things. With God in the lead, I am becoming less enslaved to things which are not good for me.

CHAPTER THIRTY-SIX:
LET'S BREATHE

As I love God with my mind, I have been encouraged to live more in the moment. I have taken on a more 'simple' approach to life. In turn this has led to me slowing down my pace of life. Living in the moment has helped me to prioritise aspects of my life. This first began during a sabbatical.

In my first week away from parish responsibilities, I literally had to slow my mind down. I even began to cloud watch. I made myself take time to watch clouds. As I did it helped in two ways.

Firstly it reminded me of God my Creator, of His awesomeness! God created something as large and fluffy and beautiful as clouds. They reminded me of my place in the universe. I am loved and valued, yes, but in the grand scheme of things, I am actually very small. Secondly, my mind was so full, it needed wringing out. It needed emptying of much which had filled it. It needed to be free. As I gazed at the clouds, so my mind became more absorbed with God.

An impromptu visit to a beach once, resulted in three children (one of whom was mine), being covered head to toe in mud. They had a great time digging, splashing and rolling, but eventually arriving home, we did have to clean up. It took five washes for their clothes to resemble clean and a lot of scrubbing for themselves to be free of mud.

As I have tried to allow my mind to slow down, I have felt at times it has been as though I am under a hot shower, trying to wash off layers of mud. Layers of busyness which have built up over the years, are gradually washing away. As they do so, there is more room for God and His love to enter and remain.

I have taken recently, to having time when my mind can breathe. This is not the same as emptying my mind, nor is it a biological term.

As an aside, I was pretty bad at biology as it happens. So bad that in every report my biology teacher, Mrs Brown, would write the same thing: *'Tracey assures me she understands but I do not think she does'.* Too right I didn't. I was terrified of her so I was never going to let on either. I scraped through which is more than my husband did in Latin. He was told if you get your name right on the paper you will get 5%. He got 3%!

Allowing my mind to breathe, is to allow myself time to rest (with God). On occasions I have taken to doing something which has not really required my mind to think or process all that much. My husband has been bemused to see me collecting fruit, making jam, collecting wood and chopping it. Still we have pots of yumminess and fuel for the fire, so it's not all bad.

I do not believe it is any accident that many people are able to rest, relax and begin to 'breathe' again outside. Being in God's creation for many people helps them to lift up their eyes. As stunning scenery is enjoyed, as air is breathed, as different sounds of nature comes to our ears, as scent rises to our noses, our heart and spirit can quite literally feel lighter.

Whilst sadly, many people do not always consider the Creator behind such beautiful surrounds, when we do, I believe our minds are able to dwell in God even more. Allowing our minds to dwell in scripture and prayer, to hear of the testimonies of other Christians all of course have a part to play. But sometimes we just need to get outside, not least to be reminded of the magnificence of God; Creator and Lord of all.

As I have picked fruit and chopped wood, I have tried to keep mindful of God. Literally to keep my mind full of God. I have also given thanks for the time to do such things. During such times I have allowed years of busyness, stress and fatigue to slowly fall off of me. This was strangely aided by a move of house.

As my husband took up being collared, we ended up moving to a house which had not been lived in for a while. The interior of the house and the garden needed a lot of work. For two months, I worked non-stop, far from happy at the filth and all the work that was required.

Looking back however, this time enabled my mind to be released from parish responsibilities and the burdens I had carried. It was a time of intense physical and practical work, yet meanwhile my mind was able to rest a little more. This has released me to be able to love God with my mind all the more.

Another important part of the healing of my mind, has been to address road rage. On my son (at the age of 4) developing road rage, I realised it was something I had to work on. I prayed into this and as I love God with my all, I have been prompted to eliminate hurry from my life. This is a work in progress as I am easily tempted back into ways of rushing and striving.

I am grateful that I seem to have been given an interior thermometer to help me gauge the pace of life. This manifests in palpitations. They are a gentle reminder to slow down. Such palpitations remind me I am pushing myself too much. For a time I called this sensation a panic-attack, but the symptoms did not always ring true. I now see that it is more like Jesus knocking on the door of my heart, reminding me of a different way; reminding me to slow down and draw closer to God.

The more familiar I have come with the Bible, the more I see how God has used different parts of different people to interact with Him. For Paul it was the constant reminder of what his thorn in the flesh was; it seems there was acute pain. As Paul experienced this, so he was reminded of God's saving grace.

For Jacob meanwhile, after wrestling with God, so he forever more walked with a limp. Having a hip out of joint was a constant reminder to Jacob of his night of wrestling with God.

Jeremiah too had his own burden to carry. Things, it is fair to say were rarely good for Jeremiah. So much so, he earned himself the title, the 'weeping prophet'. Lamentations was written by him during a particularly bad time in Judah's history. Sin and rebellion abounded, and Jeremiah was left weeping for the nation.

Jeremiah had a choice, he could just cry and weep and continue being full of despair or he could choose to see God in the situation. He chose the latter but more than this, he let 'his mind' remember God (*Lamentations 3:21-26*). As Jeremiah says;

> *'Yet this I call to mind, and therefore I have hope: Because of the Lord's great love we are not consumed, for his compassion's never fail'*
> *(Lamentations 3:21-22).*

He gave time to his mind, and this gave him hope. Through recalling who God truly is, through remembering God's love, compassion and faithfulness, Jeremiah found his mind more at ease.

Jeremiah wept yes, but also he loved God with his mind, with his all.

Trusting in God, trusting in His very nature and His promises have become key for me. For example what of the glorious promise found in *Isaiah*:

> *'You will keep in perfect peace those whose minds are steadfast,*
> *because they trust in you'*
> *(Isaiah 26:3).*

In keeping his mind focused on God, so Isaiah was being led into peace.

Earlier I spoke of Paul's encouragement for us to be transformed by the renewing of our mind. Partly this for me, has been to fill my mind with more of God. I have given more time to reflect on who God is and what He does. This starts with the Bible and continues as I seek to dwell in what I have read - meditatively.

Throughout the Bible, we can see the Sovereignty of God. We see how God *'...is the same yesterday and today and forever' (Hebrews 13:8).* God is everlasting. God is sovereign. We are not God.

> *'For my thoughts are not your thoughts, neither are your ways my*
> *ways,' declares the LORD. As the heavens are higher than the*
> *earth, so are my ways higher than your ways and my thoughts*
> *than your thoughts'*
> *(Isaiah 55:8-9).*

Max Lucado's book: *'anxious for nothing'* which reflects on Paul's words in Philippians 4:6-7, encourages everyone to look to God as Sovereign Lord in all things. As Lucado says:

> *'The mind cannot at the same time be full of God and full of*
> *fear'.* [xxviii]

This is a hard call indeed, and yet as Max reveals, with God we can do this. As we do so, so we can become less anxious and more in line with God's perfect plan for us.

Put simply, God is God and we are human beings. This does not threaten me, far from it. It brings me a sense of relief and peace. I am coming to know my place in the world and consequently I seek to come under God as Lord in all things. If anything, it makes life easier as in loving One God, I am released from divided allegiances.

The more I am able to dwell in God alone, the less reliant on human praise I become, the less dependent I am on storing treasure in worldly goods. In turn I am no longer as anxious and stressed as I once was. My mind is becoming free from that which formerly enslaved it.

CHAPTER THIRTY-SEVEN:
THE BLUE SCREEN OF DEATH!

I wrote the previous chapter truly believing it and trying to live it, and yet I am sad to admit I still try and push my mind too far. I knew as I was writing the last chapter that I needed some time just with God. I should have put the writing down and spent some time purely in God's Presence in quiet.

Rather than turning off the computer though I thought I could just do another hour. Whilst I am not saying that God then made my computer crash, crash it did. A blue screen appeared with lots of words which I couldn't make sense of.

In any computer crisis I do what I always do, I yell to my husband so loudly that he thinks I have stumbled upon a murderer! I asked him what the screen meant and he informed me it was the *'blue screen of death'!* My unsaved work of the past half hour was lost, so in a way there had been a death!

I took the hint, I turned the computer off and I went for a walk with God. It was raining. I do not like the rain and I can get cross with it - not as much as the people of Judah at the time of Ezra *(Ezra 10:9)*, but annoyed enough. On this occasion however, as the drops of rain thundered down upon my umbrella, I smiled at the second chance I had been given to live life.

Here I was even writing of being called to love God with my all, and how this is including living at a different pace, and yet all too quickly I too can forget. All too easily I can try and power through the day working just a little too hard, rather than giving myself to God. So as I walked, getting more than a little damp, I thanked God for so many good things in my life. Not least, I thanked Him that I was His child, His very own special child.

As I walked along trying to shield myself from the rain, I noticed some plants in the shade. Well, I say plants, they were more like wilted, spindly excuses for weeds. Away from both the sun and the rain they were only just surviving. As I looked at these languishing plants, I thanked God again for my second chance.

Too often we seek shade from the sun and refuge from the rain and yet these plants desperately needed both. I prayed I would not seek shelter from God's discipline or run away from His commands. They all exist so I can flourish and live the life intended by God.

Did God cause my computer crash? Who knows! As I walked though, I was reminded by God that I had been working through lunches to try and write. I had begun to strive again.

Did God last month cause Jack's computer to pick up a virus? It took even him, a computer programmer by trade, twelve hours to repair it. All I do know is that for Jack, he found a sermon out of it – not least that he needed to depend less on his computer skills and more on God.

The 'blue screen of death' reminded me there was more to life than trying to get this book finished. I am worth more to God, than this writing. I am His child. He wants me to spend time with Him – just Him. So for as long as the day allowed me, that's what I did.

CHAPTER THIRTY-EIGHT:
THE MIND OF CHRIST

During this journey of discovery, as far as I have been able, I have tried to love God with my mind. I am learning to take responsibility for it. More recently I have taken more care of my mind. I am becoming more mindful of what I put in it as well as giving it time to breathe.

At times however, I have almost become afraid of my mind, of its power and control over me and others. I have had to embrace my mind for good and for bad. I have had to acknowledge God has given me my mind to love Him.

As I come to love Him with it, so I am seeing not only how I can live with my mind, but how I'm able to live with Jesus' mind too. We are told by Paul in *1 Corinthians 2:16; 'we have the mind of Christ'*. This is not an off the cuff remark. Paul speaks of this also *in Philippians 2:5*:

> *'In your relationships with one another, have the same mind set as Christ Jesus'*.

As Paul continues to write in *Philippians 2*, so we can see the mind of Christ. A mind which allowed Himself to be a servant for us and to go to the cross. The more I have come to love God with my own mind, the more I have come to know of Jesus' through God's word. In turn, the more I sense Jesus' mind set is able to dwell within me. Thankfully this is less about me working and striving and more about allowing God's Holy Spirit to dwell within me.

As Paul comments in *Philippians 2:13; 'for it is God who works in you to will and to act in order to fulfil his good purpose'*. God longs to be at work in us, so why would we not let Him? Through God's Holy Spirit, through allowing His Spirit to dwell within us, so we are able to be drawn to know more of the mind of Christ.

God's Holy Spirit can draw us closer to Jesus, to His words, to the way He lived on earth.

For the Spirit God gave us does not make us timid, but gives us
power, love and self-discipline'
(2 Timothy 1:7).

Quite simply with God's Holy Spirit I am able to function better. Paul speaks of God's Spirit being able to give us power, love and self-discipline. The latter, 'self-discipline', is something many of us struggle with. If we had more, surely more of us would be the weight we should be and we would go to bed early enough to get our 8 hours and credit cards wouldn't be so full. If we had more self-discipline, many things we regret wouldn't have happened in the first place.

Through God's Holy Spirit, I believe He is helping me with self-discipline. This in turn is helping my mind to heal. When I commit to God's Holy Spirit all of the things I long to do, so He helps me to discern the best way ahead. This is not God taking control, rather it is me realising I need His Spirit to help in all things, including in my mind.

Within our minds dwell our thoughts. These in turn can become actions. As I love God, so I am wanting to give Him my thoughts. I am wanting to allow my thoughts, my very thinking to be influenced by the mind of Christ Himself.

On reading the Gospels, we see the mind and thoughts of Christ. Love motivated Jesus' thoughts and mind. Imagine how different our world would be, if Jesus had woken up one Thursday morning nearly two thousand years ago and thought, 'I think I'll stay in bed today'.

Imagine if Jesus had got up and gone to the Garden of Gethsemane, and had decided to not only allow Peter to cut off the ear of the high priest's servant, but He too had taken up a sword Himself.

Imagine on trial if Jesus had used His mind and thoughts to talk His way out of it.

Imagine if Jesus on the cross had leapt down or called upon angels to rescue Him.

All of these actions would have started with a thought, within His mind. Jesus may have had these thoughts (we do not know), yet He did not act upon them. His mind was made up to love us. His mind was totally focused on loving God and loving us that day. As a consequence He defeated death and became a Saviour for the world.

As I am coming to love God with my mind, so I have been encouraged more and more to depend on God's strength and not just my own. I have become encouraged to fight with God's weapons and not just rely on myself. As Paul so astutely reveals:

> 'The weapons we fight with are not the weapons of the world. On the contrary, they have divine power to demolish strongholds. We demolish arguments and every pretension that sets itself up against the knowledge of God, and we take captive every thought to make it obedient to Christ'
> (2 Corinthians 10:4-5).

I long to take every thought and not only give it to Jesus but make it obedient to Christ. I know there is a long road ahead. Furthermore I cannot do this alone and nor does God want me to. Rather we have been given a gift - God's Holy Spirit.

It is through the Holy Spirit, that my mind can be renewed and transformed. Rather than this being through my own works, it has been through making myself available to love God and to be loved by Him. God's Holy Spirit is helping me to develop a better understanding of so many things.

Time and again we see people within the Bible asking for understanding:

> 'Give me understanding, so that I may keep your law and obey it'
> (Psalm 119:34).

To understand comes from our mind. As I draw closer to God, so I can see Him giving me His understanding, rather than just my own. As Jesus spoke to His disciples after His resurrection, was it not their minds He opened: 'Then he opened their minds so they could understand the Scriptures.' (Luke 24:45).

As we love God with our mind, so it can be increasingly filled with God. Our minds can focus attention onto God. With our minds we can choose to follow God; to obey Him and His commands. It is our mind which sets the path for our heart and body. It was Jesus' mind, accompanied by His will, which kept Him quiet both at His trial and when He was hanging on the cross. Jesus' mind set the path for His will, for His heart and body.

Through His Holy Spirit, as we come to God through prayer and through reading His word, we become available to His purpose for our lives. In the past I have tried to almost master my mind, but I have come to see this cannot be done by force, but through surrender.

CHAPTER THIRTY-NINE:
HANDS UP!

To surrender is often seen as a weakness. To surrender is often seen as giving up, as being defeated. In surrendering to God however, I have found freedom to live. Rather than it being a sign of weakness, I have come to see this 'surrendering' took strength.

It took courage to acknowledge I was at the end of my resources and I needed help. I was on a downhill collision course. I could either surrender to God or give up completely.

True freedom lies in restriction: boundaries can be positive and protecting rather than restraining. Discovering what is not good for me, and what is better for me, is enabling me to enjoy the best of life.

No longer am I inclined to do things which are bad for me. Rather, I cling to the sovereignty of God. He created me, and as such knows best. I have had to acknowledge how my own willpower has weaknesses and restrictions. Paul sums it up in Ephesians:

> 'You were taught, with regard to your former way of life, to put off your old self, which is being corrupted by its deceitful desires; to be made new in the attitude of your minds; and to put on the new self, created to be like God in true righteousness and holiness'
> (Ephesians 4:22-24).

This can only be done by making myself available to God and through receiving His Holy Spirit. As we do this, so God Himself can make our minds new, renewed and transformed; to be more like Him and less like our wrongful ways.

Paul is literally saying we need to put on a new self. For far too long, I had seen this as something I had to do myself. In my exhaustion I felt it was something I did not have the energy for. God does not however, expect us to do this in our own strength. God wants to clothe us with His Holy Spirit.

Paul is calling for a partnership of our inner self and God's Holy Spirit. Through loving God with my mind I am more open to this happening. As I begin to do this, I am also becoming aware of how God is even using the fragility of my mind for growth.

Few people enjoy suffering and yet as a consequence of living in a fallen world, sadly it is a daily occurrence for many people. If you had said to me five years ago: *'Would you like to grow closer to God?'* I would have instantly said: *'Yes, of course'.* If you had also said, it would involve suffering and my becoming broken...well the conversation may have been longer.

As I look back though, whilst I wouldn't have chosen what I have endured, I am truly thankful for how I have grown closer to God in it all. Growth has come through adversity.

Even as a Christian, one does not become exempt from suffering – just ask Jesus! Sorry to all 'prosperity gospel' preachers – such teaching just seems contrary to so much of the experience of those in the Bible and in the world at large. I have come to see, whilst God does not ordain suffering, on occasions He does permit it. We see this most significantly in the book of Job (more on this later in Chapter 45).

Whilst the words of Paul may seem hard for those in the midst of suffering to swallow, I do believe in them. Paul said; *'And we know that in all things God works for the good of those who love him...' (Romans 8:28).* We may not always understand why we are going through what we are. We may not even see a way out. However, God is more interested in eternity than just our life on earth.

I have come to be thankful for what I have been through as I believe it has made me a better person, more patient, more loving and more at peace. This is God's doing, more than mine. My part was to make myself available. This has come through loving Him with my mind.

CHAPTER FORTY:
PAPER CUPS

Some people have asked why I would want to write in the style I am. They have felt it is putting my hurt and weaknesses out there, for all to see. I guess simply I am thankful for God being there for me. I am not afraid to make myself vulnerable. I am not ashamed to admit I could not do things merely in my own strength. In addition I long to share God's glorious invitation for us all.

The apostle Paul knew what it was to suffer and he shared this with many churches. His suffering puts my own to shame. Paul was whipped, beaten with rods, shipwrecked, stoned, and in danger from many people *(2 Corinthians 11:24-26)*. Throughout his afflictions however, Paul had confidence in God. To the church in Corinth he said;

'We are hard pressed on every side, but not crushed; perplexed, but not in despair; persecuted, but not abandoned; struck down, but not destroyed'
(2 Corinthians 4:8).

In a nutshell, Paul knew life was bad but it could have been a whole lot worse. He at least knew God was with him throughout it all. Before this verse, Paul wrote;

'But we have this treasure in jars of clay to show that this all-surpassing power is from God and not from us'
(2 Corinthians 4:7).

Paul knew it was all about God and less about him. We are all able to have treasure within clay jars. We are able to have Jesus, God's Holy Spirit within ourselves. I would like to be so bold to say we all have cracks too. There will be times when we are not living life to the full. Not everyone however, may admit it, not even to themselves.

I am grateful (now), for the cracks that appeared in my own life. One reason I want to share my own journey is because through these cracks, Jesus shines. His love radiates through the pain and suffering I have gone through. I have if you like been broken, but gracefully broken. God is restoring me, day by day.

As I come to love God with all of my mind, increasingly I believe this is for my own good. As I come to God with my mind, so I am encouraged to allow my mind to rest. In making myself more available to God and seeking to live according to His plans rather than just those of the world, so I am able to live more as God intends. In my own life, before this could happen I needed to discover and understand a part of me which had been crying out for too long...please let me introduce you...

***

*'**Love the Lord your God** with all your heart and **with all your soul** and with all your mind and with all your strength'*

***

CHAPTER FORTY-ONE:
NOT SO MUCH PANTING, AS WHIMPERING

After twenty years of singing songs about my soul, you would have thought I had an inkling of what my soul was. From Charles Wesley (1707-1788) to Paul Oakley (1996), with Simeon Butler Marsh (1798-1875) in between, along with millions of others, *Jesus lover of my Soul'* has been a popular theme for songs. The Psalmists had sang of and from their soul for much longer (*Psalm 103*).

Matt Redman in 1993, published an album entitled; *'Wake up my soul'*, which was roughly the time my own soul indeed was waking up. This said, I never asked anyone or have since heard anyone speak of their soul.

Perhaps no-one had spoken of their soul because it was so obvious. In learning to drive a car, you kind of know you are going to have to sit inside the car. Likewise in baking a cake, everyone knows you need a cooker. It's all rather obvious.

In all of my years of ministry, in spite of running numerous courses designed for people to ask questions, I was never asked what a soul was. Does this mean that everyone else already knew? Or, perhaps a little like me, they just hadn't given it much thought.

If I am honest the most I had ever heard on our soul, was in an episode of The Simpsons where Bart sold his soul. It is often an expression we hear; *'He's sold his soul...to the devil'*. Through some choice made or action taken, people are seen as selling their soul.

Until recently I would even have found it hard to describe what our soul is. For twenty years I had been in a relationship with God, yet the main part of me which was doing all of this, was something which I had given little attention.

In 1995, on May 6th I became a Christian. I repented of my former life, and I invited God's Spirit to live within me. Since then I have asked God for a continual re-filling of His Holy Spirit. However whilst I had been 'busy' inviting Jesus in, I had overlooked what was there all along, for God alone – my soul.

Is it any wonder, how after twenty years, (in the words of the psalmist), my soul had started to pant *(Psalm 42)*? The Psalmist pens:

> *'As the deer pants for streams of water, so my soul pants for you, my God. My soul thirsts for God, for the living God. When can I go and meet with God?'*
> *(Psalm 42:1-2).*

Actually that's not fair, my soul had started to pant many years before, but I had mistaken this for grief and then exhaustion. Losing six relatives including my father in the space of 18months, at best, is careless and at worst devastating.

Cumulative stress and compassion fatigue seemed to fit the bill for what I was going through. My mind and heart had certainly been stretched. It was only when my counsellor didn't really know what to do with me, that I realised the issue was not just of my mind or body, but of something else.

Initially I wondered if this was to do with my spirit or God's Holy Spirit, but eventually I came to see it was actually my soul. It had been crying out for far too long.

During the most difficult year of my life, I felt like a multi-layered 'pass the parcel'. Every time a layer was taken off, I thought I had got to the prize of beginning to feel better. Little did I know just how many layers I had to unwrap before I got to the 'gift'. Finally the music stopped for the last time.

My soul had had enough of panting, of whimpering and crying, instead it just roared. I am actually smiling as I write this, because on the day it truly found its voice, I endured a really noisy day.

CHAPTER FORTY-TWO:
OPENING A WINDOW

It was early September and on a rare day off, with a child at school and nothing in my diary, I aimed to spend a day quietly with God. I started off in the back garden and all was well for a moment – that is, until a chain saw started up next door and showed no sign of stopping.

So, I took off in the car to what is usually a remote quiet spot. On this day however, a rare bird had been spotted and every 'twitcher' within a 20 mile radius came to see it – curiously all in loud cars, with clicking camera's. I found no peace, just frustration and anger.

I was incensed – here I was trying to spend time with God and all I was getting was noise. My heart was racing, I had a tingling in my hands and my breathing was all over the place. I had what felt like a massive weight pressing down on me. I was tired and exhausted to my core.

Full of grumpiness, I picked up my son from school, and although he was a good antidote for a while, I knew all was not well. Even the colour he normally brought to my life was fading fast. On the recommendation of my counsellor and at the invitation of a senior work colleague, I booked to go on a Retreat. I just had to get away and be with God somehow, somewhere.

Away on my first Retreat, in twenty years, what two books fell off my shelf into my desperate hands? *'Know doubt'* and *'Soul Keeping'* by Jon Ortberg. I had not bought the latter because of any particular interest, rather it was the only Jon Ortberg book I had not yet read. I read *'Know doubt'* in a state of exhaustion. By the end of the week, with a little more energy, I started to read, *'Soul Keeping'*.

Wow, opening this book was like opening a window to my soul. Even now I am blown away by how life changing this one book was to me. It spoke of my soul, revealed what my soul is and what its purpose is. In fact, if you want to purely know more about your soul, put this book down, grab a copy and read it.

On purpose I am not quoting from it because I know if I started, I would quote from the first page and finish at the last. Any royalties I may get would then have to go to Jon! Sorry, Jon, but I have given you an almighty plug! Hey, is this product placement? If so, maybe Jon owes me some money?!

Back to my soul - as I found my soul, embraced my soul and allowed my soul to be with God, I was being opened to a new way of being. This coincided with the release of Matt Redman's incredibly popular song; 'Bless the Lord O my Soul'. I now had a book informing my mind and a song to help anchor my soul, in God once and for all.

My counsellor - I say that and it does sound like a grand term - she put up with me for only eight sessions but I am grateful. Anyway she had never wanted me to stick a plaster on what I was going through. I was desperate for a quick fix and although she could never really put her finger on what I was going through, she knew it was a process and not an overnight cure.

I don't think either us imagined this was going to involve me finding my soul and giving it a voice. Just as Bart Simpson discovered on selling his soul, how much he needed it, I came to realise our soul is not ours to sell or ignore.

Our soul is created by God for God. Our soul is not something to find or something to chase after. As our being forms, we are given the gift of our soul for our good and for God. Our role is to acknowledge it as a gift and then to care for it.

I began to listen to some part of me which I could not quite identify. My mind was weary and exhausted. I didn't have any strength and my heart didn't know which way to turn. Yet there was some other part of me, which was trying to be heard. I could tell it was battered and tired but it was quietly determined. It was the part of me which wouldn't give up, it wouldn't give in.

My counsellor on several occasions had asked after my inner core. On the whole it seemed strong. I had never wanted to harm myself; I wanted to live. I wanted to be there for my son; I wanted to be well. If I am honest I wanted to be well again so I could continue to work at the pace I was used to. God however, had other plans.

Some part of me, deep within, always believed God was in this muddle. Although I had often been hearing.... silence...I knew God had not left me, that He was still real. Even when I doubted and wondered if God was really there, my soul never gave up. As Thomas Aquinas once said:

'the neediness of our souls is a pointer to God'.

My soul would not let this go. In its neediness my soul could only find rest in God. Our souls crave to be with God.

For too long my soul had been allowed to accept second best; it knew of Jesus, but it had for too long not enjoyed knowing Jesus. My soul had been designed for more, it had been created to dwell with God forever and instead it was being left to shrivel in the ordinariness of life.

CHAPTER FORTY-TWO:
'EINE HEISSE SCHOKOLADE'

Once whilst on holiday Jack got locked in the loo! Now, having been married for several years, Jack spending a long time in the loo was not unusual, so I had gone to sit in the sun at some distance. After a while I thought I could hear his voice, but initially I ignored it.

Eventually this voice seemed to be getting louder, and even by his standards he was taking his time. As I wandered back to the loo's in the car park, the words: *'babe...BAbe... TracEY...TRACEY'* were getting louder and more fractious.

Jack had now been locked in a cramped cubicle for over half an hour. The lock had come off in his hand, and the door would not budge. The loo's had not been cleaned in a long while either. The only gap was 2 inches above the door, where I could now see his hand waving limply. I ought to say, we were also on a mini-break, as he was recovering from having had his appendix out.

By now, Jack was very hot and sweaty, and feeling quite queasy. Not only did it take quite a while for anyone to pass by, the few people who did didn't seem to speak English. We were after all staying in a remote part of East Germany.

The extent of my German, ran to 'eine heisse Schokolade', 'ein Weisswein, bitte', and 'ohne Zwiebeln'. Whilst I would have quite liked a hot chocolate, and by this time I felt in need of a glass of white wine, none of this was of much use to Jack. My final phrase of German, 'no onions', was of no use to either of us.

Through good old hand gestures, a man eventually understood I was waiting for someone trapped in the loo. It took eleven people and a screw driver to get Jack out. By the time he was freed, he looked like he'd been in a sauna.

My soul had been crying out initially limply, but then all the more fervently, until I could ignore it no more. I didn't need eleven Germans and a screwdriver to rescue me, all I needed was God and some time to listen to Him and my soul.

A challenge for our soul is that it often has to shout all the louder to be recognised. Our body lets us know when it is hungry and we can identify this. On being tired our body often wants to sleep. It over-rides all else, just so that it can rest.

Our mind too on the whole can get our attention. When our mind has had enough we may receive a headache, weariness or some other mental health alert. We can become aware of temptations which abound, by experience or through warnings.

Incidentally, as I mention 'temptation', it is important to say being tempted is not a sin in itself. What we choose to do with a thought however, can become a sin, but being tempted is not. The more however, we give in to temptation, the more it may become a habit, which can become a sin.

Back to our soul...it can be hard to locate or identify. We cannot really see it and even if it starts raising its voice, we may confuse it with other parts of us.

I also think there is a degree of individuality about our souls: each soul will speak to us in a different way. Equally our soul will be satisfied in a different way to other people. With God yes, but just as we are created with a different character and personality to those around us, so the way we draw closer to God, will be slightly different.

Every person is unique and each of us needs to work out what feeds our own soul. This may of course involve some sacrifice of other things, but actually I have only found I am better off for it. For me personally I have been drawn into more quiet, into silence. For this to happen, I have sacrificed some things which I once enjoyed.

So I watch half an hour or less of something at the end of the day rather than two or more hours! Well if it means I go to bed earlier and spend more time with God at the end and beginning of the day, well this surely has to be better.

People spend their lives moaning how rubbish television is anyway, or how social media consumes them, and yet few seem able to break free from the chains. The peace and rest I have come to experience is enabling me to become more aware of God's Presence. This far outweighs any form of 'entertainment', which in the past I had hoped would relax me.

Our souls link us with God. I have come to not underestimate this. My soul is not satisfied with mediocrity or escapism. I have now started to listen to my soul, but before I could do this I had to stop and become more aware of it. For too long I had ignored my soul, all to my detriment.

In the end my soul spoke to me through getting physical. I had originally considered the pounding in my chest, a quickening of breath and tingling in my hands, to be panic or anxiety attacks. This all said though, such 'episodes' never really made sense to me. Nor did they become completely debilitating, as I could over-ride them and function. All be it later I would be exhausted! I now think any such occurrence was actually my soul trying to get through to me.

Now of course this doesn't sound very loving or even kind, but quite simply I think my soul had run out of options. I blamed everything for how I was feeling and living. Everything that is bar the very part of me which was crying out the most. Eventually my soul made itself known.

Having spent the last year being kinder to myself and listening to my soul I have come to identify when these 'episodes' take place. They are less related to times of apprehension or stress. Rather my heart quickens and I feel a heaviness when I have not spent significant time with God. This has been a fairly recent self-diagnosis.

Believe me, in the past, as my heart quickened and my breathing became irregular, I would say to God, *'Why now?'* or *'Oh come on, please, there is no need for this. I have a really busy day and I could just do without feeling this way'*.

On every occasion when I ask God these questions of *'Why now?'*, I sense the same answer: *'Because I love you'*. It's as if my soul so wants to be with God that when I do not give it actual and significant time to do so, it rebels and yells. I have to start my day off with God in silence for a significant period – without it, the day does not go well. I say, *'have to'*, but in every sense I also want to. No longer can I just rush into the day.

Every so often during the night I still remain restless in sleep, but on the whole it is now because my soul wants to spend more time with God. This may either be because I haven't spent much time with God the previous day or more likely because something is going on which needs to be prayed over and wrestled with. Sometimes even now, it is only at night when my attention can be gained.

Such a sensation also seems to be a pointer as to when I am pushing things too far, when I am striving in my own strength and not depending on God. If you like it seems to be the thorn in my flesh, which Paul spoke of in *2 Corinthians 12:7-9*. But hey, it's a thorn which brings me closer to God, so it's a pretty good thorn. By the way in no way am I saying it is an actual thorn like Paul's, it is just a sense I have. If it brings me back to God, then this is surely a good thing.

Sometime ago, a friend had a new puppy which did nothing but bark. It was so extreme they took it to the vet. All of the barking was not only stressing the family out, but also the dog. The advice they were given was to bang a tray when the dog started barking. The idea was to startle the dog, so it would stop barking. Over time the dog not only stopped barking when she heard the bang, she stopped when she saw her owner with the tray. After several months, the dog stopped barking excessively altogether and was all the happier for it. The dog had got into such a pattern of barking, (often without reason), that it needed a shock to bring it back to reality. By jumping at the sound of the tray being hit, the dog was jolted to stop barking and to be free.

My soul (if you like), through causing a heaviness in my chest, brings me back to God. For this I am eternally grateful.

CHAPTER FORTY-THREE:
A CHILD OF GOD

On discovery of my soul, I found I had just enough energy and brain power left to look into what my soul truly was. To my astonishment, I came to see, my soul was the part of me created and designed for eternity. It was the part of me created by God for God.

Our soul is the eternal part of us designed by God for Him, to be with Him. Our soul it seems can wrestle with us and is eternally dissatisfied unless it is with God. Dallas Willard makes sense of it when he says;

'We are, all of us, never-ceasing spiritual beings with a unique eternal calling to count for good in God's great universe'. [xxix]

Our soul is always thirsty – for God. Our soul is relentless in pursuit of God. No matter how I may have tried to fill my life with other things, my soul accepts nothing other than God. Anything else may seem to satisfy for a moment but this allusion is only temporary.

We are spiritual beings and we have a soul, which for a limited time only, is bound within our body. It seems ironic how we spend so much time and money on our looks, on our body, on our hair, on what we wear, on our achievements, when all of these things will pass away soon enough. Only our soul will remain.

Another incredible aspect is how God longs for us and waits for us.

As I began to find my soul, so I began to want to care for it. The part of me created for God alone deserved to be both loved and healed. It would however, be some time before I felt able to love God with my soul. Prior to this happening, I had to discover more of what it was. I had allowed my soul a voice; now I had to listen to what it was saying. Curiously some of this came through a verse left on a card on my pillow, at the retreat centre.

The words of *1 John 3:1* washed over me with waves of love:

> *'See what great love the Father has lavished on us, that we should
> be called children of God!'*

It was like coming to God for the first time. The word, *'lavished'*, as I reflected on it, washed over me like a refreshing shower. I could quite literally feel the aches and pains of the past few years come tumbling down. My soul was beginning to...breathe more easily.

For several weeks it was like becoming a Christian all over again. I drew closer to God, enjoying His Presence and His love. I craved for my soul to be with God.

As I spent time away on retreat that week, I knew this was of God. I say this, because one evening in a highly liturgical service (one of the Book of Common Prayer no less), I sensed God's Holy Spirit upon me. I say this because liturgy usually turns me away from God, rarely towards. My soul was becoming in union with God in all things.

I felt a peace deep within, which was more than me just relaxing after a meal I had not cooked. My soul, filled with God's Holy Spirit, was breathing. For the first time in a long while holding onto promises of God, I felt my soul was lifting up its eyes to the hills *(Psalm 121:1)*...I sensed hope.

For a while all was well. I imagined my soul was like an invisible organ in my body waiting to be with God, coming alive and rejoicing as it was now spending time with God. And for a time I didn't need to know all that much more about my soul, it was enough that it was no longer crying out so much. As I turned away from other distractions, my soul was enjoying being with God.

CHAPTER FORTY-FOUR:
MORE THAN 21 GRAMS

My soul enjoyed being with God and all was well. But, me being me couldn't just let it rest there. I had to look into what my soul was and where it resided.

I came across some studies of our body after death, which claimed our body became lighter as we died. It was suggested that our souls weigh 21 grams. Dr. Duncan MacDougall led the studies.[xxx]

As our soul is not visible, in a very real sense it is hard to locate it. An X-Ray doesn't pick up the presence of a soul, yet few people would deny their existence. We can see the effects and impact of souls all around us. I knew my soul was thirsting: wanting to be made known, wanting to be heard.

In order to care for my soul, and for it to be with God as He intended, I had to understand it more. How could I begin to love God with my soul if I wasn't even quite sure what it was. Whilst understanding the soul as some invisible part of me, hidden within me for God and God alone made sense; it seemed to be only part of the picture. Do we have a soul in a body or are we a body in a soul? I needed to allow God's own word to speak into this.

In one sense I wanted to just enjoy my soul, because after all, does it matter whether you know what something is and how it functions so long as it works? I do not know how a washing machine works or a cooker come to that, but I am just grateful when I turn them on, they do.

My soul though, had been panting for such a long time that for it to be truly healed, it had to be understood. I wanted to do more than survive; I longed to thrive and to flourish.

My 'go-to' is always the Bible. Imagine my surprise to see how often writers referred to the soul. The Psalmists speak of their soul a great deal. The soul is seen as yearning and fainting for God *(Psalm 84:2)*. It is designed to search for God. It is always hungry and thirsty *(Psalm 63:1; 143:6; 33:20; 25:1; 103:1-2, 22; 63:8; 62:1)*. Our souls belong to God.

Even ordinary people, such as a fisherman turned preacher, spoke of their soul. Peter in his first letter speaks of; *'the salvation of your souls' (1:9)*, the *'war against your soul' (2:11)*, and how we should all turn *'to the Shepherd and Overseer of your souls' (2:25)*. I think for years I had read the Bible and just overlooked the word *'soul'*.

Through further study I came to see I had been suffering from 'acedia' – a weariness of soul: an inability to delight in life. In a word I was 'languishing'. I came to see the key for me was to listen to and feed my soul. This I have discovered is no easy task, but it is worthwhile trying.

Our soul is always hungry; it is insatiable, it is needy. I liken it to a new born baby who seems to be constantly in need. A baby needs to be fed, changed, fed again, changed again, loved, washed, comforted, encouraged to sleep and then everything all over again, for what seems forever!

Our soul, it is true, is demanding, but not in a bad way. It has a greater need to love than to be loved. Our soul longs to love God and it needs to be loved by God but it does not however, need to be loved by ourselves. Being loved by God is more than enough *(Psalm 42:11; 62:1)*.

Our soul in no way looks to become an idol to be cared for and worshipped. Am I bold enough to suggest this may be one reason why there is so much disquiet within us and our contemporary western culture? People may be aware of their soul and in many ways may be trying to feed it, but they are doing so from within themselves.

A Day's 'pampering' may relax our bodies and even ease our minds but it can never feed our soul. God gave us a soul for Him and it is only through being loved by Him that our souls will ever be satisfied.

Our soul longs to live in the present, in the Presence of God. Our hearts and minds often live in the future or more often the past. Our soul meanwhile wants to live with God now.

Our soul only wants what is good for us, hence it hungers and longs for God more and more. On no account will our soul ever accept second best, EVER! Our souls are living for their ultimate destination, of being with God.

Our souls are designed not to find this world perfect. They are designed for heavenly perfection. Understanding this has helped me to accept my dissatisfaction, disappointment and frustration on earth.

As Paul says in *Philippians: 'Our citizenship is in heaven' (3:20)*. I guess that's why our souls cry out a lot; the place they find themselves (in our body), is only temporary. They are always aware of somewhere better.

As well as our soul focusing on wanting to be with God, so they remind us this earth is not all there is. Equally however, our souls are not just for heaven; our souls are alive here on earth and they want to be part of our life.

Our souls help keep us heaven focused: God focused. They are totally preoccupied with God. To become content on earth or in our body is to go against their design. As Paul says;

> *'...as long as we are at home in the body we are away from the Lord. For we live by faith, not by sight. We are confident, I say, and would prefer to be away from the body and at home with the Lord'*
> *(2 Corinthians 5:6-8).*

CHAPTER FORTY-FIVE:
BEING PELTED WITH STONES

There is a curious incident in the book of *2 Samuel*. King David is weary from family strife. He faces rebellion from his son Absalom, who wants the throne. If this is not enough, a relative of Saul comes against him, pelting him and his officials with stones. Having killed Goliath in his youth, no-one more than David knew how dangerous throwing stones was!

Interestingly though King David does not allow his officials to retaliate against Shimei. Perhaps David's own conscience had been pricked. Rather than having Shimei killed, David allows him to keep cursing and pelting him with stones and dirt. King David's days of popularity seemed a distant dream.

In *2 Samuel 16:14* the writer alerts us to just how deeply life and these incidents of strife had affected David:

> *The king and all the people with him arrived at their destination
> exhausted. And there he refreshed himself'.*

The word used for *'refreshed'*, refers to more than just drink, food and sleep. It refers to the *'soul'*. The word *'nephash'* – *'the soul'*, which refers also to taking breath, to sustaining oneself. The same word *'nephash'* is used in *Exodus 31:17*, where God speaks of being refreshed, resting on the seventh day.

The longing of a soul can only be satisfied in God alone. The refreshment David needed went beyond sustenance for his body, it included his soul. There was a spiritual dimension to his weariness. Time and again David found strength (for his soul) in the Lord *(1 Samuel 30:6)*, and after yet another day of strife David's soul was weary.

Leading a busy life time and again David faced a lot of stress. He led a busy life and faced trauma, yet in the Lord he was strengthened and his soul was restored. David says:

'I remember the days of long ago; I meditate on all your works
and consider what your hands have done. I spread out my hands
to you; I thirst for you like a parched land'
(Psalm 143:5-6).

Time and again, David looked to the Lord to refresh his soul. As he did so however, he did not just expect it to happen like switching a button. David meditated on God's works. David took time to remember God, to consider all God had done in his own life and throughout history.

As I have come to listen to my soul, I can see how it too enjoys looking to the past, to events in my own life but more importantly to incidents in the Bible. My soul looks for words of encouragement and promises, which revive and strengthen it. It is God alone who can refresh me, not escapist habits.

At this point though, it is important to point out that it is okay to be downcast! It is even okay in dire circumstances to be seemingly without hope. For those who disagree, perhaps the book of Lamentations needs to be removed from the Bible. The prophet, Jeremiah, weeping over Jerusalem on more than one occasion really lets God have it:

'I have been deprived of peace; I have forgotten what prosperity is.
So I say, 'My splendour is gone and all that I had hoped from
the LORD.' I remember my affliction and my wandering, the
bitterness and the gall. I well remember them, and my soul is
downcast within me'
(Lamentations 3:17-20).

Take a look also at *Lamentations 3:21-29* and *3:40-44*.

And yet although Jeremiah sounds at the end of his tether, (after all even his soul is downcast), at least he remembers God. Time and again, the prophet pours out his anguish and despair to God, but as he does so, his soul remembers...

A gift of our soul is never to lose hope completely. Some days we may hang by a hair, but with our soul in the lead, this can be enough. Downcast or not, our soul can remember and with God it can be revived - just enough. As I look back at my life, even in times of lamenting I cannot deny how God has always been there.

As Paul says:

'We have this hope as an anchor for the soul, firm and secure'
(Hebrews 6:19).

Like the Psalmist, I now just need to remember this more quickly than not:

'Yes, my soul, find rest in God; my hope comes from him'
(Psalm 62:5).

As I reflected on David, on him being yelled and jeered at and even pelted with stones and dirt, I was thankful in my own life, those people who didn't like me had stopped at just using words. All be it through occasionally using the local newspaper. I was pelted by bird poo on a couple of occasions, but I think that was incidental...

Once on the way to a holiday club, my son and I were greatly amused, when only a hundred metres away from church, a seagull blessed me with its dinner. As I had no tissues it seemed prudent to just keep the poo there – albeit, all over my face. On arrival no one said anything so I thought they were being overly kind and polite. I quickly went to the loo and wiped the poo off before returning to the welcome desk. I was then asked where all of my fish tattoos had gone! Apparently the poo which had dropped onto my face, looked like little fish. They thought I was dressing up for the beach themed club!

Sorry, I digress...back to people being unkind and pelting me not with stones but with words. Sadly it happened too often. I am grateful it was rarely directed at me personally, and more at what I represented, at being the local priest.

Some people were against the Gospel being preached in church. Others were against the church being used for mission. Some just wanted the church for their social occasions. There were some who were just against me, for against sake! It was my turn as it were.

While I often tried to shrug or laugh it off, I have to admit within time, it did affect my soul. My soul was tired of facing ridicule and conflict. It was tired of being immersed in building projects and roof repairs. I just wanted to spread the Gospel. My soul longed to be uplifted and encouraged. It was thirsty and in need of refreshment of a spiritual dimension.

Over the years unknown to me it had also become scarred. My soul was weary of red tape, admin and leading worship in ways not natural to myself. On taking the post, I knew I had been called to be a servant of God. As such it was my duty to lead services which I would never personally have chosen to attend.

Both churches, I worked in, grew numerically and spiritually and thus in obedience and humility I led services which were not of my preference. I appreciate people come to God in different ways and I was called to serve. Whilst I was personally rarely able to engage with God through certain liturgical services, as the church was still attracting new people, I knew it was important to offer this church tradition. I also deeply loved the people and as their priest, I wanted to offer services which fed their faith.

However, what I had failed to consider (until it was nearly too late), was how the leading of such services was turning me away from God! I didn't like the way many services had to be led. I didn't like the formality of some of the symbolism or even some of the words used. This was my angst and nothing to do with the lovely people who worshipped there.

For a time I survived by merely 'going through the motions'. I tried finding times of worship to 'top me up'. I had extra time with God each Sunday morning, just to help me get through these services. After a while however, I had to admit my soul was literally wounded. I had gone a step beyond not personally engaging with God through these styles of services; slowly they were taking their toll on my soul.

It was surely time to leave and in God's perfect plan, it was also time for Jack to step up and become a stipendiary clergy person. Believe me though, I have struggled with God's timing here. The churches were growing, the buildings work was complete and the schools work had potential to flourish. The area seemed ripe for more local mission and yet I was being called out.

For years I had cried out to God to change things, but why now? Just at a time when some of the seeds planted were coming to fruition. Of course however, as in all things God's timing was and is perfect.

Job in the Old Testament, who lost everything and suffered ill health, cried out to God for understanding - for a break. God however, was silent for a long time (36 chapters) and then in *Job 38:1*, God spoke-out of the storm. God's timing is perfect. We are always too rushed.

It has taken time for my soul to become refreshed and I am aware of the wounds and scars which remain. I do believe in God's ultimate healing, but I also see scars can be for our good. They are to me a reminder of the past and a hope for the future. My soul having experienced second best for too long, was unwilling to go back…

Whilst on retreat a couple of years ago, a lady over meal times was often speaking of 'Cuthbert'. He went everywhere with her and he had apparently seen her through hard times. He was her faithful companion. She had already said she was unmarried so we assumed she was talking about her dog. It was only when she mentioned that he had come into her life in 1982 that we suspected it was not in fact a dog!

She was in fact talking about a 1982 hybrid-porsche. It was still running well, but it did not like the local supermarkets fuel. She had to go miles to fill up. 'Cuthbert' liked the expensive stuff and ran better on it. He could survive for a little distance on the 'cheap stuff' but for his full performance he wanted the best.

If you think Cuthbert was particular, our souls are even more so. They cannot take second best, no matter how it is offered, no matter how it is dressed up, no matter if it seems easier or even cheaper. Our souls are designed for the good stuff. Our souls are designed for God.

Oh to be sure we try to palm our souls off with second best. We may even begin to appreciate the spiritual dimension of our thirst, of our dissatisfaction. We may try a new prayer group or church. We may begin to start to read the Bible in a year (again).

We may attempt to pray for five minutes in the car on the way to work. We may try to allow our daily commute to become our time with God, but our soul always wants more. None of these pursuits incidentally, are bad in themselves; in fact they can contribute towards us getting the best of life. It's just no matter how much we do, our soul wants more.

Let me ask you...Are you satisfied with life? Your life, right now...Is it as good as it gets?

In all honesty, I have never met anyone who was 100% totally satisfied with their life. Even if you know God, people are rarely perfectly content. Even if they are, there is usually something just around the corner to catch them out. Sorry, that sounds a bit pessimistic, I don't mean it in that way.

I guess I rarely come across people who are 100% okay with life all of the time. Sure, some people are content and this is a good place to be, but this does not mean they are exempt from empathy with others, or illness or circumstances dictating a bad day.

To be sure some people are flourishing and this is a wonderful place to be, living with God, loving God, worshipping God and serving God. From this state of being, they can be flourishing and content even when a bad day presents itself. However, even these amazing people have wobbles.

In all honesty I don't think we are designed to be 100% okay in our life. If we were, would we really give heaven and eternal living much thought?

When I consider my soul, it really shouldn't surprise us that our being longs for more.

Let's think for a moment of where we start off in life: in the womb. On the whole it's a wonderfully snuggily place to be, and I believe it is with God. Why else would King David have been praising God from his mother's womb? David praises God for his unformed body being made in a secret place. He praises God as he considers being knitted together in his mother's womb *(Psalm 139:13-16)*.

Entering the world is a shock for every baby. My son John for instance was so reluctant to make an entrance, that he tried to stay inside by pulling on the umbilical cord. He took up campanology (bell-ringing) at an early age.

The shock of entrance into the world results in most babies crying. No wonder, it's bright, cold, noisy and there are often lots of people milling about. Above all, babies have just had several months all cosy inside the womb, with God alone for company. No wonder so many babies look worse for wear, let alone the fact they have just accomplished squeezing through the tightest of places…

In your day dreams, I wonder where your 'go to' place is? Is it back to a special moment, to a lovely holiday, to a perfect sunset, or is it to a time relaxing with friends or a great night out? Do you often look back to that day and sigh with happiness at the memories? I just wonder whether our soul is a little like this with the womb.

Except for *Psalm 139*, I have nothing to go on in the Bible of the imagery of being with God in the womb. However, just perhaps our soul looks back to the time of being with God and God alone. A time before the demands of the world, the busyness of everything, has an impact on our soul.

CHAPTER FORTY-SIX:
INSIDE OUT, OR OUTSIDE IN?

I am conscious that earlier I asked a question which I then left hanging in the air: *'Do we have a soul in a body or are we a body in a soul?'*

The Hebrew word for soul is *'nephesh'*, and it first features in *Genesis 2:7*. God formed man; God formed a *'nephesh'*, a *'living soul'*; *'nephesh'* is like *'living being'*. In reflecting on this, I came to realise rather than our soul being inserted into us like an organ, our soul is actually our whole being coming to life.

We don't have a soul, we are a soul. We are created to yield to our soul. Our soul cannot be killed, only our body *(Matthew 10:28)*. Our soul is our very being, and whilst we are on earth, it encompasses our body. In heaven it is our soul which will be united with God. Our bodies remain on earth. Our soul is created for eternity.

The most vivid picture I have had of this, was having the privilege of being with a wonderful Christian lady who died shortly after I visited her. Her family left us for a moment and as I anointed her with oil, I prayed with her. I sensed she almost needed permission to die. As she was dying, reciting words from *Psalm 42*, I held her hand. Her breathing had been faint and she had not been able to speak for several days, but as I went to leave, she squeezed my hand. I sensed what she was saying – she was leaving this world.

I left her with her family for the final moments but at their invitation, after she had died, I returned to be with them. As they continued to say their goodbyes and comfort each other, I was drawn to her face. 'She' was gone.

There was a body in physical form but the life had gone. It was more than just blood draining from her cheeks, after all it had only been a matter of moments. Rather her soul had departed.

The life that had been breathed into her in her own mother's womb was no longer there. This soul, I knew, had gone to be with God for eternity. This image is also found in *Genesis 35:18*. Rachel in her death, breathes her last and as her soul is departing, so she names her son.

Sometime later when I was seeking to be with God in quieter ways, I came across St Ignatius of Loyola of the 16th Century. Ignatius was a former soldier who after his conversion founded the religious order, 'Society of Jesus' (The Jesuits). This 'order' served the Pope as missionaries. Ignatius' reflection on our souls gave me pause for thought:

> 'I must consider only the end for which I am created, that is, for
> the praise of God our Lord and for the salvation of my soul.
> Hence, whatever I choose must help me to this end for which I am
> created'. [xxxi]

I took these words as an invitation not only to listen to my soul, but to let my soul take more of a lead. Even now when I pray for my son each night, I pray for his strength, mind and heart and all the things that are going on in his life. But above all, I pray for his soul. This is after all the everlasting part of him created for eternity. I hope and pray it may always be with God.

Even earlier than Ignatius was Julian of Norwich, whose writings have helped me to understand my soul more. Just a few quotes from Chapter 22 of her *'Revelations'*, may help you also, to embrace your soul:

> 'the Lord opened my spiritual eyes, and showed me my soul
> in the midst of my heart'. [xxxii]

Jesus sits:

> 'in the soul, in peace and rest, and He rules... [xxxiii]

> 'God wants us to pay attention to His words, and always to be
> strong in our certainty, in well-being and in woe, for he loves us
> and delights in us, and so he wishes us to love him and delight in
> him and trust greatly in him, and all will be well'. [xxxiv]

My soul is patiently but determinedly doing this for me. As my soul seeks to love God with its all, so my soul is slowing down the rest of my body, my heart and even my mind. Being 'quiet' with God is new for me but I am grateful for the gift. This book which you are reading is already too full, so my journey of becoming more quiet with God, of becoming more aware of God's Presence is for another day.

As I have come to love God with my soul, so I seek to spend more time with God. In doing so, this satisfies my soul. In addition, this has come to free my mind all the more. It has also given me a more healthy direction for my heart.

As I let my soul be in charge more, I am beginning to trust that it knows more of what is good for me than not. As I do so, I sense healing. As I rush less and as I come to God more, so I am aware of my soul growing stronger, of becoming more confident, and gaining a voice.

CHAPTER FORTY-SEVEN:
DARK NIGHT OF THE SOUL

The more I explored what my soul was, what its purpose was and how it functioned, the more sensitive I became to its leading. Above all, this has resulted in my wanting to be with God all the more.

As I spent more time praying and reading, I came across *St John of the Cross*, who coined the phrase, 'dark night of the soul'. I had heard of the phrase before, all be it, not in a theological masterpiece but through Helen Fielding who mentions it in *Bridget Jones: Mad about the Boy*. But I had never heard a sermon on it or really come across what it meant until I had truly discovered my soul.

Imagine my delight though, I had eventually found my soul and then I read of a great darkness which can befall them. I have to be honest and say I still do not know whether I did go through a 'dark night of the soul'. I think I did. I guess I am hesitant, because who am I to say God would do this for me? If I did, then it occurred even before I came to know what my soul was. Perhaps my 'dark night' was to lead me to find my soul.

Having a 'dark night of the soul' is more than having a bad time or living with depression. In recent days, I think the two have become too well acquainted. A 'dark night of the soul' is something more and comes from God Himself.

A 'Dark night of the soul' is initiated by God. It is less about our emotions, external pressures, or even our mind.

A 'dark night of the soul' is a time where God draws people closer to Himself, through darkness and silence. People are drawn closer to God through a deep wrestling of their soul, during which time they may rarely receive comfort.

I confess I wrote the next few paragraphs some time ago. As I come back to edit, after more reading and prayer, I am more confident about what I went through, however, I think my wrestling is still valid so I offer it to you...but after wards I will offer more clarity. An editor wanted me to be more bold, but I think it is important to share my initial 'wrestling'. You may be able to identify with it or know of someone who may do so.

For a long time I did not know whether what I went through was initiated by God or whether it was a combination of exhaustion and weariness of my soul. Perhaps it was merely 'acedia'. Whatever I went through and where ever it came from, I know in the midst of it, I felt far from God.

Was I beginning to believe in 'Deus absconditus'? Was the God I believed in 'a hidden God'? In 'His remoteness' was He ignoring human suffering? Even in my lower moments, this did not sit well with me, not least that during this time others around me were drawing closer to Him. God was doing remarkable things in so many people's lives – for many people He was far from hidden or remote.

I have heard of people talking about their prayers hitting a wall or a glass ceiling. If I am honest, mine for a time didn't even seem to get that far. At times they didn't even really come into being at all. During times of prayer, there were utterances, but they were not always audible ones, more like 'wordless groans'. I clung on in hope to the words of Paul:

'In the same way, the Spirit helps us in our weakness. We do not know what we ought to pray for, but the Spirit himself intercedes for us through wordless groans'
(Romans 8:26).

However, at the time I knew little of this; I was just trying to survive. In addition to St John of the Cross' words, Richard Foster's book, *'Prayer'* has greatly helped me in acknowledging what I have been through.[xxxv] He gave me words and knowledge to understand my experience. I came to see I had been stripped of dependence on exterior and interior results!

By exterior, I mean I became even less impressed with all things exterior, even or particularly things in the church. For too long I had been trying to almost manipulate 'religion' to enable people to be saved and to become part of the church. I had even done this at the expense of praying for souls. 'Church services' came to mean less and less to me – which is mighty hard when you are the one leading them!

172

By interior, I was stripped of any dependence upon interior results. I was being drawn away from 'feeling' my faith or even 'knowing' it, into something deeper. Everything for too long had become *'meaningless'*.

By being stripped of dependence on anything exterior or interior, I was forced to trust in God alone – even and especially at times when I did not even know His Presence. It's hard to explain and I apologise for making a hash of it here.

On a Maundy Thursday, in many Anglican and Roman Catholic churches, the 'altar' will be stripped. This is in preparation for Good Friday, when the church remembers Jesus on the cross. There is a time of 'less', a time of 'stripping' back before celebrating the glorious resurrection of Jesus on Easter Sunday. Perhaps this is a way for me to describe what I went through. I was stripped of everything actual in my faith, and although I didn't know it at the time, this was all for my own good.

This period was made all the harder for me, as I was still having to lead services and prayers in church. Whilst I did not want sympathy or even people being aware of what was going on in my interior, I often marvelled that not more people noticed.

Even more astonished was I, when people during this period would thank me for sermons and conversations. Apparently words from my mouth were still having an impact. I marvelled at how some people were drawing closer to God and yet I seemed to be moving further away.

I had been in times of wilderness before, 'desert times' of feeling tested and on trial. I had had times of being 'downcast' and wondering just where God was in everything, but this was something different. For one, it went on a lot longer and for a long time I could not see a way out. I also felt more alone than ever before.

I had even tried to draw close to some people, including church leaders. I met up with some, on a one to one basis, as I wanted to 'cry out' to them. I wanted to make sense of my wrestling and I hoped they could offer wise counsel. But everything drew the same response - silence. Friendships suffered, as did our marriage.

No-one seemed to understand and so slowly I withdrew all the more. Whatever I was going through, it seemed God wanted me to go through it alone. Of course looking back I wasn't alone. Throughout all of this, God had wanted me to turn to Him and Him alone.

In addition to St John of the Cross and Richard Foster, at the time of my wrestling I was helped by some letters of Mother Teresa. I had been drawn to her on many occasions, not least for her energy and zeal for God and mission. One phrase of hers is written on my heart:

'We ourselves feel that what we are doing is just a drop in the ocean. But the ocean would be less because of that missing drop'. xxxvi

This encouraged me to 'do' many things, often at a time when things seemed pretty hopeless.

It was in her death however, where I had been strangely drawn to her the most. She shared this day with the death of Princess Diana. I was always struck by these two women. They were both in the public eye and both often working for good. Yet how different their lives were, not least the reaction to their deaths.

The death of Princess Diana led to a national if not international over pouring of lament and sadness. Meanwhile, Mother Teresa seemed to die almost unnoticed.

For me as a child, the picture of Mother Teresa was always of an older tanned lady in prayer and service of God. It seemed she did so with joy and I imagined she must have been very close to God. She had after all given her life to the service of others in Calcutta and in time set up similar projects around the world.

It is the book *'Come be my , light'*, xxxvii (published long after her death), that has had the greatest impact on me. The book is a compilation of her private writings to her confessors. It reveals much of the state of her interior, of her prayer life, of her wrestling's, of her inner turmoil.

Initially as I began to read such deeply personal letters, it seemed to be prying into her private life. A life which she had only wanted a few to know of. After a while however, I took her words as an invitation for me to become more real with God. If she, Mother Teresa could have entertained such thoughts, then surely it was okay for me to have some similar ones. I also became mightily thankful, not to have experienced the inner darkness she herself had endured for decades.

As I read of her inner wrestling and of her darkness, I was humbled at her honesty, but also at her remarkable strength to carry on. Her willingness to submit her all to God, to Jesus - to her *'spouse'*, was truly inspirational. I marvelled at how even at her lowest points, rather than seeking to be spared of the 'darkness', she came to embrace it as a gift. She continued with all of the missionary activities and love which she is well known for. Few, until after her death knew of her 'darkness'.

Mother Teresa participated in corporate prayers and encouraged her 'novices' to do likewise. In her private devotions however, she rarely experienced the light she knew to be true. It seems she grew closer to God through His apparent absence.

I had not experienced the depths of her anguish, nor the longevity of the time of her darkness. At no point either had I sought it. I guess that is one of the many reasons why I would never be beatified, as she herself was (on 19 October 2003). Mother Teresa was sold out for Jesus, 100%. Her soul belonged to Him and yet rather than receive the light she longed for, she lived more often in darkness.

This as a consequence strangely strengthened me. Not just because there was someone who had had life a lot worse than me, but because her testimony showed how God was there in the darkness.

I sensed I was being given a choice; I could either see God in 'this', or I could walk away. The latter was tempting but my soul knew it was not an option. Inspired by Mother Teresa's faith and resolve I chose to continue to wrestle with God.

One aspect of Mother Teresa's darkness was identifying with Jesus on the cross when He says; *'I thirst' (John 19:28)*. She came to see this wasn't Jesus asking for liquid to quench His own thirst. Rather Jesus' thirsting on the cross was thirsting for lost souls.

This made sense, as Jesus on the cross said He was thirsty, but then He did not accept the wine vinegar which was subsequently offered to Him. His thirst seemed more than what a drink could quench.

It was this thirst for souls, that Mother Teresa longed to satiate. It was this thirst of Jesus which encouraged her to go into the slums, to fight politics, to set up projects around the world, to counsel novices and to work the hours she did.

She longed to satisfy the thirst of Jesus on the cross, to bring more souls to Jesus. But even Mother Teresa could not do this by herself. Only through Jesus, only through the Holy Spirit ministering within her and through her, could such acts be accomplished.

If doing things in her own strength was not an option for Mother Teresa, it was hardly an option for me either. Her soul cried out for the souls of others. For Mother Teresa this was made all the more of God and God alone, through her having to live in an interior darkness.

Rightly or wrongly, I took comfort in Mother Teresa's experience. God was there even when people did not 'feel' or 'sense' it. Through listening to my soul more and through surrendering myself to God, I was brought closer to Him. A quick skim of the Bible, looking for others who may have entered into some 'darkness' also helped.

CHAPTER FORTY-EIGHT:
ELI, ELI, LEMA SABACHTHANI?

The phenomena of the 'Dark night of the soul', goes back further than St John of the Cross. What of Abraham *(Genesis 15:12)*, where we are told a *'thick dreadful darkness'* came upon him? At a first glance this doesn't seem to make a lot of sense. God had just made a covenant with Abraham which had to be a high point. Yet as Abraham came to sleep, rather than encompassed in light, he was enveloped in darkness.

What of Jesus? On the day He was baptised, heaven was torn open, a voice was heard from heaven, the Holy Spirit came upon Him – this is an amazing day. Rather than being able to enjoy this moment though, He is led into the wilderness to be tempted by the Devil.

It would never naturally be our way that we could go from something amazing to something so testing in an instant. To go from light to darkness so quickly, seems all wrong. But then we are not God and we do not always understand His ways.

Life didn't make sense for me in the Parish either. On many occasions when ministry was going well, it was on these days when I felt most alone and far from God.

How could God's Holy Spirit be working in the Parishes and through me? Only for me to feel...nothing; to sense...silence.

I took comfort in others who had felt such apparent abandonment. David for example, in *Psalm 22:1* cried out:

> *'My God, my God, why have you forsaken me? Why are you so far from saving me, so far from my cries of anguish?'*

And yet it was Jesus Himself who in saying these words gave me some curious comfort. Jesus went through times of darkness; sometimes as a consequence of people and sometimes purely of God, but all for our sake *(Luke 22:53)*. Who can read the words of Jesus on the cross, without feeling wretched?

> *'My God, my God, why have you forsaken me?'*
> *(Mt 27:46).*

To be forsaken is to be left, to be abandoned at a great point of need. Jesus knew God more than any other. Jesus had been in heaven with God. Jesus was God's Son. Jesus had previously said the words; *'The one who sent me is with me; he has not left me alone' (John 8:29)*. Yet at the time of intense pain and isolation, all Jesus could say was; *'Eli, Eli, lema sabachthani?' (Matthew 27:46)*. Even for Jesus on His worst day, it seems there was... silence.

Perhaps it is not for me to reason why? Rather I am now grateful for the what...that is, being brought closer to God. I took comfort from the words of one of His prophets;

> *'But what can I say? He has spoken to me, and he himself has*
> *done this. I will walk humbly all my years because of this*
> *anguish of my soul. Lord, by such things people live; and my*
> *spirit finds life in them too. You restored me to health and let me*
> *live. Surely it was for my benefit that I suffered such anguish. In*
> *your love you kept me from the pit of destruction; you have put all*
> *my sins behind your back'*
> *(Isaiah 38:15-17).*

I can then testify that an everlasting blessing and benefit of my wrestling; of experiencing the darkness I went through, is I am now more at peace. Spiritually yes, because my soul has found a voice and I try to listen to it, but also peace in my heart, mind and strength.

At times I had wondered if I was losing my soul, but with Jesus' words in mind, I knew I did not want to forfeit my soul, nor was anything as precious as my soul *(Mark 8:36-37)*. My soul belongs to God and even though at times I wasn't sure if my soul was in union with God; I wasn't going to let it be in union with anything or anyone else either.

At the height of my 'wrestling' with God, in those low moments of wondering if God was still there, I would have given anything for an 'exit'. As I look back however, although I felt God was absent and I was abandoned, I was anything but. God was there for me in the deepest of ways. God loved me so much, He let me wrestle, shout and stomp. I was drawn into loneliness and despair all for my own good. I can now even thank God for the time of darkness; for drawing me near.

I have also come to know myself more, what I can and cannot do and also what I am willing to do and not do. Knowing myself, my limitations as well as my strengths, protects me from becoming too involved or pushing myself too far. This does not mean I am becoming lazy, far from it, if anything I am able to achieve more, but the motivation is different.

Hopefully my actions flow from God's love rather than running towards to it. My priorities have changed. I have spent time considering my legacy. If I had died a few years ago I am likely to have been remembered for being a worn out grumpy priest and perhaps a mum.

With God's leading, I now hope I am a child of God first, a disciple, a mum and a wife. Being a priest could no longer keep muscling in at first place. I hope now to be even more open to God's voice, to His leading. I am grateful for time given to consider my legacy, before it was too late.

CHAPTER FORTY-NINE:
SOUL, SPIRIT AND SPIRIT

As I discovered my soul, so I talked about it where ever I went. It wasn't long however, before I realised there was quite a lot of confusion within the church over what a soul is. Many people were using the terms 'spirit' and 'soul' synonymously. Was this correct? I had discovered my soul was something we are born with and it belongs to God, but what was our spirit? Was it a term for our soul?

I knew it wasn't the 'Spirit' as this was God's Holy Spirit which could be invited into our being. Paul himself confirms this;

> *'Now it is God who makes both us and you stand firm in*
> *Christ. He anointed us, set his seal of ownership on us, and put*
> *his Spirit in our hearts as a deposit, guaranteeing what*
> *is to come'*
> *(2 Corinthians 1:21-22).*

The Spirit is from God and is given to us as a gift to help us live with Him. The Holy Spirit is something external to be invited in, whilst our soul is internal and present without an invitation; it is part of who we are.

It is impossible to do justice to describing the Holy Spirit in this book. Many books have been written on this subject alone. In the briefest of synopsis, the Holy Spirit has existed from the beginning of time and was present at Creation. During the history of God's people, the Holy Spirit came down upon people at particular times for particular tasks. During Jesus' lifetime He promised the gift of another to help His people *(John 14:15-17)*.

From the time of Pentecost *(Acts 2:1-13)*, God's Holy Spirit has been available for all who call upon God. God's Spirit can dwell within us. The Holy Spirit gives us gifts for His service and is able to renew our inner selves: *'the fruit of the Spirit is love, joy, peace, forbearance, kindness, goodness, faithfulness, gentleness and self-control' (Galatians 5:22-23).*

As Jesus returned to heaven, so the Holy Spirit is available to all who turn to Him. It is God's Spirit which can lead us *(Romans 8:1-17)*, comfort and encourage us *(Acts 9:31)*, convict us of sin *(John 16:8)*, help us to pray *(Romans 8:26)* and give us gifts *(1 Corinthians 12:1-11)*. We are not left in this world by ourselves, far from it. God through His Holy Spirit longs to be with us in all things. God's Holy Spirit longs to be called upon.

You only have to look at Jesus' disciples to see the power of the Holy Spirit. Literally overnight they went from being a group who lacked understanding and faith, to being transformed into extraordinary people who spoke and lived God's word. Their fearfulness was transformed into courage and strength, even taking many of them to their deaths. This was God Himself, the Holy Spirit dwelling within them.

Sadly too often even as a Christian, we can depend on ourselves rather than on God. This is not God's intention or will. For me personally I have been given cause to remember the words of Zechariah to Zerubbabel:

> *"Not by might nor by power, but by my Spirit,' says the LORD*
> *Almighty'*
> *(Zechariah 4:6).*

God's gift, the fulfilment of Jesus' promise should never be overlooked. This is the Holy Spirit, capital 'S'.

Within the Bible, there is another spirit, no capital 'S'! At times writers of the Bible used the term 'spirit' to refer to a human spirit, that is to an inner force which motivates someone to move in one direction over another. For example, the writer of *Numbers* records God saying of Caleb:

> *'But because my servant Caleb has a different spirit and follows*
> *me wholeheartedly, I will bring him into the land he went to, and*
> *his descendants will inherit it'*
> *. (Numbers 14:24).*

This implied 'spirit' was something within Caleb which was a motivational force of some kind. My difficulty came that the Hebrew word for *'spirit'* used in Numbers is *'ru•ach'*, which is actually the same word used for the *'Spirit'*.

Furthermore, on investigation I realised the Bible used the terms of soul and spirit interchangeably! Timothy for example, says; *'The Lord be with your spirit' (2 Timothy 4:22)*. Before I knew it I had gone down several rabbit warrens. Rather than being enlightened like Alice (Alice's Adventures in Wonderland), I only became more confused.xxxviii

In the end the Apostle Paul shed some light as he says:

> *'May God himself, the God of peace, sanctify you through and through. May your whole spirit, soul and body be kept blameless at the coming of our Lord Jesus Christ'*
> *(1 Thessalonians 5:23).*

Paul on this occasion was clearly identifying three separate aspects of ourselves. Our spirit (πνεῦμα-pneuma - the Greek for the Hebrew word ruach). Our soul (ψυχή-psuchē - the Greek for the Hebrew word nephash). Our body (σῶμα-sōma – the Greek for the Hebrew word 'bädē).

This wasn't a one off for Paul, as in Hebrews 4:12 he also separates the soul and spirit, as does *Isaiah: 'My soul yearns for you in the night; in the morning my spirit longs for you' (26:9).*

Without boring you further, (after much wrestling) I have come to see our spirit is something within us which is a motivating force; it is part of who we are.

I will be honest and say, I still do not completely understand it all. Of more importance however, I have become aware of different aspects of myself. This helps me not only to understand and then seek to care for them, but also how I can bring so many different aspects of me to love God and in turn others.

I have come to see our soul is created by God *(Jeremiah 38:16)* for God. Our souls on our death, outlive our body. They depart from the physical body *(Genesis 35:18)*. If we have chosen to come to know God and belong to Him, then our souls are able to be with God forevermore – in heaven.

Our soul is something other than the physical body and yet it is part of us. God breathes His breath into us *(Genesis 2:7)*, giving us a soul, making us a living being. Our soul is separate from our heart:

> *The LORD your God commands you this day to follow these decrees and laws; carefully observe them with all your heart and with all your soul'*
> *(Deuteronomy 26:16, compare also 30:6).*

For a while I had the image of our soul almost being like the 1980's 'Ready Brek' advert.xxxix A boy having eaten the cereal has an orange glow around his body. I envisaged that our souls surrounds us; it was as if our souls encompassed us. Our physical body was inside our soul.

I am no longer comfortable with this image but for a time it gave me pause for thought, not least to remember my soul being part of my being. Do I have an image nowadays? Not so much actually, but I am okay with this. As George Macdonald famously said in 1892; *'You don't have a soul, you are a soul. You have a body'.*xl I am now less interested in the actual make up of it, rather I am grateful I have been made more aware of my soul and its voice.

I rejoice in the knowledge that Jesus promises to look after our souls; *'For 'you were like sheep going astray,' but now you have returned to the Shepherd and Overseer of your souls'. (1 Peter 2:25).* Jesus offers rest for our soul *(Matthew 11:29).*

On earth, God longs to refresh our souls *(Psalm 23:3)* and He is able to be with us even through the darkest valley. We are not told our souls, even with God, can avoid trials and dark times. Yet, we are shown that God can go through such times with us *(Psalm 23:4).* Such times may even be initiated by God as He comes to teach and even discipline us; as He draws us closer to Himself.

My soul is something which dwells within me, for God. Everyone has a soul and although it is designed to be with God, every person has a choice whether theirs does or not. God gives us all a choice. Our soul is there whether we ever come to acknowledge it or not.

The Holy Spirit meanwhile longs also to dwell within us, but this only comes at our invitation. The *'God-shaped hole'*, I had heard people speak of was a metaphor for a place within me which belongs to the Holy Spirit. St Augustine began such thoughts with:

> *'You have made us for yourself, O Lord, and our hearts are restless until they rest in you'.* xli

Blaise Pascal, later developed this saying:

> *'There is a God-shaped vacuum in the heart of every man which cannot be filled by any created thing, but only by God the Creator, made known through Jesus Christ'.* xlii

When invited, God the Creator promises to come into our lives through His Holy Spirit *(John 14:16-17)*. God's Holy Spirit can live with us and in us. This is quite remarkable. The Spirit lives within us, resides, remains, abides and somehow lives with God.

Whilst our soul already exists within us, it is up to us whether we invite the Holy Spirit in. The soul if you like, longs, thirsts, desires and needs to be with God. The Spirit, however on our invitation, dwells *(1 Timothy 1:14, compare 1 Corinthians 3:16)*. My soul rejoiced on the day I invited God's Holy Spirit into my life and from that day this Spirit enables me to commune with God.

My soul and my spirit both commune with God's Holy Spirit. On the day I became a Christian some twenty or so years ago, I knew of none of this. To be honest it has taken all of these years to really come to some understanding of it all.

Even now I realise I have glossed over a lot of deeper theology, and there are holes in my understanding. I am however, as my husband reminds me, 'not John Stott'.

I could probably have lived another twenty years without knowing all the ins and outs of what my soul is, but for me I now see this knowledge as a gift. God not only made a soul for me which lives within me and makes me the being I am, but through a relationship with Jesus, I can invite His Holy Spirit to live within me. This is all pretty remarkable for someone who messes up every day.

God loves me; I am His child and He longs for me to love Him with my all, including my soul. I find it interesting that Jesus did not include spirit, as He spoke of our different parts coming to love God. It is one of the many questions I have when I get to heaven. In all honesty, I do not understand it all. I mean why did Jesus in His last moments in a loud voice say: *Father, into your hands I commit my spirit (pneuma)'*. As Luke records, *When he had said this, he breathed his last' (Luke 23:46).*

Why did He not say *psuchē'* (soul)? Are the spirit and soul interchangeable after all? In all honesty I remain uncertain as to the exact meaning. Did Jesus know His soul was already with God and He was thus committing His spirit also? But, why would Jesus' soul leave earlier than His spirit? Was Jesus, rather referring to the Holy Spirit which came upon Him in His baptism? To be honest I am not entirely sure. If I do find out, I will try and let you know (somehow). All I know is that I have invited God's Holy Spirit into my life and I have become aware of my soul.

My soul and spirit work in partnership for my good as they both long to be with God. Several people have gadgets on their wrists at the moment, monitoring their heart rate. I have considered the need of a similar 'app' for my soul, a monitor of how much I am in the Presence of God. After musing on this, I realise I have one; it is the Holy Spirit.

As I consider my 'all', my very being, so I see there is so much more of me to love God and to be loved by Him. By coming to know of my mind, soul, heart and strength and even my spirit, so I am able to love God more fully. This is all possible through being loved by God first and through allowing His Holy Spirit to dwell within me.

Don't despair, the next chapter helps this make more sense...

CHAPTER FIFTY:
ARE YOU THIRSTY?

Forgive me if the above section has left you more confused than not! Let's look at our soul, spirit and God's Holy Spirit in a different way. I have spoken of my soul being thirsty without really giving an explanation. Here goes...

Throughout the Bible, one of the most popular forms of imagery is 'water'. The image of water which strikes me most, is when it alludes to the Holy Spirit coming into our lives; flowing over us, through us and in us. The image is almost of a flowing river. Rivers are mentioned over 150 times in the Bible.

The Bible even begins and ends with a river. We do not know much about the Garden of Eden, but there was a river running through it. In *Revelation 22* we are given a picture of the river of life, a river as clear as crystal flowing from the throne of God.

Rivers are seen as a picture of spiritual life, perhaps with good reason, as after all Israel was a desert. God's people throughout the times of the Bible lived and breathed dust! When the Psalmist wrote of the deer panting for water, that was literal as well as metaphorical. Animals and herdsmen walked miles for sources of water. There were no taps. Everything depended on wells or streams. No water meant dying. God's people knew what it was like to long for water.

A trip to Rwanda, not long after the Genocide, alerted me to just how precious water is. The fervency of prayers for just a cup of tea put me to shame. Often having to walk miles for it, no-one ever took fresh water for granted.

As I write, this last week after a lot of snow, many water pipes in England started bursting. This resulted in water shortages, which was rather ironic considering at the time it was raining heavily outside. My husband, (who had not heard the news), on entering a kitchen filled with vessels of water, thought I had finally gone mad.

We had been encouraged to fill vessels in case the water got turned off. After a few days however, this water was no longer fit to drink. Fresh living water is imperative for survival.

Isaiah, the prophet, would have known what it was like to have living, fresh water and what it was like to be denied it. In *Isaiah 55*, we are given an invitation to come to God:

'Come, all you who are thirsty, come to the waters'
(v.1).

For all whom are thirsty, for those whose souls are panting, there is an invitation to come. To come to God.

Our souls more than any other part of us, know what it should depend on - God. Our minds and hearts can try to survive by themselves, on knowledge, on achievements, on money, or with the help of others. Our souls however, know of only one source to turn and that is to God. Jesus reveals how this is possible:

'Let anyone who is thirsty come to me and drink. Whoever
believes in me, as Scripture has said, rivers of living water will
flow from within them'
(John 7:37-38).

Jesus through God's Holy Spirit can revive our thirsty souls, our parched bodies. Jesus in these words revealed Himself to be the fulfilment of the promise of Isaiah.

For years the Jews had looked forward to a Messiah, to a Saviour, and here Jesus (a Carpenter's son from Galilee), was in effect saying: I am the one who can quench your thirst, it is through me. I will leave the Holy Spirit for each of you to turn to. Come, come to me, invite me.

I do not know of any Christian who has not at some point acknowledged their thirst. It is how God has designed us. We are designed to crave. Without being thirsty for more, for more of God, we would after all be satisfied with our lot on earth.

By the way, it was no accident that Jesus chose to speak of *'living water'* at the time He did: at the Feast of Tabernacles *(John 7)*. During this feast, Jews celebrated God's gift of water and life. The chief priest would dip a golden pitcher into the pool of Siloam before leading a parade up to the temple. It was a festival of great joy.

Within Israel, water was scarce and precious and you did not waste a drop. Yet during this feast the chief priest would pour out water onto the ground, almost wasting it frivolously. This symbolised how God one day would satisfy the thirst of His people.

God was going to satisfy thirst, giving more water and more life than anyone had ever experienced. Jesus announced to the crowds that He was the fulfilment of this long awaited promise. Some believed Him, others did not.

God longs for our lives to also flow with rivers of living water. This is a wonderful invitation. We have a choice whether we accept it or not. God knows it is best for us, but He leaves it to us to decide.

I had been thirsty for so long, my soul was parched and on receiving the invitation to drink, I have never looked back. My writing may not always convey it, but I am so much more at peace in all things. My life has become less about doing and more about being, of being with God in all things.

For too long I had made the Christian life about me, about works. I had never tried to earn salvation as I knew this was impossible, but on receiving the gift of new life, I had certainly tried to work too hard. Perhaps I was trying to 'pay back', as one does on a loan. I failed to see the gift was free - no strings attached.

I am grateful for this second chance of being invited to come to God through His grace, through Jesus Himself. As we encourage our soul to come to God, to drink, to receive, it is then and only then that we can become the people God created us to be.

We are created to live with the Spirit of God flowing through us, like a river of living water. It is when we try and live without God's Spirit, that life gets harder. God designed us with a mind, heart, body and soul, but He also created us to be filled with His Holy Spirit. God longs to come alongside us in our life. We were after all created for His glory, for His love, for Himself.

Now for another outrageous plug for one of Jon Ortberg's, books: *'the me I want to be – becoming God's best version of you'.* This book is a wonderful invitation to allow God's Spirit to flow through us. As Jon reminds us, this is less about effort and more about being available and open to God's Spirit working through us.

Now I forget to do this about 23 hours and a half every day. Yet when I do remember to *'let Go and let God'* I can literally look down upon myself and give God thanks. I love it when I see myself doing something I wouldn't naturally do, because that is God's Spirit flowing through me...it is not of me, but God's Spirit. It is such a blessing to see God at work within little ole us.

God's generous Spirit chooses to dwell within us. We are like clay jars, expendable vessels, but God longs to dwell within us, to shine through us. Now more often than not, because of my bad habits, through my being grumpy and selfish, this doesn't happen, but God invites us to let this happen.

When I see me being, the me I am not so keen on, I try to remember to say to God, *'let your living waters flow, let your Spirit flow through me'*. *'God, please more of you and less of me'*. In fact I spend time each morning praying this over and again, just so I have a little more of God within me, *'making me the me God wants me to be'*.

CHAPTER FIFTY-ONE:
A NATURAL SPRING

I wonder, when you have ever been at your most thirsty? After a hot curry? Within a desert? During a long walk? I have to admit, I am always thirsty. I even drink 3 litres during the night. And before you kindly suggest I have diabetes, I have been checked out; I am just always thirsty. I try to avoid deserts.

A year ago, out running I fell over and nearly ended up in a local creek. I got covered in mud, all over my legs, clothes and hands. Of course I then wiped my face and that too got covered in mud. There was water all around me but it was dirty creek water. I knew this water would have been worse for me than to have none at all. Incidentally, our souls thirst for living water – to accept anything but this, is to do them damage.

I hadn't taken a drink so after this incident, I had a choice, turn around and limp home or continue. I chose the latter because I knew there was a natural water source a mile on.

I knew this was slightly risky as I was now running further away from home. Eventually however, I got to the natural spring. I was thirsty and filthy and in need of a drink and a clean-up.

Just as I arrived, it started to thunder so I was left thinking, *'Do I stop and drink and clean up or should I head home?'* I decided I had to stop and have a drink. In the end I didn't want to leave. The water was cold, clear, good to taste and satisfying my thirst as well as cleaning my muddied self.

This source of water on that day was doing more than just quenching my thirst. I felt refreshed and strangely at peace. I marvelled as it sprang from the ground, this natural source of water.

The clouds in the sky however, were turning ever blacker. The thunder was rolling and I was now a long way from home. As I ran back, greatly refreshed, I had the impression God was saying, *'Let my living waters flow...Let my living waters flow...Come to me...now'*.

At this point in my journey, I still had a long way to go but I knew I was being invited to stop and to come.

It's too easy to keep on going, to do so in our own strength when actually God wants us to be in His Presence, to receive His Living Waters, to be blessed by His Spirit. Too often we try and be God, rather than letting God be God and us be us.

God invites us to allow His living waters to flow in our life. He longs for us to allow His Spirit to flow through our lives. He wants us to come to Him to be refreshed, to have His Holy Spirit flowing through our lives...

I was fortunate enough a year or so ago to visit my brother in Canada. During our stay we spent some time on the lakes. Never before have I been surrounded by so much 'living water'. Streams ran into rivers which ran into lakes. It was quite breath-taking. I loved the early morning. As the sun began to rise and warm the day, so I was able to watch the mist hovering over the lake.

On the whole we enjoyed incredibly sunny weather, so much so I wondered just how there could be so much water around. I was aware of snow which had melted earlier in the year but even so. On one occasion though, it rained for 24 hours non-stop. Several inches fell in just one day.

I happened to go to church the next day and I was amused at the Pastor's reaction to the rain. We in England would have lamented such 'bad weather'. The Pastor meanwhile was praising God and shouting *'Hallelujahs'*. He knew they had desperately needed rain. (Writing in July 2018, the hottest summer since 1976, my oh my, do we ever need the rain too).

After the 24 hours of rain, it was incredible to see the impact of the rainfall. With the blessing of that rain, the river changed shape and aspects of the lake were transformed. Dried up ravines once again began to flow joining up with the river, which flowed into the lake. I marvelled at rocks which over years had changed shape as the power of the water had rushed by. I knew even then I needed to change. I knew also, only God could be trusted with my formation.

During that stay of just a week, within an area of less than two acres, I saw fish, terrapins, snapping turtles, eels, crayfish, beavers, squirrels, otters, ducks, geese, toads, chipmunks, turkey eagles, dragon flies, frogs, blue jays, humming birds, an elk, and even a bear. All of them were gathered to this natural water source. All when they were thirsty came to the lake.

As I walked one day up-stream, I was grateful for some time to let my mind breathe, my heart slow, my strength be restored and my soul live. As I ventured further up-stream, I saw parts where the river was wide and others where it was narrow and flowing faster. As I reflected on my own life a little, I marvelled at the ever changing nature of it.

As I looked back over the past few years, there were times of fast pace, of wallowing, of being formed, of bumbling along, of hitting rocks, of making dams, of peace and calm, as well as times of chaos.

My family commented a lot, that week, how perfect the place was, of how it was heaven itself. Whilst I could see its attraction – it was beautiful, I know heaven will be even more than the most perfect thing on earth.

Later on during that holiday we visited Niagra Falls. I am afraid I was a little underwhelmed. It just didn't do it for me. The force of the water and the natural source was impressive, but for me it was too noisy and almost too powerful. Standing behind the falls, seeing the water thundering over, with spray in our faces, I remained unmoved. After a week of being by calm streams of quiet water, I knew my preference.

In my own soul and spirit, I was also seeing that I wanted less of the big, less of the impressive, less of the powerful and more of the still calm quiet. Within the Bible God does speak of rivers, and yet in the Psalms the song writer speaks more of streams. It was the streams of God's Spirit which my soul was longing for.

Before you have had enough of this imagery, just one more picture. Whilst at the cabin, John was enthusiastic to have a fire. Up until this point the area had not had any rain for weeks. The advice was to surround any camp fires with water, to thus limit any spread of fire.

After spending a day collecting wood we were filthy and it was fun to hose each other down around the fire, thus killing two birds with one stone. After a few minutes John got a little over enthusiastic with the hose and I was drenched. Pleading to his kinder nature, I said we had to stop otherwise we would run out of water.

He looked at me with a bemused look and said; *'Mumma, the water is being pumped up from the lake. Does it look as though it's running out?'*. Hmm, good point! The lake was bigger than any reservoir in England.

As I chuckled, I also wondered how often in coming to God's living streams of water, I had limited His outpouring. What was I afraid of? Why time and again was I limiting God? Was I fearful of not being in control? Was I lacking faith?

Why at times of knowing God's peace, did I often then want to rush off and do something else? Was God seeking me to live in His Presence more; to live in the moment? Was God inviting me to be blessed yes, but also equipped for His paths? Time was not just mine, but God's.

I now see we are created to be thirsty. To be created otherwise would mean missing out on our thirst being quenched. We could miss out on the glorious gift of the Holy Spirit. My soul had once longed for the Holy Spirit and it had received it. My soul was now longing to love God in a new way and this too was beginning to happen. My soul as it was learning to love God with its all, was equally learning to come to God to be loved by Him first.

*'**Love the Lord your God with all your heart** and with all your soul and with all your mind and with all your strength'*

CHAPTER FIFTY-TWO:
HEART BY ANY OTHER NAME...

A challenge with reading the Bible and not knowing Hebrew and Greek, (which accounts probably for 99.9% of Christians) is we have to depend on translations. Just as the English word, 'love' is rather limited, so is our understanding of the word, 'heart'.

On the whole, the word 'heart' within the English language either refers to the physical organ within the body, or to the seat of our emotions and feeling. *To love God with all our heart* is unlikely however, to suggest we are being called to love God with a muscular organ. Perish the thought. Thus many may assume, *'to love God with our heart'*, means to love God with our affections.

Such love however, by its very nature would surely be dependent on feelings and circumstances. Thus on a bright sunny day, a person in good health, with money in their pocket, holding hands with their loved one, may profess God is good and they love Him a lot. On the next day however, as storm clouds gather, as they are struck with illness, and made redundant, they may no longer feel any love for God.

Would God really be asking us to love Him in such a fickle way?

Within the ancient world, there was an emotional sense of the heart. In *Proverbs 12:25*, the writer speaks of a heaviness in the heart. This understanding continued in the writings of Paul who said; *'I have great sorrow and unceasing anguish in my heart'* (Romans 9:2). However, the heart in the Hebraic sense, referred not merely to emotions, but more to the core of a person - to their inner being. Thus the heart, unlike today, was not limited to feelings or emotions.

The Hebrew word, *'lebab' - (heart)*, is our *'will'*, it is the very essence of our being. It refers to behaviour, to action, to the seat of the intellect, and not merely to an emotional state dependant on circumstances. Lebab – (heart), relates to one's character and morals - it shapes a person. Our heart gives orientation for all we do.

From the time of Moses when Israel first received the command to love God with their 'heart', included their minds (this as I have explained previously). The heart was seen as a 'conscience', as seen in *Job 27:6; 2 Samuel 24:10*.

To love God was with their brain – with the thinking part of themselves, as well as with their feelings. We see this in *Luke* as he records Mary's response to shepherds and angels being visitors at the birth of her son;

> *'But Mary treasured up all these things and pondered them*
> *in her heart'*
> *(2:19).*

Wow, this young Jewish girl was something else – she was incredible. Personally, having given birth, all be it, in a hospital, it was all I could do, to welcome my mum and best friend to see me, let alone smelly shepherds and angelic visitors.

I love Mary's reactions to everything she faced. An angel says to her: *'Do not be afraid, Mary; you have found favour with God. You will conceive and give birth to a son, and you are to call him Jesus' (Luke 1:30-31)*. She says, *'How will this be, since I am a virgin?' (1:34)* followed by, *'I am the Lord's servant. May it be as you have said' (1:38)*. If I had been an unmarried girl some 2000 years ago, who could have faced being stoned to death for being pregnant outside of marriage, I do not think I would have been so understanding.

I believe my reaction would have been a wide range of expletives. I realise God sent His number one messenger in the Angel Gabriel, but I still would have had a few more things to say. I guess that's why the Son of God was born to Mary and not to me!

Back to Mary and a pondering of everything in her heart. After having given birth myself, all I wanted was peace and quiet. Mary did not have that option, but neither does she moan when she is kept awake half the night by singing angels. She remains questioning and yet obedient. The fact she has no bed to lie in, and nowhere better than a food trough to lay her son does not seem to upset her either. She doesn't even moan about the smell of the shepherds or of the animals nearby.

As a farmer's daughter I am very aware of what animals do around a food trough? They poo! On this note, I was once given a 1 minute slot to share a message at an open air carol service. I sense for some people reading this book, you may just need to hear it too. If, however you just want to press on, please skip to the next chapter.

My offering at the Carol service was:

'What smells do you like at Christmas?

Christmas pudding? Mulled wine? Turkey?'

(I then opened what looked like a box of chocolates for people to smell, but actually the box contained poo!). I continued speaking:

'So what smells do you like at Christmas?

How about Poo? Yes, you heard, Poo?

That first Christmas would have reeked of it.

Jesus was laid in a food trough, we know this.

And what do animals do as they eat, they poo.

What of the shepherds as they came to visit?

Smelly shepherds, living with the sheep,

they too would have smelt of poo.

The wise men went to find the King of the Jews

and ended up at Herod's Palace, where it was clean

and yet Jesus wasn't there.

God's son was a tiny baby in a food trough

surrounded by poo.

So if in this last year you have felt life has been a pile

of poo, it may just be, that Jesus was there with you.

No matter what life throws at us, poo and all, if we

choose, Jesus can be there too. Poo and all'.

CHAPTER FIFTY-THREE:
NO HALVES HERE PLEASE

So where was I? Oh yes, 'Mary pondered things in her heart'. This has less to do with emotions and more to do with the thinking part of herself. The Hebrew *'legab'* by this time, was replaced with the Greek word for heart, *'kardia'*.

Like *'legab'* however, this word refers to the innermost centre of a human being. We have this understanding today when we have to get to the 'heart of the matter'. The heart is the centre.

Some thirty years later when Mary's son grew up and said; *'Love the Lord your God with all your heart',* He was referring not merely to an emotion but also to our thoughts and our will, to our innermost being.

We are called to love God not merely with affection dependent on feelings, but with our choices and our behaviour – all of which comes from the heart, the seat of knowledge and wisdom. It is therefore with our *'inner being',* that people have a choice whether to love God or not.

Emotional love is a variable. Love from the will is a constant. Of course when emotions get involved it may be harder to love, but to love is to make a conscious decision to do so. I almost wish this was not so.

To love anyone or anything with one's emotion is hard. People fall in and out of love, but at least in part, we can blame our feelings. We can say our love tanks are empty without too much guilt – it's just how it is! We may say we have fallen out of love because our partner no longer pleases us. We may have changed and we expect our partner to have changed too.

To love however, with all our heart, which involves our will, our inner being and our choices - well this seems to give us less room for manoeuvre. Jesus calls us to love with more than emotion and feeling. We are being called to love with something stronger - our core being.

John Flavel, a seventeenth-century English Puritan recognised the challenge of loving God with our heart:

> *'The human heart is the well-spring of all human action... the greatest difficulty in conversion, is to win the heart to God; and the greatest difficulty after conversion, is to keep the heart with God...'*[xliii]

On the whole, even at my low points, I know on the surface, it looked as though I was still loving people. I was certainly listening to them and when required I would offer a response. Too often though, my heart simply was not in it.

Whilst many people may not have noticed, over time I did. I began to feel as though I was lying, to others, to myself and to God. It began to eat me up and I became resentful and angry. I knew I had not been created to live this way but my pattern of behaviour seemed stuck in a rut. In the end I had to make a choice, to stop! To stop pretending, to stop seeming as though I was loving with my heart, when in fact I had little capacity to do so.

CHAPTER FIFTY-FOUR:
RESTORE TO FACTORY SETTING

As I acknowledged God wanted me to love Him with all my heart, for a while I wondered just what this entailed. After all any quick skip through the Bible, focusing on our heart, rather than heartening me, made me feel even more despondent.

I encountered less than encouraging glimpses into our heart. Ours is naturally wicked *(Genesis 8:21)* and deceitful *(Jeremiah 17:9)* and a place where sin is first committed *(Matthew 5:28)*. As Jesus warns us, out of the heart come: *'evil thoughts — murder, adultery, sexual immorality, theft, false testimony, slander' (Matthew 15:19)*. Yikes! Where did this leave me?

It seemed Jesus also saw through our words into our heart. *Luke* captures a story of Jesus to illustrate this *(18:9-14)*. We encounter a Pharisee who seems on the surface to be 'good'. The Pharisee in going to the temple to pray, claimed not to steal and not to do wrong. The Ten Commandments looked as though they were being obeyed.

The Pharisee was disciplined, fasting twice a week, and he took his tithing seriously. Yet Jesus knew this man's heart. Outwardly this man was doing everything right. Inwardly he was smug and self-righteous and rather than being 'holy', he was being holier-than-thou.

Meanwhile, Jesus looked to a tax-collector, who with his head bowed low, cried out to God; *'God, have mercy on me a sinner'*. We do not know this man's sin, but we can guess he had broken more than one of the Ten Commandments. Being a tax-collector, he had probably lied and stolen money most days of his life, yet it was this man who Jesus praised. It was this *'sinner'* whom Jesus said: *'returned home justified before God'*.

The Great Wall of China is visible from space. This man made accomplishment is visible from the lower part of the low Earth orbit, all be it, only under very favourable conditions. I am grateful as God looks at us from heaven, He looks less at our accomplishments and more at our heart.

God's heart is for us and He longs for ours to be for Him. Our words reveal the content of our heart *(Matthew 12:34)* and our actions reveal what truly lies in our heart. There is no room for hypocrisy with Jesus and He warned against it *(Luke 12:1)*.

The very people who were to uphold and teach the Law, (the Pharisees) had become hypocrites. It is interesting to note, it was Jesus Himself who first used this word with reference to our inner-self. He meant being different to that which we present.

In classical Greek, *'hypocrisy'*, spoke more of acting, of someone who practises deceit, but Jesus used it as a warning. God looks deep into our heart. He knows what lies behinds our actions and words.[xliv] Titus in his letter, found in the New Testament, also began to understand this:

> *'To the pure, all things are pure, but to those who are corrupted and do not believe, nothing is pure. In fact, both their minds and consciences are corrupted. They claim to know God, but by their actions they deny him. They are detestable, disobedient and unfit for doing anything good'*
> *(Titus 1:15-16).*

At this I was beginning to lose heart, right up until I came across the writer of Proverbs, who began to give me some hope:

> *'Above all else, guard your heart, for everything you do flows from it'*
> *(Proverbs 4:23).*

God longs for me to love Him with the very core of me; the deepest part of my identity.

Just as the disciples had to become aware of their hearts being hardened, so do I *(Mark 6:52)*. I found hope in us being able to guard our heart, but I have come to see that even this is not done in our own strength but in God's. As I look at people such as Mother Teresa who daily chose from her heart, from her will, to love God and others, so there has to be a way for all of us of orienteering our hearts for good.

For a while I supposed to *'guard your heart'*, just meant trying hard, striving all the more. After all did the writer of Proverbs not encourage the reader to:

'Keep your father's command and do not forsake your mother's teaching. Bind them always on your heart; fasten them around your neck'
(Proverbs 6:20-21).

By keeping God's commands in my heart *(Proverbs 3:1)* so it seemed all would be well. However, this overlooked the rather frustrating element of life, which is, I am human.

No matter how hard anyone tries to keep God's commands, so we end up breaking them. I know in part this keeps us close to God. Having commands and laws helps us to acknowledge that we do sin, and thus we are brought closer to God as we seek forgiveness. But in being asked to love God with all my heart, was I being set up for a fail? This seemed kind of cruel!

I even found that as I tried all the harder to guard my heart and love God with my heart, so I ended up failing all the more. I took some comfort that I was far from the first to have struggled with this. Paul, the apostle, knew of it and confessed as much to the church of Rome:

'For I do not do the good I want to do, but the evil I do not want to do - this I keep on doing'
(Romans 7:19).

But there had to be more. I later came across St Augustine who seemed to understand the complexities of loving God with our heart. He wrote:

'Follow humbly this simple stirring of love in your heart; I do not mean in your physical heart, but in your spiritual heart, which is your will'. xlv

Paul also referred to the spiritual element of our hearts, as he spoke of our heart being where the Holy Spirit and Jesus can dwell *(2 Corinthians 1:22 and Ephesians 3:17).* I came to see God longs to dwell in our hearts, in the seat of our will. My condition therefore, was as much spiritual as it was of choosing to love. For now I was setting my emotions to one side.

I have come to see for me personally, it is impossible to love God with my heart, or others by myself. I can only love through God loving me. Only through the strength and power of His Holy Spirit, can I love and live the way I am intended to.

God therefore was not asking me to do something by myself, rather He wanted to come alongside me – even to love Him. I began to seek the promise God had given to Ezekiel and His people:

'I will give you a new heart and put a new spirit in you; I will remove from you your heart of stone and give you a heart of flesh'
(Ezekiel 36:26).

To love God with my heart, with my inner being, with my will, has helped me to become more honest, both with myself and God. I have come to see that as I cannot hide anything from God, there is no point even trying.

No matter how well we may be hiding the truth from others, God can look into our hearts. At times such as in the case of a young boy called David, He does so and sees good where others cannot *(1 Samuel 16:7)*. Everyone else on the day when Samuel asked Jesse to assemble his sons, was looking at the outward appearance. Not God though; He was looking at the heart. God saw within David, a heart which far surpassed that of his more experienced and able brothers.

At other times God looks into our core and sees reality. We cannot hide anything from Him - ever. Although nowadays the Pharisees of Jesus' day have a bad press, at the time of Jesus they were often well respected. They knew the Law and spoke of it.

Jewish leaders of Jesus' day were seen to be keeping the Law and were held in high esteem. Jesus however, was less interested in their external keeping of the Law and looked at their hearts:

'I know you do not have the love of God in your hearts'
(John 5:42).

I sought for a long time to love others and to function as a Parish Priest. It took a long time before I acknowledged that I could not do this in my own strength. I longed to love God and to love others, but my heart had grown cold.

Love can only come from a pure heart *(1 Timothy 1:5)*. I have come to see I can only truly love with all my heart, through God's love flowing through me. My heart, my will, can over-ride even the best of intentions. I have to purify my heart, I have to allow God to take the lead.

Just as I had come to God with my mind in an attitude of surrender, so I realised this was required of my heart also.

Through surrendering my own way of doing things, I was becoming more open to God's ways. As I was drawing closer to God, through His word and in prayer, I hoped like the first disciples that my heart might burn within me with a passion for Jesus *(Luke 24:30)*.

To love God with my heart, was not centred purely on my will-power, rather it involved God's love and forgiveness. I had heard and even preached many times of God's unconditional love, of how God longs to forgive us and is always there for us. I now needed to start living this for myself.

In the midst of darkness however, lies can come to us. It is too easy after a time of being away from God, or after a time of sin to begin to believe the lies of the devil. Namely that what we have done is too awful to be taken to God. Instead of turning to God at such times, we turn our backs, ashamed of our actions and life.

King David can perhaps give us hope in this. The same young boy who was chosen by God because of his heart, ended up committing adultery and murder. I am sure as he came to God in repentance, he did not say the following words lightly:

> *'Create in me a pure heart, O God, and renew a steadfast spirit*
> *within me'*
> *(Psalm 51:10).*

David knew what it was to sin but he also knew what to do when he was at the end of his resources. As he called upon God that day, so he was forgiven and loved. Yes, there were consequences of his sin but he was given a new heart. God became his strength as he confesses later:

> *'My flesh and my heart may fail, but God is the strength of my*
> *heart and my portion forever'*
> *(Psalm 73:26).*

David acknowledged, as a human being he was prone to sin but with God he could be renewed. He also did not shy away from allowing himself to lay metaphorically naked before God:

> *'Test me, LORD, and try me, examine my heart and my mind'*
> *(Psalm 26:2).*

Through allowing God to examine his heart, David was surrendering his all and as he did so, he could begin to love again.

As I mentioned earlier, when I asked my mum, when I started being independent, she replied: *'as you came out of the womb'*. This independence and strength for a long time, served me well, but this was not how I was created to be. As I have come to surrender myself to God, so my state of being is gradually being restored.

It's if you like as if I am going back to, 'restore to factory settings'. For too long my personality and circumstances had resulted in my not including God in everything. I now long for the words of Solomon to be tattooed in my heart:

> *'Trust in the LORD with all your heart and lean not on your own understanding; in all your ways submit to him, and he will make your paths straight'*
> *(Proverb 3:5-6).*

As I do this however, I have almost had to re-learn how to live.

I have had to become less independent so I can be who God has created me to be. This has at times been painful, and there have been moments when I have tried to flee. However, the more I embrace, being loved by God and loving Him with all my heart, the more I see this is the only way for me.

God does not force this upon me. God has made me a human being, not a robot. Rather I have come to see the best way of living life is His way. As I seek to fulfil the command to love God with all my heart, there is a partnership.

My role, from my inner being, from my will, is to love God. God's part is to strengthen me to do so. Through the power of His Holy Spirit, through Jesus and His word dwelling in my heart *(Psalm 119:11)*, so I am strengthened and empowered to love with Him. His love is able to flow through me.

At times I sense God's leading is very practical, for example while I am called to love others, not all 'others' may be good for me. Thus on occasions I have felt it important to remove myself from certain situations and people. At times, their attitude and behaviour has had a negative influence on me. I am all too aware we are called to be 'salt and light'. However, at times of my strength being weak, of being overwhelmed, I have come to recognise my limitations.

At other times, now more mindful of my emotions, during low times, I try not to rely on them alone. Rather I try to be subservient to what I know of God. Loving God with my heart, involves the knowledge I have of Him.

Crucially, I now acknowledge my intellect is involved in loving God through the power of the Holy Spirit, through the word of God. I seek to be led less by emotions, but by my *'lebab'* - my *'kardia'*. I seek for my will, to be that of God's will. I do not underestimate how hard this can be. The more I come to God though, the more I know this is God's best way for me.

CHAPTER FIFTY-FIVE:
MARVELLING AT THE HEART OF OTHERS

As I consider the heart, and the call to love God and others with it, I honestly marvel at the great capacity human beings have to love. Many quite incredible people have forgiven others after great atrocities. I can only imagine that such love comes not merely from an emotional response, but from their inner being making a choice. At times the love and forgiveness which flows from a person's heart can only come from God's Holy Spirit enabling them to act so powerfully.

Corrie Ten Boom, a Christian, who was deported to Ravensbrueck concentration camp in September 1944, could not forgive her guards. Is this any wonder? Over 130,000 female prisoners passed through this camp, with some 50,000 women and children dying. Forced labour, medical experiments, inhumane conditions and starvation abounded.

Corrie Ten Boom, unlike her sister Betsie, survived the camp. On her release she spoke on forgiveness at a church service in Munich. This was incredible enough, but then she came face to face with a former prison guard who asked her for forgiveness. Corrie had just preached on it and she knew it was right to forgive, but she also knew she could not do so in her own strength. In prayer she found strength from God alone to forgive and she accepted his extended hand.

Corrie loved God with her whole heart, she knew it was right to forgive but without the power of God within her, she also knew it was impossible.[xlvi]

Chained to a basement wall in solitary confinement for five years, Terry Waite confessed, during this time, to not having felt particularly close to God. He repeatedly said a prayer from his youth; *'Lighten our darkness, we beseech thee, O Lord...'* Incredibly on his release he was able to forgive his captors. His love of God and God's love for him enabled him to forgive.

What of the mother of 18 year old Anthony Walker who was murdered in 2005? She testified it was only her Christian beliefs which enabled her to forgive. As she did, so she was helped to release her feelings of anger and revenge.

Likewise of the wife of a church organist in 2013, whose husband was bludgeoned to death on his way to Midnight Mass. She testified that she had no feelings of hate and un-forgiveness for his murderers. Rather Maureen Greaves spoke of praying for the killers, hoping, *'God's mercy will inspire them to true repentance'*.

It is incredible how our hearts can love and forgive. With God's love flowing through us our capacity to love can know no bounds. Jesus lived and died as an example of this. Even on the cross the words He uttered were:

'Father, forgive them,
for they do not know what they are doing'
(Luke 23:34).

Loving God with our heart is dependant not on our emotions and feelings, but on our will. Loving God is a choice. Loving others is also a choice and made easier if it is done through God's love flowing through us.

We must however, always remember we are sinners, so even if we choose to love and our will is obedient to our desire, we still need God. From God's love we are able to love. It is not about us coming to God through good actions. Rather as we are loved by God and love Him in return, so from this we are able to love ourselves and others. This can then manifest itself in good works.

At times God's people in the face of extreme adversity, have known they have had no choice but to turn to God with their heart, with their will. Habakkuk was one such person. At a time of great hardship, as he waited for a neighbouring nation to invade God's people, at a time of famine, Habakkuk made a decision to love God. He says:

'yet I will rejoice in the LORD, I will be joyful in God
my Saviour'
(Habakkuk 3:18).

Habukkuk knew on that day that he could not love God because of an emotion or because of his circumstances. On that day and on many others, Habukkuk and God's people have loved God from their will. I always wonder what day the Psalmist was having when he said:

'This is the day the LORD has made;
We will rejoice and be glad in it'
(Psalm 118:24 New King James Version).

This verse is common in Anglican liturgy and believe me there were many days when I have said the words with a hollow heart.

There were times when I only just made it out of the house to church, let alone had the energy to believe these words. In time however, I came to see these words needed to be said even more on the very days I wondered if they were true.

In saying them I was almost asking God to reveal Himself, to show these words were true. Furthermore these words were an invitation to my will to take control and chose to love God, rather than my waking up and being in the mood to do so.

Back to Habakkuk, a prophet who knew of this too. In a very short book of the Old Testament, we see almost a telephone conversation between Him and God. Habakkuk complains and God explains. Habakkuk incidentally lived up to his name, which means *'wrestler'*. After a long conversation, Habakkuk concludes saying:

'I will rejoice in the LORD, I will be joyful in God my Saviour.
The Sovereign LORD is my strength'
(Habakkuk 3:18-19a).

By this response, you may imagine Habakkuk has received good news. Well, not exactly!

As you can read in chapter *3:16-17*, his heart pounded, his lips quivered, *'decay crept into his bones'*. There were no figs, grapes, olives or crops, along with no sheep or cattle. Yet, in spite of all of this, still Habakkuk trusted in the Lord and was able to rejoice in Him. He knew the Lord was His strength in spite of the current circumstances.

By the way the irony is not lost on me, that one of the physical symptoms I had during my darker days was of either a pounding in my heart, or an inability to catch my breath. As I have said I considered these palpitations, to be anxiety, until I ruled this out.

Either way this knocking of my heart was ironic because inside my heart felt dead. As someone whose family has a history of heart disease I do not say this lightly. My heart often felt dead inside and yet 'my heart – my will' was there, at the core of my being, along with my soul trying to make itself heard.

'For where your treasure is, there your heart will be also'
(Matthew 6:21).

I guess it's fair to say for a long time my heart was in the wrong place. My treasure should have been found in loving God, but it had got lost along the way. By the way, have you ever considered what God treasures? It is us *(Deuteronomy 32:9)*.

CHAPTER FIFTY-SIX:
EGGS AND BACON

As I considered loving God with 'all' my heart, I was drawn to the prophet Ezekiel. This prophet spoke of God being able to give His people not only a new heart and a new spirit, but an *'undivided heart'* *(Ezekiel 11:19)*.

I knew in my life, my loyalties had long been divided into four areas.

I knew God and I sought to serve Him.

I had a Parish ministry with many responsibilities.

I had a family and a son whom I adored and wanted to be with.

Finally there was me – whoever me was.

Too often I compartmentalised these areas, more often than not, resulting in not doing a great job in any of them. Through coming across *'Loving God with my all...'* I knew this is what I wanted, what I needed and what I was created for.

Increasingly I was seeing with God coming first in everything, then everything else could flow from this source of love. I couldn't keep dividing life into 'God' and 'everything else'. As Jesus Himself said:

> *'No one can serve two masters'*
> *(Matthew 6:24)*.

In addition, in the New Testament I came across James who spoke of people who were *'double-minded'* *(1:8)*. On closer inspection as I came to *chapter 4* of the book of *James*, I came to see being *'divided'* or *'double-minded'* was not just of this world. James says:

*'Submit yourselves, then, to God. Resist the devil, and he will flee
from you. Come near to God and he will come near to you...
purify your hearts, you double-minded. Grieve, mourn and wail.
Change your laughter to mourning and your joy to gloom.
Humble yourselves before the Lord, and he will lift you up'*
(James 4:7-10).

It has been said the greatest lie the Devil convinces people, is that he does not exist. He does. This said it is so important to get a balance here. On the one hand I do not want to give too much glory to the Devil. To speak of him can lead people to attribute too much to him; it can generate an unhealthy interest in him. On the other hand, to deny he is at work in this world can result in us not protecting ourselves against his schemes.

In these verses from James, it seemed to me that as much as I wanted to submit to God, I had to also admit the Devil, at times, was at work. I knew through the works of Jesus I did not need to be afraid, but I did need to become alert to the Devil's tricks.

Through learning about surrender, I knew I wanted to submit to God. This it seemed, involved humility. I wanted to come near to God so in turn He could come near to me. As I came to love Him with my all, so I was coming closer to God. In humility I was sensing less of me and more of God.

In the name of Jesus I now wanted to resist the Devil: his lies, schemes and tricks. This it seemed was made possible through purifying my heart. The fact that James used the word *'double-minded'* after the word heart, reminded me of how our hearts are not just an emotional entity but our will.

As I looked back at the past few years I had endured many lies and tricks. The Devil will often work in our weaknesses; he will attempt to distract us from what is important and most of all he loves to waste our time. Whilst it is a privilege to be involved in people's lives, for a period of 18 months, the amount of people who sought 'help' from me was more than normal.

In addition to a number of people facing significant mental health issues, there were a number of people who had been involved in the occult. Whilst I worked with other agencies, a lot of this, understandably was of a confidential nature. In addition the Devil hit me in my weakness: in administration and building works. As the Archdeacon frequently remarked, it was *'unprecedented'*. Over time all of this took a toll on my heart, as well as my mind and soul.

Over time, I recovered from such an onslaught and as I did, I wanted to be all for God; kicking the Devil's schemes away. In addition to praying Paul's prayer of *Ephesians 6:10-18* over myself and the parishes, I wanted to flee from the Devil and come near to God.

Rather than having a divided heart or being double-minded, I wanted to be wholehearted. After all who in the Olympics has ever received a gold medal through giving anything less than 100%.

In my own life I knew I was guilty of not always doing things wholeheartedly. Often this was because I was exhausted and too busy, but sometimes I just scraped by because that was all I wanted to give. My mum's phrase of, *'a job worth doing is worth doing well'*, would often resound, but not always abound.

How often do we do just enough to get by? Does it matter? Surely if the job gets done, that's what matters. Well it seems not.

In *2 Chronicles 25*, there is an account of the reign of Amaziah, King of Judah. Starting at the age of 25 years, he ruled well for 29 years. His feats in battle were commendable, he raised an army and fought well, and he secured peace for Judah. He acted in accordance to the Law of Moses and he was seen to do *'right in the eyes of the Lord'*. So all in all a pat on the back...except no...

The writer of Chronicles reveals three words which undo all the good aforementioned. Amaziah; *'Did what was right in the eyes of the Lord, but not wholeheartedly' (v.2)*. You would have thought success in battle was enough, but no, God saw into Amaziah's heart. Amaziah's failing was to bring back gods of the Edomites, to bow down to them and to offer sacrifices to them *(v.14)*.

Amaziah had been listening to God, to His laws and even to God's prophets, but for some reason the temptation to turn to other gods was too much. In this action, Amaziah was saying, 'God is not enough'. In that instant Amaziah was double-minded, his heart was divided; he was not wholehearted and the Lord's anger burned against him.

God commands us to love only Him; no other deity is to be loved. He commands this by His very nature. He invites us to love Him with our all, so we can have the life designed for us. Amaziah had done well, but then he turned to something other than God. God created us for Himslef alone and

213

we have to trust God, as our Creator, that He knows best.

Meanwhile, another King crops up in the book of Acts, who is heralded by Luke as being *'wholehearted'*. Yet this same man was a liar, an adulterer and a murderer. Surely Luke had got the wrong man!

> *'God testified concerning him: 'I have found David son of Jesse, a*
> *man after my own heart; he will do everything I want him to''*
> *(Acts 13:22).*

You have to wonder how Luke could have recorded such a thing about a man, who did so much wrong, who lived a lie for so long.

This seems all the more unfair if you take into account a later king, a younger king, the young Josiah. He was recognised as being a king, like no other. The writer of *2 Kings* said of Josiah, he:

> *'turned to the* LORD*...with all his heart and with all his soul*
> *and with all his strength, in accordance with all the*
> *Law of Moses'*
> *(2 Kings 23:25).*

Surely King Josiah, who loved God with his all, who initiated magnificent reforms for Israel, deserved the title of being a man after God's own heart?

Yet, no! The title of a *'man after God's own heart'*, was reserved for David – an adulterer, murderer and liar. Yes okay we may know of David's great Psalm of repentance (Psalm 51), but this only came after the death of his son with Bathsheba.

David had had over nine months to be sorry and to get his act together, but no. Instead during those months of deceit, he added to his crime of adultery - murder. Bathsheba's husband Uriah, at the request of King David, was put in the front line of battle and killed.

In fact to be honest David's sins started even earlier than adultery. Where was Bathsheba's husband at the time when David was lusting after Bathsheba? He was away in battle. *2 Samuel 11:1* sets the scene:

> *'In the spring, at the time when kings go off to war, David sent*
> *Joab out with the king's men and the whole Israelite*
> *army...David remained in Jerusalem'.*

David had decided not to go war that year, instead he had sent others. David already negligent of his duties, kicked around his palace, so he got bored and ended up chasing another man's wife.

Yet, this same man, King David, is seen as being *'a man after God's own heart'*. Perhaps I don't want anything to do with God after all!

Through this terrible episode we see how God does not seek perfection. He knows we sin. He would of course much rather we did not murder and steal another man's wife. At the same time however, God is after our heart.

God's primary interest is in the desire of our heart. He knows we mess up and He longs for us to turn to Him when we do. God longs that our heart *'wholeheartedly'* belongs to Himself - this is His desire.

David was not always a great husband or father, but His life was immersed in God. In His love and worship He put God first. He made some catastrophic mistakes, but on realising them, his reaction was to confess, to turn to God, to repent, to seek God to create in him a new heart.

God knows who we are; fallen human beings. God is more interested in our intention, in our desire, rather than perfection.

David got it wrong, big time, but God is a God who forgives; a God who longs to forgive. God cannot forgive what has not been confessed or repented of. For our part we need to know this, remember this and turn to Him. It is our love God seeks, being sold out in our love for Him, not perfection.

We cannot do this alone and nor does God expect us to. Paul as he wrote to the Galatians reminds us, Christ can live in us *(Galatians 2:19-20)*. Everything is less about us and more about God working in us, in all things. I liken it to the death of our will, so it becomes nearer to God's will.

By the way, why eggs and bacon? Well, as the hen lamented to the pig that she was sick and tired of having to lay eggs every day for her master's breakfast, the pig replied: *'At least it's just your eggs he's after'*. The hen gave from what she had, the pig meanwhile had to give of his all. God gave us His all and for our own good, He longs for us to do the same.

CHAPTER FIFTY-SEVEN:
RIVERS FLOW DOWNWARDS

As I continue to reflect on *'wholeheartedness'*, let's return to Jesus' interaction with the Rich man *(Mark 10:17-31)*. As the man asked Jesus who can inherit eternal life, he more than likely thought he was in with a chance. After all he had kept many commandments since he was young.

Unlike King David, he had apparently not murdered, committed adultery, stolen or even lied. He had even honoured his parents. Jesus looked at him and loved him...surely this guy was going to fast track to eternal life.

Yet, Jesus knew there was something which kept this man back from being wholehearted. As Jesus looked at this young man who during his entire life, had done so much good, Jesus could see His heart was divided. His wealth was a stumbling block.

This does not mean that rich people cannot love and worship God and inherit eternal life. Rather Jesus was asking what was first in this man's life. Would God ever be able to be first in this young man's life or would wealth always make his life divided?

Jesus ensures that we know which people He met were wholehearted. A widow giving her all, even though it was only a few pennies, was commended *(Luke 21:1-4)*. Mary in pouring perfume over Jesus, gave a lavish gift; it was worth three hundred denarii, which was an average year's wage *(John 12:3-5)*. In today's money (2018) that would be £28 500. I do not limit wholeheartedness to money, but to anything which can be put first above Jesus.

I spoke earlier of how I had begun to see my son as number one. During the toddler years of my son, in many ways I had begun to put him first above God. In my disenchantment with my job and my dislike of who

I was becoming, all I wanted to do was spend time with him.

A lot of this was because I loved him and enjoyed his company. Some of it was that I liked the person I was around him. He always brought out the best in me. It is really only now, as I am beginning to live life in a new way, that I can see however, this was not always healthy. There is nothing wrong with having a close relationship with your child, but sometimes I was seeking a 'love' from him, which only God could give.

More recently, I have seen that this wasn't good for my relationship with God either. Only now, as I am being drawn closer to God, is the balance being restored.

In no way does this mean I love John any less. Nor does it mean he has done anything wrong. In fact I think my relationship with him is all the more healthy for it. As I put God first, everything which flows from God's source of love is improved.

Incidentally my husband is fine with this too. He had read the small print on the contract and on us having a child, he knew he was sliding further down my list. He was now fourth, that is after God, my son and the cat! Since writing this, the cat has died so for the first time in seven years Jack is back in at number three.

Too many people however, can be unsettled by the notion of putting God first. Some words of Jesus in the Gospel of Matthew have left many people feeling uncomfortable:

> *'Anyone who loves their father or mother more than me is not worthy of me; anyone who loves their son or daughter more than me is not worthy of me'*
> *(Matthew 10:37).*

Many people want their marriage, child or pet to be first. As I wrote earlier, my son understood it. John knew God was first and he was not threatened by this. Coming second to God should be more than good enough.

From loving God with my whole heart, I am able to love people all the more. Such love comes from God's strength and not just my own. Only through loving God with my all, can I truly love others. I am then able to love from love I have first received. Some things just have to be in the right order.

Rivers naturally flow downwards. Yes, they can flow upstream but only with considerable engineering. God wants us to love others, but through

His love. There are times in all relationships, when the natural love we may have for another, is put to the test. This may be through sleep deprivation, the stress of a job or having to care for someone when they are ill.

My Grannie was a remarkable woman. She was gentle and loving and she had a good word for everybody. Sadly her last few years were hijacked with dementia and she became a changed person. She was still at times lovely, but her degenerative state meant caring for her was a lot harder.

Loving Grannie, for my family, was no longer merely a feeling, it became an action. With the cruelty of dementia, Grannie was no longer the lady we had always known, but my family chose to love her wholeheartedly through their care until the end.

When it comes to wholehearted love, God designed us for this. Our heart is to be directed to Him. This may include sacrifice, but God never asks anything of us, that He has not modelled.

Jesus gave His all, He gave His life. Jesus was not a people pleaser; He was pleasing to God. This is the wholeheartedness which God commands. To not love God with our whole heart means we are open to other influences, which are not for our good but harm.

How many people put their ambitions, desires or jobs, first? This can not only harm their family and their own well-being, but it can also affect a relationship with God, as everything gets out of kilter. In saying this, living life loving God with all our heart is not easy. Jesus Himself recognised this.

After Jesus' interaction with the rich man, speaking to His disciples who were confused about who could be saved, Jesus said; *'With man this is impossible, but not with God; all things are possible with God'* (Mark 10:27). In coming to God with my whole heart, I am coming to the source whose very nature it is to love. In God and God alone all things are possible – this includes being able to love Him with my heart and indeed all of me.

CHAPTER FIFTY-EIGHT:
HOME IS WHERE THE HEART IS

As we are invited to love God with all our heart, so God makes it possible for us to find His heart. This heart of love resulted in God sending His Son to earth for us, to enable us to have a relationship with Him. In putting God first, we are exalting God in our hearts, with our all. Let's for a moment consider the Disciples.

In reading with my son this past week, he was pretty put out by Peter and the others for letting Jesus down on the days of His arrest, trial and crucifixion. Their failings are well documented.

I'm looking forward to reading Acts with my son, because there he will see this same group of people doing remarkable things. Within Acts, we are witnesses to a group of scared, despondent people becoming incredible people of God. From divided hearts, from double-mindedness we see wholeheartedness.

Through the death and resurrection of Jesus Christ; through the forgiveness of Jesus and the gift of His Holy Spirit - we see in the early church remarkable things; miracles galore, followers in abundance and churches multiplying. There were days of wobbles, beatings, shipwrecks, persecutions, imprisonments and deaths but in their love the disciples had become wholehearted.

In fact tradition suggests all but one was martyred for their faith. The apostle John, it is widely believed, was the only one who had a peaceful death. Even this death however, was on the island of Patmos, during which he received the book of *Revelation* – so perhaps not all that peaceful after all.

The disciples who became apostles, along with millions since, lived wholeheartedly and at the core of this they were loving God with all their heart. This included sacrifice which resulted in them choosing to put someone or something over themselves. God, for the apostles, became number one.

Such 'whole-heartedness' did not come without a cost or without hardship, but they knew their life on earth was not all there was. The crown they pursued was not of jewels of this world, but of righteousness *(2 Timothy 4:1-8)* and eternal living. In the New Testament letters we may not read much about *'loving God with our heart, mind, strength and soul'*, but their lives testify they were living it.

Now of course we can be wholehearted over many different things. Some people are sold out for the sport they play, or the job they have, or in their pursuit of enjoyment. A tale of caution however...

One soldier on his return from an operational tour was wholehearted in wanting to have a good time. In fact he spent all of his Operational Tour allowance (all £6000 of it) in one night! Twelve ladies helped him spend his money – less said. He ended up in jail that night not because of spending the night with prostitutes, but for not having enough money left to pay for a bottle of champagne. He ended up in a fight with the bouncers and came to regret his wholehearted desire to have fun that night!

Another soldier, (bless him) wholeheartedly became addicted to cocaine, or at least he thought he was. He ended up losing everything and started stealing to fuel his wholehearted desire to sniff! In the end it was found in fact that he was not addicted to cocaine but rather to 'Vim' – a powder used to clean sinks!

His (charming) wife was not buying cocaine as he thought, but mixing Vim with flour, making what looked like cocaine. She was pocketing his money in a personal account. The soldier lost his family, his home, his job and landed up in prison because of his wholehearted addiction.

Being wholehearted and being called to living wholeheartedly encompasses everything. Increasingly as I look at the four parts of me which Jesus' invitation speaks of, I see my soul as deep within me, designed and created purely for God; my mind as something which can surrender to God for my good; my strength is all I have to give and the way in which I do so, is in God; finally my heart wraps everything up.

I am not there yet, but I hope and pray as I love God with my all, I may be led by His Holy Spirit into wholehearted discipleship. From love, from becoming more aware of God's Presence, I hope to be led further down the path of understanding of what wholehearted discipleship means.

Paul knew and makes reference to our hearts in this:

> *'Therefore, as God's chosen people, holy and dearly loved, clothe yourselves with compassion, kindness, humility, gentleness and patience. Bear with each other and forgive one another...Forgive as the Lord forgave you. And over all these virtues put on love, which binds them all together in perfect unity...And whatever you do, whether in word or deed, do it all in the name of the Lord Jesus, giving thanks to God the Father through him'*
> *(Colossians 3:12-14, 17).*

I wrestled with these words for many years. The last part in particular made me work all the harder and strive all the more; life became about 'doing'. Whatever I did, if in the name of Jesus, had to be good. Nothing less than 100% was acceptable.

I guess I had overlooked, *'And over all these virtues put on love'*. We can never be expected to do everything in the name of Jesus by ourselves. Rather God longs for us to be loved by Him first. From here flows my ability to do all He asks of me.

As I seek and trust God, I am already experiencing the blessing of God but this is not why I am submitting to God. I submit and surrender because this is God's way. With the leading of His Holy Spirit, I am seeking wholeheartedness. In turn I am discovering more of what it means to be whole in every sense. In being invited to love God with all our heart, I see this as returning home.

The popular phrase, *'home is where the heart is'* perhaps has something to say after all. As I have come to love God with my all, so I am finding where my home is, that is in God Himself. Where we put our heart, our will, our being, there is our home.

In all honesty I have spent too little of my life considering my 'home'. By this I do not just mean 'heaven' – a place to go when life on earth has ceased – although I do look forward to this. No, I mean home, as in being with God, an eternal home which starts from the moment of coming to know God as Lord and Saviour.

Busyness took my eye off the ball for too long. I was accepting second best because that is all I could see. From becoming more aware of my heart, and in turn being led to living more wholeheartedly, I am in fact being led 'home'.

I am increasingly becoming aware of being called to 'eternal living'. I used to refer to being called to 'eternity', but for too long this referred to something which happened on my death, to a new life in heaven. However, in being drawn closer to God, 'eternal living' reminds me living starts on earth before heaven.

I could now identify a feeling deep within me was of being 'homesick'. There is within each of us a longing deep within, to be somewhere other than this world. This I believe is our heart and soul crying out to be with God – to be home.

Ultimately yes, this will be with God in heaven, but for now whilst on earth, I am being drawn 'home' in every-day living; being with God wholeheartedly, with my heart, mind, strength and soul. The author of 'the cloud of unknowing' puts it better than I:

> 'Through the will we love God, we desire God and finally come to rest in God'. [xlvii]

***

'**Love the Lord your God** *with all your heart and with all your soul and with all your mind and* **with all your strength**'

***

CHAPTER FIFTY-NINE:
WITH ALL YOUR BODY?!?

When I first came across the verse to Love God with my all, I was a little daunted at the prospect of having to love God with my 'body'. My body was certainly the weakest part of me. For several years I had suffered what I would consider low level ill-health. To consider loving God with my body was something which at times I could not imagine.

Yet even as I write this now, I wonder what led me to believe God was asking me to love Him with my body. The verse actually uses the word 'strength' or 'might', not 'body'. Where had I heard the word 'body'?

Perhaps without realising it, I had been lured to the modern phrase; 'mind, body and soul'. Nowadays the phrase is common and all sorts of things can apparently feed our 'mind, body and soul'. Spa's, retreats, books and even shopping experiences all seem to offer what is good for them. Some even add the word 'spirit' as well.

I have now come to see within the New Testament, the word used was 'ἰσχύος', as in 'strength' or 'might'. The word, 'ἰσχύος', 'strength' can of course be perceived as our body, as strength often refers to the state of someone's physical-ness.

Imagine my surprise therefore in deeper study to discover just as the word, 'body' was not the meaning of the word 'ἰσχύος' – 'ischuos', it was likely 'strength' and 'might' may not be totally accurate either. However, before we get to what I think is the most wonderful understanding of 'ischuos', I would like to skim over how I came to God with my 'body' and 'strength' and 'might'.

Rightly or wrongly, as I first came across this verse, the thought of loving God with my body had a massive impact on me.

Some days it was enough for me to be up and about, let alone loving God with my body. Being ill, all be it low level, always annoyed me and led to a constant wrestling with God. I could never reconcile being ill with mission and my vocation.

How was being ill helpful, when I had three funerals and three school visits this week? It also frustrated me on a personal level, because I am someone who enjoys or at least feels the need to do some form of exercise every day. Not to exercise, brings on irritability.

I would wrestle with God, saying: *'surely it is better for the Kingdom of God and for me, to just stay well'*. Eventually on coming across this verse, just as I had given over my weakened heart, mind and soul, I put up my hands and said, *'Weak though it is, take it. My body's not great, but it's the best I can give – have it'*.

My own body had weakened physically, so although I had little to give, if God wanted me to love Him with my body, well I would give it a go. For a while I actually felt that by giving my body to God in love, perhaps this was to be part of a healing process. Over time I had to learn to come to God with what I had, rather than with what I did not.

CHAPTER SIXTY:
LET'S ALL SING A LITTLE OLIVIA NEWTON JOHN; 'LET'S GET PHYSICAL...''

I am sorry if you have seen the video to that song, the image of all of those rather unfit men is now flooding back to me as well...moving swiftly on!

The challenge with our bodies, (or at least what I find), is I rarely give it much thought, except when it does not function as I expect. Unless you are a body builder or have a job like a sports person whereby so much of your life revolves around your body, I think in the main, we just potter along in our shells.

Talking of which I find it incredible what people can achieve with their bodies in their own strength. The mountains people climb, the distances people run, the weights lifted, often defies what we consider the human body to be capable of. Within each Olympics, records are broken time and again.

One athlete I marvel at is Rebecca Romero; an Olympic medal winner at both rowing and cycling. She is far from having gained the most medals and yet her story is nevertheless impressive. After just 6 years of taking rowing seriously, she got a silver medal in the 2004 Olympic games at Athens. Disappointed however, with her achievement and disillusioned with rowing, Rebecca switched to cycling.

She became the first British woman ever to compete in two different sports, let alone to win a medal in both. Rebecca sped to gold in the women's 3000m individual pursuit race. Her achievement was attributed to her driven-ness and her determination.

I equally marvel at Sir Steve Redgrave who after having won five gold medals at consecutive Olympic games (1984-2000), on retirement from the sport, he had to run a marathon – just to calm his body down! Most people have to train and give their all to run a marathon. Sir Steve meanwhile, ran one as a way of reducing his training regime.

Rebecca and Sir Steve are amongst thousands of sports people who have pushed their bodies and strength to the limit. However, injuries befall even the best of people, old age creeps up and eventually every person's body and strength fails.

For most of us though, we go through life rarely giving much thought to our body, well that is until our body hurts, or becomes ill. It is often only then that we truly give it some consideration.

For me, so long as I could do my job and go for a jog most days, I am guilty of having given my body little thought. Even when I was unwell, I did not always give time to it. When I was ill, I found its inability to perform a hindrance, an annoyance, especially if it made me become more dependent on someone else.

I am grateful that any illness has only been chest infections and the like, as I am aware so many people suffer so much more. Yet for me, chest infections have always hit at my core, often resulting in a loss of voice, something which a minister can find hard to work through.

I always felt to take a day off sick, was weak, it was being lazy and it was letting others down. There was more than one occasion when even with no voice I was still trying to do services. Sometimes I used extra power point slides, whilst on one occasion I printed off sermons for the congregation to read. During one funeral, with little voice, I even looked around to see if I recognised anyone who could possibly read the eulogy.

God created us in His image *(Genesis 1:27)*, but He also gave us a body. Human beings were not created as angels and nor were we merely created as a soul or spirit. We have been given bodies.

Furthermore, (whether I liked it or not) we were created to be dependent on each other and on God. The words, *'Our Father'* in the Lord's prayer, as I said earlier, reveal we are part of something bigger than ourselves. We are called to be with others and are invited to come to God with our needs.

In saying *'Our Father'* we recognise God is not just our Father, but He is the Father of many. Jesus did not start what has become known as the Lord's Prayer with, 'My Father', it is *'Our Father'*. As we ask God for our daily bread, God invites us to come to Him with our needs (note I say needs and not wants!).

Even Jesus Himself was created to be dependent on others. As fully human, He was born and placed within a family. Joseph and Mary had the responsibility of bringing Him up, of watching over Him, and of providing His day to day needs.

Even as a grown man, Jesus allowed others to take care of His daily needs *(Luke 8:2-3)*. Mary (called Magdalene) from whom seven demons had come out, Joanna the wife of Chuza, the manager of Herod's household, Susanna and many others supported Jesus' ministry by providing for His physical needs. Jesus was not too proud to allow others to tend to Him.

Throughout the Bible we see attention given to the body. Jesus may have said; *'Man does not live on bread alone'*, but equally He gave time to feeding over 5000 and 4000 hungry people.

As a quick aside, last week I was trying to get toast into a child who was in no hurry over breakfast. My encouragements were knocked back by the words, *'mumma, man does not live on bread alone'*...

After teaching all day, Jesus did not have to feed the hungry crowds, He could have sent them away, but He didn't. Rather He had compassion on them and fed them, not just with a snack but with enough food that there were left overs *(Mark 6:30-44)*. Jesus having healed a young girl, who everyone thought was dead, was also concerned that she should have something to eat *(Mark 5:41-43)*. God created us with bodies which need to be fed and looked after.

This also happened in the Old Testament: Elijah was used by God to feed the Widow at Zarephath. Elijah himself knew of the miracles associated with food, as just earlier he had been fed by ravens *(1 Kings 17)*. God provided manna and quail during the wilderness years *(Exodus 16)*. Time and again, we can see God's interest in people, in their bodies, but it was not just to do with food.

Consider on how many occasions Jesus Himself was concerned with the bodies of others. On coming to Jesus, people could see, hear, walk, be cured of leprosy, be freed of evil spirits and even come to life again.

Jesus Himself, as well as being fully God, was fully human and we see the effects of His ministry on His own body. The Gospel writers record when Jesus Himself was tired, hungry, thirsty, troubled and in pain. Even after His resurrection from the grave, He asked for food *(Luke 24:41-43)*, and ate it.

Jesus chose to take on a human body, with a brain, mind, heart, lungs, even a 'stapes'. Do you know where your 'stapes' is? It's the third bone of the three ossicles in the middle ear. The reason I mention it, is because it is the smallest bone in your body! Jesus as a human, was created like any other.

Jesus took on a body to identify with us, to understand what it was to be human, but also to show us how we can live in our human body. Ultimately through His life, He can show us how we are to love God with our all.

We were created by God with a body and through my own weariness I came to see we were created to be dependent on God and others. It was only as I recognised the limitations of my own body, that I allowed myself to stop being so independent. As I came to love God with my body, so I saw that I was created to depend on God more than I had been doing.

In considering how to love God with all of my body, I was drawn to Paul who spoke to the church at Corinth:

> *Do you not know that your bodies are temples of the Holy*
> *Spirit, who is in you, whom you have received from God? You*
> *are not your own; you were bought at a price. Therefore honour*
> *God with your bodies'*
> *(1 Corinthians 6:19-20).*

Paul wrote of this in context of sexual immorality and how our bodies are for the Lord. As a believer in Jesus Christ, as someone who has invited God's Holy Spirit into my life, I am realising I too have a responsibility for the whole of my own body.

CHAPTER SIXTY-ONE:
KEEPING AS WELL AS WE CAN

God Himself through His Holy Spirit dwells within me, and I have a responsibility to take care of my body. In addition I need to remember my body belongs to God. This is actually for my good. As Creator of my body, it stands to reason He knows what is best for it.

In coming to love God with my body, I have come to submit my whole being which includes my body. This is not a new thought. The author of, *'The cloud of unknowing'* from the late fourteenth century, encouraged those to whom he was writing to, *'keep in good health as an aid of being with God, as an aid to prayer'*. xlviii

Now please do not hear me wrongly. In no way am I suggesting only those who are in good health can be with God. By no means. Paul the apostle himself revealed times of his own ill health. One of the most inspirational ladies I have ever met was confined to a wheelchair and suffered much ill health. This lady's gift of prayer was incredible. She would pray for at least 8 hours a day.

Personally, on many occasions, my own ill health was incredibly well timed. I am not suggesting God made me ill, but I know that He often used times of illness to draw me closer to Him. For example, after I had announced my resignation from the Parish I ended up with flu, 'real flu' and it knocked me out for two weeks.

Initially I was so frustrated as I had had so much planned in the wake of the announcement. Instead, I had two weeks of being ill, of being withdrawn from parish responsibilities. There was time to pray, time to be with God and time to rest. The added blessing of this time was that by the time I returned to work, everyone had got used to the idea of my leaving. Thus I was saved a lot of questions and pastoral engagement.

Here too though, please do not read me wrongly...I am not saying God gives illness, nor am I saying illness is always for some greater higher purpose. Hospital visiting, coming alongside those who are terminally ill, and being called to the bedside of a young child will always makes me wrestle with God.

Seeing how some people have to struggle during their life seems intolerably unfair. Having to do the funeral of any baby will have any minister questioning God and life. I know we live in a world of sin and I know this world is not all there is, but still, it is impossible not to wrestle with God as one stands beside a tiny coffin.

For my own self, sadly I learned a little too late that at times I pushed my own body too hard. Whilst I may have thought I was loving God in service and ministry, at times I expected too much from my body. Looking back I should have given my body more rest. I was often pushing it far harder than it was capable of going.

I am grateful in my current lifestyle, to be able to now make more time to listen to my body and to give it more rest. I try to allow it to function at a pace which it is more designed for. A very practical measure is to go to bed earlier. Too often late nights are just spent watching, 'drivel'. Studies are showing too much 'blue screen' time is affecting our ability to sleep.

As I seek to rest more, so I am able to love God with more of my all. Loving God, I have come to see, is less about pushing myself to my limits and beyond. Rather it is about listening to what God and God alone wants from me. As I love God, so I am spending more actual time with Him. As I do so, I am becoming more aware of how He has created me and for what purpose. In doing this I try not to be the cause of my physical weakness.

A warning though. At times this may involve removing certain aspects of your life which may not be healthy for you, such as an addiction, whether this be with, alcohol, excessive exercise, caffeine, nicotine, over-eating or unhealthy working practices. Few of us like to admit such failings, let alone do something about them. To become more disciplined is never easy. There are spiritual disciplines too.

Fasting is one such well-known discipline. To absent from foods or other substances for a time, such as during Lent or Advent, or to do it on a more regular basis, can help people to love God with their all. Richard Foster writes well of this in, *'Celebration of the Disciplines'*.

As we abstain, so we can focus less on our self and our intake and more on God. Such a discipline which first affects our bodies, can renew our minds, transform our hearts and nurture our soul. Throughout history there have been other forms of denial or even harm to our bodies in an attempt to draw close to God.

On occasions these may be motivated by an attitude of penitence, as seen in the film, 'The Mission'. Rodrigo Mendoza, (played by Robert De Niro), a former slave hunter, seeks forgiveness through accompanying a Jesuit Priest on a journey. He does so, by carrying a very heavy awkward bundle, which serves as a reminder for all the wrong he has done. Other people have used forms of flagellation as a religious discipline.

I make no judgement on those who have sought to draw closer to God in such ways. I am merely grateful God invites us to come just as we are. It is God who forgives and He longs to do so.

CHAPTER SIXTY-TWO:
'THIS IS MY BODY...'

As I considered loving God with all of my body, I cannot escape the awareness Jesus had of His own body, nor how He quite literally loved God with all of it. There is the occasion in a bustling crowd when a lady touched Him for healing and He felt His power go out from Him *(Mark 5:25-34)*. On this occasion Jesus shows not only how He was aware of His own body, but also of the plight of the woman's.

Jesus could easily have let this woman just go on her way. She was healed. There didn't actually need to be a conversation – except Jesus knew one was necessary. To have been bleeding for twelve years, to have spent all of your money looking for a cure, would have meant this woman was now not only poor, but she would also have become a social outcast.

To be bleeding so profusely would have alienated her from her society. Jesus knew this and as such He wanted to talk to her, He wanted to restore her mind and heart as well as her body. He could have quite easily have just let His power pass through Him and let the woman go on her way, but No! Jesus wanted her to be restored in all aspects of her being. He even went one step further and called her *'daughter'*. With this word, He spoke tenderly; lovingly. This great teacher, Rabbi, healer, stopped and welcomed her into His family.

As an aside, I marvel most days at just what made it into the Bible. First through oral transmission and then through the faithfulness of scribes, men throughout the centuries have kept alive an account of a woman who suffered continual menstruation. It's not the first time a lady's 'period' has come under scrutiny.

What of Rachel, Jacob's wife? In a bid to hide some family idols which she had stolen from her father Laban, she sat on them. I mentioned this in passing earlier, but in her own words, Rachel said: *'Don't be angry, my lord, that I cannot stand up in your presence; I'm having my period.' (Genesis 31:35).* Such language also features in *Isaiah 30:22* who talks about *'menstrual cloths'*. Moving swiftly on...

It is perhaps the day Jesus was on the cross that He showed most awareness of His own body. Quite frankly, on this day, He gave His all in love, for God and for us. As I consider Jesus' body, the very body which He spoke of at the Passover Supper which was to be broken, I wonder whether perhaps we have all become over familiar with it all.

In services of Holy Communion we are called to remember the life, death and return of Jesus. We are called through His Holy Spirit to be in communion with God. On the first occasion however, of Jesus saying His body was to be broken and His blood was to be shed, I can only imagine there would have been a lot of open mouthed stares.

The disciples were familiar with remembering acts of the past, after all this is the primary function of the Passover Supper – to remember the acts of God during the flight from Egypt. However, to be asked by their Rabbi to remember His proposed death through eating bread and drinking wine, must have sounded barbaric at best and perhaps even ludicrous.

As an aside, this is one reason why the early church faced persecution. To an outsider, to be drinking blood and to be eating Christ's body, must have come across as nothing less than cannibalism.

Jesus wanted His disciples to remember His body and during the Passover meal He asked them to do so. The day after this very instruction of Jesus, what must His followers have thought?

Rather than looking like the Son of God, Jesus must have seemed weak. Jesus was arrested, flogged and crucified. At no point did He even try to escape. Jesus' body went through tremendous pain. He was mocked and encouraged to leap down from the cross. Those around Jesus wanted Him to prove He was indeed the Messiah. Instead His response to such insults was to keep quiet.

This was hardly the political Messiah they had spent years looking forward to. Did Jesus really want His disciples to remember His body? It must have looked rather weak on the day of His death. Why on earth would the disciples want to remember this body? Although rather than being weak, Jesus showed His 'strength' and it is to this word I would now like to turn.

CHAPTER SIXTY-THREE:
IT IS FINISHED

As I seek to love God, I have come to value and appreciate my body more. I now appreciate its limitations and as I seek to love God with my all, so I try not to over-do it! In seeking to treat myself better, I see this is valuing myself as a child of God.

I have come to see the meaning of *'ischuos'* is not our actual physical structure which includes our bones, organs and flesh. I do not believe I am heretical in advocating a desire to love God with all of my body, as I believe God wants us to love Him with our all, our very all.

Just as Jesus did not say love Him with our 'spirit', it would be foolish to try and love God with our all and leave out the 'spirit' part of us. Likewise with our 'body'. Are we to love God with our mind, soul, heart and strength, but then abuse our body and the body of others? As God commands our whole being to love Him, this must include our body.

In believing the word *'ischuos'* should be translated more as *'strength'*, or *'might'*, I have had to try and understand what this may mean. If I am being asked to love God with all my *'strength'*, it stands to reason that I should know what this entails.

Back to Jesus. As He shared the Last Supper, as Jesus was arrested and hung on the cross, many can be forgiven for thinking this was Jesus at a time of weakness. Being led by soldiers, Jesus was given over to the Chief Priests, to Pilate, to Herod, and back to Pilate, before finding Himself dying on a cross. After His death, His body was carried away and placed in a borrowed grave. Jesus' followers could be forgiven for thinking Jesus had become weak.

I would like to suggest however, that Jesus was far from weak on this day. Rather Jesus was displaying strength of a supernatural quality. In being mocked and encouraged to jump down from the cross, the temptation to do so, to allow God's angels to rescue Him must have been enormous. To have escaped the arrest in the first place, to flee from Jerusalem would surely have been the easier option. Jesus was far from weak; He was strong.

On the cross Jesus said the words: *'It is finished!' (John 19:30)*. Now these words could refer to, 'Phew, thank goodness for that. It's all over'. Alternatively, and how I prefer to look at them, these words were said in a tone of triumph: *'It is finished!'*

Jesus in saying these words was doing all He had been asked to do. Heaven sent, He had come to take on a human body, to live on earth and then to die. As He breathed His last, so He accomplished all that He had set out to do - *'It is finished!'*.

Jesus entered this world through a young peasant girl, Mary. Jesus, with a human body, had grown up as a carpenter's son. In His last breath, with the words, *'It is finished!'*, as one thing finished another was beginning. As His physical body died that day, His resurrected body would return.

Okay when He did rise from the dead, He was not immediately recognised, not even by those closest to Him, but with His new body came something new. Power over death. With Jesus' resurrected body and the coming of the Holy Spirit, came a new way of being, a new faith, a new way of living, a new way of loving.

Jesus' strength was displayed in His obedience, to even death on the cross. Paul writes of this beautifully to the church in Philippi. In encouraging followers of Jesus to have the mind-set of Jesus, Paul writes:

> *'Who, being in very nature God, did not consider equality with God something to be used to his own advantage; rather, he made himself nothing by taking the very nature of a servant, being made in human likeness. And being found in appearance as a man, he humbled himself by becoming obedient to death - even death on a cross!'*
> *(Philippians 2:6-8)*.

Many consider it to be the first Christian song composed. It may not have several million hits on youtube as Matt Redman does, but it gives us a picture of the strength of Jesus. It shows how Jesus Himself loved God with all of His strength.

Jesus, *'humbled himself by becoming obedient to death - even death on a cross!' (v.8)*. To have humbled Himself to do this, not only took physical strength, but also strength of His mind and heart.

The Romans incidentally devised crucifixion as a means of inflicting the most excruciatingly painful death of slow suffering on law breakers and prisoners. To remain obedient to the commands of His Father, to have willingly gone to the cross, must have taken every ounce of strength Jesus had. No sacrifice comes without incredible strength. Jesus loved God on that day with all of His strength and showed complete trust in His Father.

In Jesus, what was first perceived as weakness was actually strength. It is important we do not always see weakness as being merely a negative trait. If we are open to allowing God to turn our weakness into strength, we can see our original weakness as being an opportunity for growth. At times God has been able to use someone because of their very weaknesses.

Time and again, throughout the Bible we see God using those who are seen as weak, rather than using those who are naturally confident and strong. We have to ask why? The initial résumés or C.V's of David, Saul or Gideon were far from impressive.

David was considered by his own father to be young and insignificant. Saul as he came to be anointed to be king, was so unsure of himself, he was found hiding behind the baggage. Gideon was a weak, fearful person. As an angel came to Gideon and called him a *'mighty warrior'*, you have to wonder whether the angel got the wrong person.

Far from being brave, Gideon was hiding from the battle, in a wine press, threshing wheat. The angel, I am sure could have found braver people that day. What did Gideon have that others did not? Perhaps it was that he was weak and he knew it! God knew that with God by Gideon's side, this weakness could become a strength.

Even as God called Gideon a mighty warrior, He did so with a pre-cursor - *'The LORD is with you, mighty warrior' (Judges 6:12)*. When the Lord is with us, we can indeed become whatever and whoever the Lord wants us to be.

God strengthened Gideon and called him to raise up an army, but even here God reminded Gideon that it was God alone who was the strength. Gideon ended up with an army of 33 000, but God reduced it to 300. Why? Because then they would rely on God's strength rather than on their own.

Time and again God called His people to depend on Him alone. What of Moses bringing His people out of Egypt? What of Joshua and the battle of Jericho? On each occasion it was God who was to strengthen the leaders and His people. He made this clear to others as well:

> *King Jehoshaphat and all who live in Judah and Jerusalem! This is what the LORD says to you: 'Do not be afraid or discouraged because of this vast army. For the battle is not yours, but God's"*
> *(2 Chronicles 20:15).*

Okay it was King Jehoshaphat who was on the ground fighting, but actually the battle and its outcome was down to God. What of Israel's battle against the Amalekites? So long as Moses raised his arms, Israel was winning but if he ever lowered them, the Amalekites started to win *(Exodus 17:11)*. Such a visual image reminded God's people to whom the battle belonged – to God.

In loving God with all of our strength, mind, heart and soul, so I have seen we too are invited on an incredible adventure. In loving God with our all, so God can turn our lives upside down for good. God can call the weak and make them strong. With God we can achieve the most remarkable of feats. God continually calls the ordinary into the extraordinary.

Many of Jesus' disciples were living fairly ordinary lives before He came along. They fished, collected taxes and lived their lives. On meeting Jesus however, their lives became extraordinary adventures. They experienced extreme sports, such as walking on water. They participated in feeding thousands. They witnessed healing's in abundance and even saw Demons flee.

After Jesus returned to heaven, in the power of the Holy Spirit, the disciples saw thousands of people become followers of Jesus. None of the extraordinary occurrences in the early church were accomplished in their own strength.

The disciples had proved at the time of Jesus' trial just how weak their own strength was. Blessed with the Holy Spirit, as they came to live in God's strength, so their lives were turned upside down for good.

What of countless other followers of Jesus? What of William Wilberforce? As the son of a wealthy maritime trader and later as an English politician, he could have lived out a comfortable life. However, on becoming a Christian in 1785, his life was never to be the same. In spite of on-going ill-health, as a philanthropist and leader of the movement to stop the slave trade, he worked tirelessly for God. This was in God's strength and not in his own.

What of Michael Luther King? Better known perhaps as Martin Luther

King Jr. Coming from a line of pastors, becoming one himself was perhaps to be expected. Who would have thought however, he would become such a visible spokesperson for civil rights? Martin Luther King's strength was in the Lord. He not only had a dream, he shared his dream and lived his dream...

What of Elizabeth Fry? At Just 12 years old, with her mother dying, she ended up taking care of her family. She ended up marrying well and could have lived out of a comfortable life. Who would have thought she would have established an institution to train nurses: the 'Nursing Sisters of Devonshire Square', let alone had the 'strength' to become so involved in prison reform. A mother of eleven children herself, she opened schools for children who accompanied their mother's in prison. According to her diaries, through the preaching of another and after visiting a prison, she was moved to initiate reforms in prisons. Of devout Quaker stock, the 'strength' of God became her strength.

What of Anjezë Gonxhe Bojaxhiu? She could have stayed in what is now known as Macedonia, but no, her adventure led her to the slums of Calcutta. God's love and strength resulted in dozens of communities being set up all over the world. Hundreds and thousands of people have received medical treatment, water, food, shelter and love through her love of God, by His strength. You may know her better by the name of, Mother Teresa!

More recently, what of Jackie Pullinger as she has ministered amongst drug addicts, prostitutes, and gang members in Hong Kong? What of David Wilkinson and Nicky Cruz, as they work amongst New York City gangs? The list continues, with many people only being known to God. Within each of their lives, any biographer can pick up how God turned weaknesses into strengths. As they loved God with their all, with the power of the Holy Spirit, so any weakness in God can become strength.

Each of these people ended up pretty busy in their lives for the things they campaigned and worked for. They were not however being asked to do such things in their own strength. Each in their own way, had to take Paul's words to heart: *'for it is God who works in you to will and to act in order to fulfil his good purpose' (Philippians 2:13).*

Jesus never asks us to do things merely in our own strength. Jesus is not expecting manic religious activity done purely by ourselves. Rather, Jesus longs for us to give of ourselves to Him, so He may work in us and through us for His purpose and for His glory.

Yet I am sure, that each of these people just mentioned, rather than rejoicing in their accomplishments, heeded the advice of Jesus. In speaking to the seventy-two whom He sent out, on hearing of their adventures, in hearing of even demons submitting to them in His name, Jesus said:

> *'do not rejoice that the spirits submit to you, but rejoice that your*
> *names are written in heaven'*
> *(Luke 10:20).*

The seventy-two had returned from their adventures full of joy and perhaps had the beginnings of pride. Jesus gently reminds them, exciting though everything has been, no matter what may be achieved in this world, the most important thing is to rejoice in our names being written in heaven. The joy of the Lord was to be their strength. God's strength enabled them to do incredible feats.

God is bigger, so much bigger than little ole us. God is God and sometimes He has to remind us of this. Throughout history, time and again when ministry, even in God's name, seems to be flourishing it can suddenly stop.

On a human level it doesn't make much sense that the Apostle Paul and his companions were stopped from preaching in the province of Asia *(Acts 16:6)*. God however, had other plans for them...

The story of Dr David Cho does not seem to make much sense either. As a young man he was a Buddhist, living in poverty, with tuberculosis. He had heard of a Christian God who healed. In desperation he called upon 'their' God and he was healed.

By 1964 he had 2 400 members in his church, which is pretty good going! Unsurprisingly, he was then taken to his bed for several weeks with nervous exhaustion. His doctor advised him to give up ministry.[xlix] This made little sense, after all his church had grown from 300 people in just a few years, why would God let him become ill? Surely for God's Kingdom, such growth and increased growth was good.

Long story short, after some significant rest, Dr David Cho became the pastor of one of the world's largest churches (Yoido Full Gospel Church) in Seoul, Korea with 730 000 members, in some 25 000 cell groups. What looked as though it was a disaster for the Kingdom of God, grew into something even greater. How? Through God doing it His way.

Dr Cho became broken before he could minister again. Dr Cho was given another opportunity to minister, but not until he had learned it was not to be in his strength, but in God's. Sadly this story is far from ended, as in 2014 Dr Cho went to prison for embezzling church funds, some $12 million![l] We wait to hear what may come from this weakness, but we cannot deny the growth of his church. All I know is that God calls the broken, God calls sinners, God calls me, and God calls you.

William Wilberforce incidentally suffered a lot of ill health. Mother Teresa suffered much in her interior life. Elizabeth Fry, due to financial problems of her family, nearly didn't return to the Prison's after her first visit. Jackie, David and Nicky all faced their own trials and tribulations.

Many Christian writers at one point of their lives have also testified to going through darker times, either of depression or weariness; of times when their 'body' and 'strength' was weak. Jo Swinney,[li] Joyce Hugget, Philip Yancy, Jon Ortberg, Charles Spurgeon and Tozer all share in their writings of times of weakness. Yet within each, God's strength reigned and as they began to depend on God's strength alone, so they each began to thrive and minister in His name.

CHAPTER SIXTY-FOUR:
STEAK OR OFFAL?

Jesus was fully God and fully human. Jesus in His humanness, knew what it was like to lack strength. In this I believe Jesus not only identifies more with us, but we in Him. In Gethsemane we see a man greatly troubled. The day before He was to die, He was hardly at His peak of physical or mental strength.

As Jesus was whipped and scourged, so He bled. On the cross whilst His soul, heart and mind may still have been strong, (after all He stayed there), yet physically He was spent on that day. Physically Jesus died, His physical strength was exhausted.

Even before this though, we can see how Jesus' physical strength was tested. It is no accident that the Devil knew exactly where to start his attack on Jesus in the wilderness. Jesus had gone forty days without food. Where did the Devil start? With food! Of course Jesus was hungry and so the Devil strikes there; tempting Him to turn stones into bread.

Sadly, I am all too aware, I rarely have the kind of strength Jesus exhibited. All too often, I try and do things in my own strength and I have even tried to do things for God in my strength. I guess the problem with this has been the pronoun, 'my'. If I am starkly honest here, I also see on occasions, my strength became an idol.

I relied on myself rather than on God. Perhaps, I even put what I could achieve before God. My personality, my high work ethic and my dominant 'will' would drive me on. I depended on my strength rather than relying on God. Some words of Hosea, initially directed at Israel, spoke starkly to me one day:

> *'But I have been the Lord your God ever since you came out of*
> *Egypt. You shall acknowledge no God but me, no Saviour except*

me. I cared for you in the wilderness, in the land of burning heat.
When I fed them, they were satisfied; when they were satisfied,
they became proud; then they forgot me'
(Hosea 13:4-6).

I do not think I am alone when I admit that there are times when I have depended on God, but after a while my focus has changed and I try to do things in my own strength. Pride kicks in, independence abounds and without even realising it, I forget God. Sometimes I even think, God doesn't need to be bothered with this, I can just crack on. I get on with my day and I do not involve God.

Now you may be thinking, but what's wrong with this? Surely God lets us get on with our life. Well yes and no! Yes, God does give us choices, yes God does want us to live our life, but also He created us for Himself. God longs for us to make choices with Him, to live the best of life, which is to love Him with my all and to live in His Presence.

I have come to acknowledge that although I may have often tried to love God with my strength, even with all of my strength, this is not enough. For years I was despondent at this, frustrated even that my strength was not equal to the task.

I am grateful that in my wrestling I have been brought to a place where I am now actually okay with this. As much as I am indeed called to love God with all my strength, I am not called to do this merely in my own strength.

I have been encouraged to see I am created as a dependant being, dependent on God and on others. Thus in being called to love God with all my strength, it is actually only in God's strength that this is possible. The Psalmist understood this far better than me:

'My flesh and my heart may fail, but God is the strength of my
heart and my portion forever'
(Psalm 73:26).

Together, in union, I am called to offer my strength with God's Holy Spirit. This includes both the big and the small. In addition, heaven is closed to my strength, closed to my flesh, it is only open to my soul.

Even something as simple as playing with my son, is an opportunity to bring to God. On the days, I remember to pray, our time together seems all the more precious. Why would God be interested in this? Why do I need to be prompted to pray about this seemingly inconsequential thing? Quite simply because God is interested in absolutely everything.

Time with my son is precious, it is consequential. God longs to be just as much a part of my time with John, as with anything else I have to do that day. For all of us, God is interested in the people we meet, in the meetings we attend, in the emails we answer, in the loo's we clean, in the meals we prepare, in everything we do.

God longs to be our strength in all things. As we come to God's love and strength, so we too are enabled to love and to be strong in Him. I cannot describe 'how' this happens, that is down to God. All I know, is it does.

To be sure there are many things which I can rely on myself for. I can do many things in my own strength. The difference is, I no longer want to. I want to do things in God's strength because I know this is God's best way for me. When I let God's strength flow through me, rather than merely depending on myself, everything goes better.

Who, having driven a car with power-steering would choose to go back? Who having used an automatic washing machine, would rather wash by hand? Who having a slow cooker, would prefer to hang a pot over a fire? Who having tasted steak, would prefer offal?

Time and again in the Bible we see those who were perceived as being weak, accomplishing great tasks. This was never in their own strength but in God's. In humility I have had to see this to a lesser extent for myself. I cannot love God by myself and even more so, I cannot love God with my own strength. I need God's love and God's strength to love Him.

I spoke of Gideon earlier. He may have become a mighty warrior, but in his calling, he self-confessed to being of the smallest family of the weakest clan. The fact, he was hiding in a wine press also shows he wasn't even the bravest of this small gene pool.

Repeatedly God used people who were weak. Being old, ugly, a stutterer, young, suicidal, a liar, a drunk, a prostitute, an adulterer or a murderer was never a weakness too much for God; for His glory. He used Abraham, Leah, Moses, Timothy, Elijah, Noah, Rahab and David for His purposes. God turned people whom the world perceived as weak into people of strength. Such people gave birth to a nation, had many children, led a nation, led churches, killed hundreds of Baal prophets, saved humanity in a boat (all be it a big one!), helped spies escape and led Israel for over forty years.

Isaiah and Paul seem particularly conscious of God's strength rather than merely relying on their own. Isaiah knew God:

> *'gives strength to the weary and increases the power of the weak...those who hope in the Lord will renew their strength'*
> *(Isaiah 40:29 and 31).*

Through hope in God, strength can be renewed. Paul above all, knew what it was to be weak, whether this was in his own stature, his failing eyesight or from wounds from his afflictions. Yet in all of these he came to be content:

> *Therefore I am well content with weaknesses, with insults, with distresses, with persecutions, with difficulties, for Christ's sake; for when I am weak, then I am strong'*
> *(2 Corinthians 12:10).*

I too have come to embrace this idea. When I am weak, then I am strong. It is no longer all about me, about what I can achieve, accomplish and fit into a day. It is all about God. I am grateful for His patience in my weakness and for His promise to help me in all things, even in prayer.

If I am honest I cannot even talk to God without some help. On occasions I do not know what to say or how to phrase things. Thankfully even in prayer, Jesus is there to help me out:

> *'In the same way the Spirit also helps our weakness; for we do not know how to pray as we should, but the Spirit Himself intercedes for us with groaning's too deep for words'*
> *(Romans 8:26).*

It is in God's strength and in reliance on God's Holy Spirit that my strength is not only renewed but sourced. In humility, I have had to learn *'to love God with my strength'*, involves me having to give myself completely to God. In doing so, God resources me; God's love in effect is the source of my strength.

CHAPTER SIXTY-FIVE
'AS I RUN I FEEL THE LORD'S PLEASURE'

Before this all sounds rather over spiritual, let's come down to earth. As much as God wants us to be filled with His Holy Spirit, to be renewed with His strength and to live the best life we can, God also gives us things on earth which we can enjoy.

Eric Liddle (featuring in the film Chariots of Fire) famously said, as he ran he felt the Lord's pleasure. Eric, who later became a missionary in China, felt God's pleasure and experienced God's love, as he ran. Eric enjoyed running but even in this he wanted to honour God. Eric did this by not running his favoured race of the 100 metres in the 1924 Olympics. The heats for this race were held on a Sunday and to run on such a day to Eric, was to break the Sabbath. Instead he ran the 400 metres (which was held during the week) and he won.

Different people find pleasure in many pursuits. For my husband it is steam locomotives, for others it can be in sport, music, gardening, knitting. So long as these pursuits are not bringing dishonour to God or put above Him, many people can be strengthened and blessed in seemingly ordinary activities. The key is to invite God to be part of all things.

If people are blessed enough to have an opportunity to go on a 'Retreat', they often return all the better. You could say people come back being refreshed after a few days, because of extra sleep, nice food, or time away, and yet there is more. God is there and longs to renew our strength and refresh our souls.

Now I am ashamed to say my experience of 'going on Retreat' is less than it should be. Priests are encouraged to make an annual one, not least to revive them. I took my first, 'real' one after twenty years of ministry – I cannot imagine why I grew a little tired! I have now trebled my 'Retreat' experience.

By my own testimony and that of others, it is rare to go on a Retreat and not experience, in some way or another, becoming more aware of the Presence of God. Through the guidance of those who may lead the Retreat, through additional time to be with God, many people come away having experienced a little of the peace of God. This is just a foretaste of so much more. It is as Paul says:

'For here we do not have an enduring city, but we are looking for
the city that is to come'
(Hebrews 13:14).

Every so often, we may just be given a glimpse of life in heaven with God.

At times, as we draw close to God, we may even be given a picture or a sense of heaven; of our ultimate home. This world is not all there is. At the moment, due to our limitations, I cannot truly comprehend what is in store, but in faith I wait expectantly. Any glimpse of 'something more' strengthens me. I am given hope of so much more, not least of being with God Himself.

As I consider our body and heaven, perhaps a paragraph or two should be devoted to our body getting older. I currently have a six year old who for the past three months has been counting down to his seventh birthday. He has another three months to go – I wonder at times whether he will make it!

As a young child we often long to be older and then before we know it, we long to be younger! There are many verses which seek to encourage us as we grow into our old age. Solomon has a go: *'A grey head is a crown of glory'* *(Proverbs 16:31)*, as does the book of Job: *'Wisdom is with aged men, With long life is understanding.' (Job 12:12).*

Different Psalmists presented other views of ageing. On a good day the words: *'They will still yield fruit in old age; They shall be full of sap and very green'* *(Psalm 92:14),* were sung. Perhaps on a bad day though, when getting up was just a little more difficult, the following words were croaked: *'Do not cast me off in the time of old age; Do not forsake me when my strength fail' (Psalm 71:9).*

We may be aghast at the thought of living 969 years, as Methuselah is said to have done, but we all hope to live long enough – however long, long enough is! The wisdom of the older generations was once something to be revered. Experience nowadays however, is often second to creative youthfulness.

As someone nearer to fifty than thirty, I am choosing to take to heart the words of Paul:

> 'Therefore we do not lose heart. Though outwardly we are wasting
> away, yet inwardly we are being renewed day by day'
> (2 Corinthians 4:16).

These words remind me once again that this life is not all there is. Grey hairs should remind us of our ultimate home, in heaven with God. Our strength may not be what it once was, but in the Lord our strength can be renewed.

Our bodies are for this world only, there is no place for them in heaven. As our body begins to lose some of its functions, rather than always being disheartened, perhaps we can pause to rejoice! Our soul is looking forward to a new way of being, and our body is its home only for a short while. Heaven takes souls only. But for those to whom the body is important, we will have one, it will just be a heavenly one, not an earthly one *(1 Corinthians 15:40 & 2 Corinthians 5:2-3)*.

So for anyone over the age of forty, who may be feeling a little old, take heart and rejoice. Every time you see a grey hair or your bones may creak, give thanks that these remind us of our ultimate destiny, of our final alighting, in heaven.

As we approach this last stop, perhaps we should be preparing ourselves more for this destination. We often spend so much time investing in 'stops' along the way, that we forget where we are going. As our physical body fades, so heaven approaches. I do not believe, as some say, that life begins at forty. Rather, I consider we will only truly know life in death.

As we come to be with God in heaven, so we will truly know what it is to live. Heaven, a place of eternal blessedness, a perpetual Sabbath.

Too often though, we live our life trying to do things in our own strength. Quite simply God loves us so much that He wants to do things with us. We were not created to go it alone. The prophet Isaiah understood this:

> 'Surely God is my salvation; I will trust and not be afraid. The
> LORD, the LORD himself, is my strength and my defence, he has
> become my salvation'
> (Isaiah 12:2).

Peter did too and he reminded his readers of it:

'If anyone serves, they should do so with the strength God
provides'
(1 Peter 4:8-11).

Recently I was cooking. Not only was the smoke alarm squealing loudly; all of the windows were misted up. The boys took the alarm as a signal that tea was ready – rude! A burning pan however, suggested tea was going to be late.

Once the pan was off the cooker, to get rid of the moisture, I began trying to wipe the windows. With this, Jack came in and just opened all of the windows. Not only did this help the alarm to stop ringing, but within a few minutes the mist had disappeared.

Too often we try to do things in our own strength or we try to get rid of things by ourselves. We try to wipe things from our lives, in earnest maybe, but often abrasively and in our own strength.

God longs for us to open the window, to allow Himself to be our strength and for us to see another way of being. I am eternally grateful for Jesus, for not only wiping away all of my sin, but for making my paths straight.

CHAPTER SIXTY-SIX:
RUBBLE AND STONES

As I come to rely on God's strength, so I have also been introduced to the *'joy of the Lord being my strength'*. I came across this in the book of *Nehemiah*. Initially, I looked at this book in the Old Testament because of Nehemiah's passion for prayer. I was also attracted to him, as at the time I was involved in two building projects. I thought he could help lead me through.

Nehemiah, at the time of exile, was a cup bearer to a foreign king. In general chit chat one day, Nehemiah discovers the walls of Jerusalem are in ruins. He is devastated. The ruined walls symbolise more than just tumbling stones. To Nehemiah and God's people it symbolises how a once great nation is crumbling. The rubble does not honour the Lord their God.

With no Heritage Lottery funding, with no local architects on hand, Nehemiah has to raise the funds, source the materials and even become a builder himself. The walls at least were not Grade 1 listed and nor was there a need for 'faculty applications' or 'planning permission'.

As the walls are mended, all be it with a lot of opposition, Nehemiah builds up God's people as well. All of this activity is immersed in prayer. First he prays for four months, before even approaching the king for permission to go and inspect the walls. Just as he is about to reveal his anguish to King Artaxerxes (a non-Jewish king), he sends up another quick prayer *(Nehemiah 2:4)*. Nehemiah then leads a massive building project which is often under attack, but at all times and in all things he remembers God.

Nehemiah engages in personal prayer as well as leading the people into confession and corporate prayer. Along with Ezra, he also got the Jews to listen to the Book of the Law, making God's people stand for hours listening to it. A synopsis of the book of *Nehemiah* may not whet many people's appetite: it's a building project! And yet it is a book soaked in prayer.

Within this short account we encounter a man with a secular job who embarks on an amazing mission for God. Nehemiah knew what it was to live in the Presence of God and as he did so, he became more aware of who the source of his strength was. On an occasion of festivity, he said:

'This is a sacred day before our Lord. Don't be dejected and sad,
for the joy of the Lord is your strength!'
(Nehemiah 8:10).

Not only did Nehemiah know God was his strength, he knew such strength was deeply rooted in the joy of the Lord.

Joy is not a feeling, it is not to be happy. Happiness, after all, dependent on circumstances, can come and go. Rather, 'joy' is acquired by the anticipation of something. Joy is to know God, to know salvation and to know of eternal life with God. Joy is of God. Joy is less about us; our circumstances and feelings. Joy is more about God and His promises for us. As the Psalmist says:

'The Lord is my strength and shield. I trust him with all my
heart. He helps me, and my heart is filled with joy. I burst out in
songs of thanksgiving'
(Psalm 28:7).

Now I admit, I am very typically 'British', so there are rarely times of bursting out in song or for that matter *'leaping for joy' (Luke 6:23)*. I have nothing against others doing it, but I am unlikely to have joined King David on the day he leaped and danced before the Lord *(2 Samuel 6:16)*. The joy I have been given is there, it's just very deep within.

On this note, as I was jogging the other day, I passed a lady, who looked at me and said, *'cheer up!'*. I have two points to make. Firstly, runners rarely grin widely when running. It would look odd to start with. In running, you tend to concentrate on giving all of your energy into getting your feet to go forward.

Secondly, until she said, *'cheer up'*, I was actually in quite a good mood. The writing was going well; it was sunny and I was enjoying the fresh air with God. Just because I wasn't grinning madly did not mean that I was not happy nor not full of joy. My face does not naturally smile – you only have to look through 600 wedding photographs! I did smile on one, but Jack had his eyes closed!

To depend and to live in the joy of the Lord is not about whether we can smile or not; it is to trust ourselves to something greater than just us.

Joy is to have faith in the one who created us; the one who sustains us and the one to whom we should come in all things. My strength is in the strength of God. To have joy in the Lord is to know on whom I can depend.

Nehemiah had some touch and go moments. He faced criticism and attack; the hours were long and the rewards seemingly few. Yet Nehemiah was successful, because he lived in God's strength and not merely in his own. Nehemiah knew loving God with all His strength, meant relying on God's own strength all the more.

For too long I had been living in my own strength, which consequently had had a negative impact on my body. As I further considered who I was, I found myself wanting to get back to the origins, back to the roots of my created being. As I did this, I was drawn to *Jeremiah 18* and the image of God being the potter.

CHAPTER SIXTY-SEVEN:
GOD THE POTTER

I know originally, the image of the pot referred to Israel, who at the time (roughly 600's BC), were being particularly disobedient and unfaithful. Israel had become proud and were taking their God for granted. They thought God would be theirs, no matter what their behaviour. God's prophets were rejected and true worship abolished. As I read *Jeremiah 18*, sadly I could identify with some of this in my own life.

Perhaps I had taken God for granted. There were times when I depended on myself rather than on God. Whilst I wasn't abolishing true worship, my heart was not always in the services I was leading. All I knew, was the life I had been leading wasn't working.

I was attracted to the idea of God being a potter, who if He was willing, could re-shape me. I liked the picture of God being a potter, of throwing the raw material - the clay and making a pot *(v.8)*. Any defects could be reformed and reshaped into some other pot.

On acknowledging my being 'broken', I was willing to become something other than what I had become. I had come to a point where I wanted to be re-formed. I was willing to submit to God, to become like clay in His hand.

In the time of Jeremiah, the God of Israel, as Creator, had a choice. He could either put up with the people as they were; disobedient and unfaithful or He could do something about it; like throw them away, or have them destroyed. As *Jeremiah* reveals, God could do what He liked with Israel because they were like clay in His hand *(18:6)*.

Throughout the book of Jeremiah, we see the sovereignty of God and how He chooses to operate according to certain principles. Time and again throughout the Old Testament we see God's people sinning. Will they be destroyed once and for all, or saved?

Only after acknowledging their wrong-doing and having a time of repentance, (true heart-felt repentance), does God refrain from a punishment which could have wiped them out. This held true not just for Israel but for others. Consider Ninevah, who heeded the warnings of Jonah, and how the people of this city repented and were saved.

Some may argue, who is God to be able to judge our actions? I would reply He is the ultimate Judge. In addition though, God only seeks what is best for us. God only sent prophets to condemn disobedience and evil because He could see His people were not living life as best as they could. God's people had taken to accepting second best which often resulted in hardship and depravity.

Ultimately, there will come a day when all of our actions and words will be judged. On this occasion I am thankful I can look to Jesus who promises to take all of my sin. When a list of sins and wrong doings are about to be read out, I am grateful that Jesus will stand in place of me.

Meanwhile, whilst on earth I turn to my Creator, to the Potter and I hope God will show me mercy and re-form me. For too long, I had gone my own way in my own strength and quite simply it wasn't working. I longed for the *'joy of the Lord to be my strength'*.

CHAPTER SIXTY-EIGHT:
DECEIVER TURNED WRESTLER

God knew His people Israel: He had created them, saved them and led them out of Egypt. God gave them the promised land. God gave them the Ten Commandments, the first of which reminded them to have no god before Him. If this wasn't enough, in the second commandment He told them plainly to have no graven image; to have no idols.

Many centuries passed and as His own people time and again turned to false idols, God was faithful. God had sent prophets with warnings. At times under some kings there was even great hope. Josiah ascended the throne young, yet he initiated incredible reforms throughout the land *(2 Kings 22 & 23)*.

More often however, God's people, not helped by wicked kings, turned to other gods. In the end, God took away from them the one thing they were so proud of: their land. Being in exile was Israel's ultimate punishment: they lost their promised land. This traumatic event was part of God's plan, to bring the people to repentance, so finally they would turn to God in both sorrow and hope. In effect God loved His people so much, He knew for them to return to Him as LORD, they had to be allowed to be in exile, they had to almost experience being away from Him.

I knew in my own life this had also been true. At some of my darker times, I had in effect been in exile, almost away from God. My exterior was seemingly with God, after all I was still a parish priest. My interior however, had been in exile for some time.

In our families and society, we know that sometimes punishment is necessary for our own good. A child to learn what is right or wrong needs discipline. At times plainly the word 'no' has to be said. On other occasions, there are 'time out' steps, reward charts or the loss of privileges or toys. All of these are encouraged to motivate and guide our children to live better lives.

I believe God to be our Heavenly Father and so I see He does the same to us. We sometimes become so obsessed with this world and ourselves, that we simply forget about God. In the case of Israel they often needed a shock to turn them back to God.

On occasions during our life, things may just go pear shaped. This may sometimes be a consequence of our actions. Occasionally it is at the result of the actions of others. Sometimes we may not understand the life we live. Every so often however, God may allow things to happen so we stop relying on our own strength and turn to His.

As Paul concedes, God loves us so much that like an earthly father, He disciplines those He loves *(Hebrews 12:5-6,* taken from *Proverbs 3:11-12)*. God disciplines us for our own good...why? As Paul says: *'in order that we may share in his holiness'* *(Hebrews 12:10)*. Paul is not naïve, he is aware of the agony this may entail:

> *'No discipline seems pleasant at the time, but painful. Later on,*
> *however, it produces a harvest of righteousness and peace for those*
> *who have been trained by it'*
> *(Hebrews 12:11).*

In my own life, in humility, I can testify this to be true. On many occasions I cried out to God wanting everything to stop. I wanted, the fatigue to cease, my mental anguish to decrease, the busyness of life to lessen.

I shouted to God, I cried out to God time and again. It wasn't that God wasn't listening...He was. Rather, I wasn't listening and more pain and separation was required before I was willing to do so.

As someone who loves to wrestle in all things, it is understandable that I should be attracted to Jacob who once wrestled with God for a night. I am not attracted to Jacob the character; I have always found him hard to warm to - a mummy's boy who stole his brother's blessing. Even after he wrestled with God he had some serious flaws, not least showing favouritism to Joseph and Benjamin, over his other 10 sons.

Rather, what attracted me to this strange incident recorded in *Genesis (32:22-32)* is how Jacob lived to tell the tale. Okay he ended up with a hip out of joint and a limp, but if I had wrestled with God or His angel all night, I would have expected to have come off even worse.

As they wrestled, it seems God would not let go of Jacob, but neither would Jacob let go of whoever was wrestling with him. After the wrestling,

Jacob ended up being blessed by God. From this day, Jacob's name was changed to Israel meaning to 'struggle'. God's own people were named after a man who wrestled with God. Jacob, who had lived his life being known as the one who had grasped his brothers heel, of being a deceiver, is now given another name, another chance. Okay the name 'to struggle' isn't much better than 'deceiver' but at least he would never forget the day he wrestled with God and in the end received a blessing.

The aspect that attracts me to this story, is that whilst it may not be wise to wrestle with God, if you do find yourself wrestling, God will not let go. As I have found myself 'wrestling' with God, like Jacob, God has allowed me to wrestle until my natural strength was exhausted. In the end, like Jacob, all I could do was surrender and cling to God's love and His grace. Note I do not say give up, I say surrender.

I surrendered to someone greater than I. God wanted what was best for Jacob and so I believe God wants what is best for each of us. This never includes second best, we are after all designed for Him and Him alone. Sure, there may be times when we become broken, but this may not be to destroy us, but to renew us.

John, my son, last year ended up having four of his toes broken. He had been born with congenital curly toes which meant several of them curled under each other. When he was little they were a feature; they were cute even. As he grew they became more uncomfortable and in turn they would limit his ability to walk. Through breaking them, they have now re-set and are renewed – all for his good.

Looking back in my own life, God's timing was perfect. Through the dark times, through the times of languishing, during my time of being in the pit, I was being disciplined. Such 'discipline' was always in love and always for my own good. I am grateful to God for not giving up on me and for showing me a way back to Him:

> 'For I satisfy the weary ones and refresh everyone who languishes'
> (Jeremiah 31:25).

Just as God did not leave His people alone, so I have not been left alone and neither are you.

God's people were given the promise of a Messiah, a Saviour who would restore the relationship between God and His people. I am eternally grateful to live in a time after Jesus has come to this earth, so I may turn to Him. There is still a time of waiting; we wait for His return. However, some of our present experience of exile is the inevitable state of living here and now on earth where we struggle sometimes to feel Jesus' closeness to us. Even if we are living eternally; we are not in heaven yet. More of this later.

CHAPTER SIXTY-NINE:
DISPOSABLE CUPS!

On occasions, we can become hard pressed and perplexed. Paul wrote of things we face in this world, using the image of a clay jar *(2 Corinthians 4:7)*. Clay jars remind me again of God being the potter. As I return to this image I actually stop in awe.

God created us, God formed us. God gives us the image of Himself being like the potter. This should actually give us tremendous self-worth. God formed us and in spite of how we may behave, God has not left us. When life can seem to overwhelm us, we can be tempted in our despair to forget this. If this is so, the image of 'clay jars' comes to our rescue.

In the time of Jesus and Paul, clay jars were ten a penny, they were almost as disposable as a plastic cup – without the environmental concerns. The important part of the clay jar however, was not the vessel itself, but rather what it contained. Clay jars held water, oil, wine, and some were even used for hidden treasures such as money or jewels. Their role was to contain.

I think one problem with the human race, is human beings either think too little of themselves, or they think too much of themselves. Thinking too little of yourself may result in someone believing that they are not worthy of God's love or indeed of any other love. Considering too much of yourself, either in a narcissistic or bombastic way or just in the sense of being too independent, can lead to a person believing everything which happens in life is about them. We can be too anthropocentric.

Recently we have had some very strange weather in England. We are used to rain of course, but in the last month (September) we have had temperatures ranging from minus 7 degrees to 12 plus. Some parts of the South East have had six feet of snow, which was followed by floods and then curiously (after burst pipes), water shortages. This was followed by high winds and glorious sunshine. All of this however, was preceded by an earth quake which was strong enough to nudge my chair.

I am not great with uncertainties and I remarked as much to a friend. Her reply was the opposite. She said: *'I love extreme weather. It reminds me, we are not in charge!'*. Whether such weather was of God or a consequence of our treatment of His world, is not for me to say. However, the weather can be a timely reminder of how we are not in control of everything, no matter how we may think otherwise.

As I reflect on my strength, I concede we are if you like, 'clay jars'. With the advance of technology, we may think we run the world and we can depend merely on ourselves. In truth however, we are more like clay jars. Some people think they are indispensable and yet after the death of great leaders, popes, singers, footballers, dancers, carers ...the world continues... The saying: *'The King is dead. Long live the King'* rings true.

Human beings are created by God and this gives us great worth, but also we are but vessels which come and go. The important part of us, as a vessel, is what we hold and here we are reminded it should be God Himself, in His Holy Spirit. God longs to dwell within us to give us strength. To enable us to love. God's Holy Spirit longs to be an all surpassing power within us.

With this understanding, I began to realise, we are important yes, we are created by God, we are of God but we are not God ourselves. Thus as Paul observes, when we feel *'hard pressed, let us remember we need not be crushed' (2 Corinthians 4:8)*. Sometimes it may feel as though we are crushed, but actually we can survive again and again.

Sadly for three years in a row, at New Year I said to Jack, *'Well this year cannot be any harder than the last'*. At times I felt we could not withstand much more. Would our marriage survive? Yet by God's grace, we can now look back and see we have been hard pressed yes, but not crushed!

In fact our marriage is all the stronger for the times of having been hard pressed. I have been tempted on many occasions to spiral into despair but as Paul says:

> *'Perplexed but not in despair, Struck down but not destroyed'*
> *(v.8)*.

At this time of writing some of my dearest Christian friends are being struck down and hard pressed, much more than I have ever known. I am almost fearful to become friends with anyone, lest they too should end up going through terrible trials and anguish.

Seeing my friend's pain, at times is quite literally breaking my heart. I cling however, to my own testimony of the past few years that even though we may feel struck down, I and they will not be destroyed. God is for the long haul.

God looks to our ultimate home, to heaven. Sometimes the best I can offer are some words from Solomon. Believe me though, it takes a person strong in God to take this verse as comfort:

> 'God has also set eternity in the human heart; yet no one can
> fathom what God has done from beginning to end'
> (Ecclesiastes 3:11).

Simply, we do not know why some things happen. We do not know everything, but God has set eternity in the human heart. This is my hope, my joy and my strength. We are as Jude writes to persevere:

> 'But you, dear friends, by building yourselves up in your most
> holy faith and praying in the Holy Spirit, keep yourselves in
> God's love as you wait for the mercy of our Lord Jesus Christ to
> bring you to eternal life'
> (Jude 20-21).

It is less about us and all about God.

CHAPTER SIXTY-EIGHT:
ALAN MASTERS

In talking to some people of my thoughts and beliefs, they have been alarmed at how I have come to a place of 'surrender'. I have come to a place where I am looking less at my own strength to love the Lord and depending more on His alone.

Some have considered I am giving in or worse I am giving up. Perhaps until recently I would have thought this too. I know I once feared submitting wholeheartedly to anything or anyone, as I feared losing control. Nowadays though, I long to give myself to God. I long to surrender and to submit. I choose to give myself to God.

Consider for a moment: on whom do you depend? Perhaps a family member, a friend, a colleague, yourself? Or, in what do you depend? Your job, your retirement plan, an addiction, your role in society? Whom or what is your strength?

My dad was known by many within our family as, 'the rock'. Alan Masters was always there for us. He went out of his way for any of us. I cannot remember the amount of times he helped me move house. If anyone needed running to the hospital or an airport, Alan Masters received a call.

My dad's funeral bore testimony to how many people either depended on him or thought well of him. He did not lead government, he did not discover a cure, he did not invent anything. He was not great at public speaking, he wasn't a great cook and he wasn't even well read - he was in fact a farmer.

Yet at his funeral there were over 400 people, all crammed into a local village church. There were people of all ages, from all strata's of society. Such was his impact on people that even the post man came along, as did people from his insurance company. His hairdresser attended and come to think of it, even my mum's hairdresser was there.

People came to pay their respects to a man who was as happy in his own company, as in the company of others. My father had a great inner strength, he knew himself, he liked himself, he was honest and he was someone you could turn to. His death was a great loss not just for his family, but for many others too.

My father was a great source of strength for me also; in fact he was the greatest strength for me for most of my life.

Perhaps therefore, it was only at his death that I realised some of my strength had been misplaced. I do not regret relying on my dad or for the time I spent with him, but on his death the gap, the void was great and I knew no earthly person could fill it.

Only God alone could now be my strength in all things. As I began to turn to God all the more, I saw curiously I was being offered the opportunity of becoming a slave of Christ!

CHAPTER SIXTY-NINE:
SLAVE, FREE OR BOTH?

Few people would like to say they are slaves. To speak of being a slave, infers being the legal property of another. It is one person being forced to obey another, namely their master. So, why would the Apostles seemingly refer to being, *'a slave of God'*, as being a good thing? (Just check out *Philippians 1:1, Ephesians 6:6, James 1:1, Jude 1:1, Revelation 1:1 and 1 Peter 2:16*).

The word; *'δοῦλος', 'doulos', 'slave'*, is in fact used at least forty times in the New Testament. The answer perhaps lies in *Colossians 3:24*, where Paul reminds us, the reward of being a slave is that of *'inheritance'*! Not an earthly inheritance but that of eternal life. The latter part was the same of actual slaves of the 1st Century and indeed of us today – inheriting eternal life.

Followers of Jesus Christ are called to serve Him and not man alone. We are called to obey God *(Romans 6:16-18)*, who only has our best interests at heart. No longer do we need to be slaves to sin, but rather slaves to goodness, to God.

Sadly the term slave today has only negative connotations and with good reason. However, in the day of Jesus to be a slave in many ways was to be better off than a hired worker. After all, in being a slave you were guaranteed bed and board. It was your Master's responsibility to feed you and to look after you. In response to this, slaves were called to submission and devotion.[lii]

In serving God, in becoming a slave of God, we see how God is responsible for us, that He is Lord of our lives. Coming to God as my Lord and Master, I am relieved I now only have one Master to please. As I consider the Greek or Roman gods, there were so many gods to try and please!

It is for my good and pleasure that I have come to know God, that I have been invited to serve Him, to become dependent on Him and to love Him. As I spoke earlier, I am called to live an undivided life.

We were *'bought at a price'* *(1 Corinthians 6:20)* and we were not cheap; it cost Jesus His life. We are designed to be dependent on God, to honour God with our bodies. We were not created to merely please ourselves or even others, we are created to be pleasing to God. In coming to God in this way, rather than my freedom being restricted, I have only known peace.

For too long I had been striving in my own strength. In resting and living according to God's way, I am being restored to the way of life which I was created for. Becoming a *'slave of God'* has given me greater freedom to live and to love. A slave yes, but also forever God's child; His heir. With His Spirit within me, I am blessed to be able to call God *'Abba – Father'* *(Galatians 4:6-7)*. I would even go so far as to say this renewed thinking, and my coming to understand loving God with my all, is leading to *Shalom*.

CHAPTER SEVENTY:
SHALOM

The word 'Shalom' is more than just a salutation. It is more than merely, 'hello' or 'goodbye' or even 'peace'. The biblical 'Shalom' means an inner sense of wholeness, of completeness. It is peace; wholeness. It speaks of your whole well-being.

The term well-being has become increasingly popular in the West. Everything it seems can contribute to our well-being: positivity, healthy eating, good mental health, exercise and so on. Whilst I do not deny all of these things in life can help people, I want more, I want to return to the source – to God, to the Creator and Sustainer of all.

Shalom in its purest sense, can only be found in God Himself *(Numbers 6:24-26)*, the author of peace *(1 Corinthians 14:33)*. As I have come to love God with my all, so I am beginning to understand Shalom a bit more.

In coming to God, in loving God with all my mind, heart, strength and soul, so I can testify an inner sense of wholeness is developing. I do not encourage people to come to God with their heart, mind, strength and soul just for what they personally can gain. However, I cannot deny that as I come to God with my all, I am more complete in myself. This does not mean a perfect life – far from it – such perfection is reserved for heaven alone.

Rather in the midst of trials and difficulties, in the thick of life, knowing God loves me and commands me to love Him – well, it's enough. In spending more time with God in love rather than merely out of obligation, so I am more at peace. This has come by becoming more aware of the four parts of me specifically cited by Jesus.

Shalom: I cannot deny as I come to love God with my all, I am becoming more at peace with myself, God and the world. With God as my guide and His Holy Spirit as my strength, I am becoming more of the person whom God originally intended me to be.

For me to function best, I am designed to be loved by God and in turn to love Him. To try any other way, no matter how attractive it may seem, is second best. No matter how well those ways may work for other people, to me anything other than God is second best.

Actually no that is wrong, to imply second best suggests they can still work. For a while maybe but ultimately no. My soul was created for God, forever. To allow my soul to miss out on this is hardly second best – it is death for my soul. To merely focus on my mind, or physical health is not enough. To have the perfect athletic physique or the most brilliant mind only, will not do my soul any good.

My husband one day, through filling up our car with fuel has helped me to understand what I am trying to get at. Forgive me, if it sounds crass to liken God's Holy Spirit to fuel, but please bear with me.

Jack is a motorbike man. To use the car is always second best. Already late for a friend's wedding, we had to stop for fuel. With his head on other things, he filled our car with petrol. This would have been okay if we didn't have a diesel car. To an uninformed user, surely fuel is fuel! Not only did we have to pay for the petrol, we then had to get assistance to drain the petrol from the car. Some four hours later, we then had to re-fill the car with diesel.

This has always been an expensive memory. Quite simply, petrol is not second best for a diesel car. Not only would it not work as well, if we had used the car, it would have ruined the engine. We too are not designed for second best.

We are designed for Shalom; we are designed to be God's children. I say it again...I believe I am designed by God for God and as such I hope to rely on His strength rather than on my own.

On the theme of 'fuel', within the Army, there was always a different take on the word. Food was seen as 'fuel'. If you dared criticise what was on your plate or the contents of a silver bag (a ration pack), you were reminded: *It's fuel, eat up'*. On exercise or on an operational tour, it was just that: 'fuel'. Lumps of food, covered in different coloured sauces, in a bag, sometimes heated, more often not - it was 'fuel'.

I always marvelled how a small bag of porridge could really consist of over 1400 calories! Nor was I ever enamoured by the 'best before' dates.

Seeing a date five years ahead on a packet of scrambled eggs and beans, always made me wonder whether there was anything nutritious in there at all!

However, this was food and it kept you going, but only physically. It never blessed your soul, or even your heart and mind. It was fuel for your body – end of. God's Holy Spirit longs to be 'fuel' for more than just our physical body. God's Spirit longs to bless our mind, soul, heart and strength.

CHAPTER SEVENTY-ONE:
NO MORE 'BEST BEFORE DATES'

As I have looked at loving God with our *'ischuos'*, I have looked at the words *'strength'* and *'body'*. As we seek to love God with our all, each I believe have their own merit. For many years I had only ever understood loving God with our *'ischuos'*, as referring to our strength. This was until I came across Christopher Wright's understanding of the original word from the *Deuteronomy 6:5*.

Wright spoke of the word strength meaning, *'very-muchness'*. Ordinarily referring to the meaning, *'greatly'* or *'exceedingly'*. He points out, in the earliest Jewish versions (including the Targum) it was translated as *'your substance'*.

With reference to the words, heart, soul and strength, Wright concludes: *'it may be that this third word is simply intensifying the other two (heart and soul) as a climax'*. Thus God's people were being asked to, *'Love the Lord your God with total commitment (heart), with your total self (soul), to total excess'*.[liii]

Strong's Lexicon confirmed this and I came to see, to love God with our *'ischuos'*, or as in the original Hebrew; '־ךָ֖דְאֹמ' *'me•'o•de•cha'*, was to love God with all of our *'abundance'* or *'might'*, or indeed *'muchness'*. I love the imagery of loving God to total excess, to almost become over the top in our love for God.

It is perhaps a little similar to when you are freezing cold and dirty and you eventually get to have a shower. As you allow the water to tumble over yourself, you only need the first minute or two to clean and warm yourself up. However, it is often lovely to stay for a little longer, to just have the water tumbling over you to excess.

In coming to love God with our *'ischuos'* I have to say, I love the word, *'muchness'*. Until looking at this verse, I had never really come across the word *'muchness'*. *'Muchness'*...it just has such a lovely sound. To love God with all our *'muchness'* kind of sums up everything. We are to love God with our all in abundance.

King David often expressed such love, both in the songs he composed and also in his actions; on one occasion he danced before the Lord and the ark with all of his might, if you like with his very 'muchness' *(2 Samuel 6:14)*. This didn't go down too well with his wife who ended up despising him, not least that as he danced he did so semi-naked! King David could not help himself though – nothing else mattered than to express his love for God with all his 'muchness'.

'Muchness' is an awesome word in how it sounds but also it what it means: to give your very all, everything you have, absolutely everything. So when Jesus said, *'Love the Lord your God with all your heart, soul, mind and strength/muchness'*, we are being encouraged to love God, with every part of ourselves.

Just as God longs to fill us to overflowing with His love, so He longs us to love Him likewise. I have a picture of a waterfall tumbling down, giving of its all, overflowing in every way, never drying up.

God formed all of us for Himself and longs that all of us, every part of us, all of our 'muchness' will be loving Him always. As Tozer succinctly says:

> *'God wants us all, and He will not rest till He gets us all. No part of the man will do'.* [liv]

I believe Jesus named our heart, soul, mind and muchness for our own good. In doing so, Jesus helps us acknowledge every part of us. God does not want just a part of us, He created us, all of us, every part for Him; our mind, soul, heart, spirit, body, strength and our muchness.

To give of all of ourselves in muchness...what a wonderful desire. God after all gave of His muchness, in the life and death of His Son. As we come to God and allow Him to love us in His muchness, so we can be loved by God and in turn love Him with our muchness. From all of this muchness, in turn we can begin to love each other, not just in our own strength but in the strength of the Lord.

I realise due to our sinfulness, as God's love flows through us, it may become tainted, (after all we are human), but even so, it is God's love that longs to flow through each of us. This surely has to be better than merely relying on our own.

Just as ration packs had 'best before' dates, so I believe human love does. Our love can run out according to feelings, circumstances, and our own well-being. God's love never does. God's love never fails.

CHAPTER SEVENTY-TWO:
TO BE A PILGRIM

As I seek to wrap up thoughts on loving God with our mind, heart, soul and strength, a thought from one of the Psalmists reminds me of two things:

'Blessed are those whose strength is in you, whose hearts
are set on pilgrimage'
(Psalm 84:5).

Our strength is to be found in God yes, but also our hearts are to be set on pilgrimage.

This wonderful verse reminds me I am a pilgrim, my heart is set on a journey, no, in fact an adventure. I am travelling towards a sacred place, towards God Himself. Jesus was heaven sent and I am heaven bound. The one way ticket has been purchased by Jesus. I couldn't afford it. All I have to do, is keep hold of it, living for God and loving Him with my all.

***

'Love the Lord your God with all your heart and with all your soul and with all your mind and with all your strength'

***

CHAPTER SEVENTY-THREE:
MIND, SOUL, HEART AND STRENGTH OR SOUL, HEART, STRENGTH AND MIND, OR HEART, STRENGTH, SOUL AND MIND AND SO ON...

Part of me wanted to finish the book on that last chapter. In many ways it felt conclusive. A cold spring is turning into summer and I would prefer to be sat in the garden reading and praying, than beavering away. However, there is still much to say, so for good or bad, the journey continues. You would have thought that perhaps I had even devoted enough time to the invitation of loving God with our mind, soul, heart and strength. Yet, I believe there is still more.

The more I become aware of these four aspects of myself, created to love God, the more in tune I am beginning to be with them, both individually and together. They are after all, wrapped up in one package – ourselves, our very being, but there is also something distinct about each of them.

I have come to value the importance of separating the aspects of myself, of my mind, soul, heart and strength. Equally however, as I come to love God, I do so with my whole being, united as one. There is an inter-connectedness of our mind, soul, heart and strength.

Our life with God is not just about any one aspect of us, God is interested in all of us. All too often we may limit Christianity or God's interest to just our mind. I do not stand alone in the conviction of God being interested in every part of us. Martin Luther said; *'Christianity is concerned with the 'entire human person', not just the human mind'*. [lv]

As I look back, it took courage to stop and assess. At the time I thought I was being weak. My mind and even my heart were on a downhill collision course, a battle of 'doing' raged within me. My strength was failing and my soul, which was weary, had gone from panting to screaming. I am grateful for my soul and for the time I had to begin to listen to it.

As I look back, I see different parts of myself at different times took the lead. I have come to see in my own life that it is actually important for me to recognise this, and to learn from it. Confused? So was I for some time.

My heart, (my will), when I feel strong often likes to take the lead. This is an employer's dream. My heart likes to do; it likes to work hard; it likes to finish a task and then start another. My heart also loves to multi-task so in many ways the role of a Vicar was perfect, lots to do and lots of balls to juggle.

However, my heart driving me is not always good for me. My heart has a great belief in itself and at times it has pushed me too hard. This of course has an effect on my strength as well as my mind; both become weary as they seek to catch up with my heart. My poor soul can sometimes struggle to get a look in, as my heart, strives for achievement and accomplishment.

In defence of my heart though, it has often only strived because there has always seemed so much to do. Whilst the motivation of my heart may be good, after all things often do need doing, my heart has not always been kind on myself. I have come to see my heart tends to drive me harder than what I am designed for.

Occasionally, my heart may have been less bothered about what was being asked of me, so it took a back seat. At such times, my mind (for good or bad) seems to have taken the lead. My mind can work very fast. In a single moment several thoughts can have raced through it. My mind is also creative and it does not like to rest. It prefers to be thinking – or over-thinking about everything.

The challenge of having an over active mind is, it is frankly…exhausting. I am aware many great things can come from our minds. Consider how many discoveries have been made and inventions created, through someone having a good idea. From an idea of the mind, the heart is required to follow it through to make it a reality.

Our minds however, can also focus on things which are not good for us. How many mistakes in life can be attributed to a single thought? Giving into temptation usually starts in the mind.

In seeking to fill our mind more with God and His love, this in turn can have a positive effect on our behaviour. Our heart can be more motivated to do what is good rather than bad. Consequently this can have a positive effect on our body.

Our mind, heart and soul all currently reside within our body. Our body is the most visible part of us. Wrapped in God's love, each part can all have a positive effect on each other.

What of the 'strength' part of me? In all honesty my 'muchness' does not necessarily take the lead, rather it gains momentum. A good idea from my mind or something to do from my heart, will motivate my 'strength' to go one step further than always necessary.

It is perhaps my strength and body, over time, which have caused me the most unease. Its 'healthiness' affects all the other parts. When my body is physically ill, all other parts of me suffer. Well, at least that's what I thought for a long time. In fact when I became physically ill and unable to work at the pace I was used to, my soul often ended up rejoicing.

As I said earlier, I am not saying God made or makes me ill. Having periods when I have had no choice but to stop has however, given me space to spend a little more time with God. My heart always wants to do and sometimes through the grace of God, (through the generosity of God), my body closes ranks and shuts down. In turn this often gives my mind time to breathe.

I often saw being ill as weak, as being an excuse to be lazy. This was my heart speaking, the core of me which likes to be strong and take the lead. I praise God indeed that my soul has been given more of a voice, and I have now been given ears to hear.

Increasingly I am learning to listen to my self and know what is achievable and what can be left. This is a massive learning curve for me. Let me give you an example...my mind will think of something to do, my heart jumps onto this and wants to run with it, even before the idea is completely formulated. In the past my strength would go for it, no matter what else was in my diary or how I felt physically. I am learning however, to listen to all parts of me and at times I have now, even said 'no'.

Saying 'no' does not come naturally to me. In the past if I have had to say this to others, I immediately felt weak or guilty. I usually ended up saying 'yes' in the end anyway. I am now however, becoming more comfortable with saying 'no'. This is for my sake, for my family's, but also for God.

Too often I have put things before my relationship with Him. Often such acts were in service of Him, but they were not done with the right heart, or the right strength. Activities were often done in my strength rather than in God's.

The first person I have had to learn to say 'no' to is actually myself. As I am learning to say 'no' though, so I am able to say 'yes' to other things. Not least to spending more 'actual' time with God. This not only strengthens me for whatever I may end up doing but the flow is right. I am able to love others from a place of love, from God's love rather from frenetic busyness.

I am learning how I have a responsibility to allow my strength, my muchness to focus on God and not to be distracted. Allowing anything but God to be our all, is sadly too easy. Thankfully my soul is there to help me.

For many years my soul panted, it whimpered, but as I did not really know what it was, it was overlooked for too long. Over time my soul found its voice and through God's blessing I have come to acknowledge it for what it is. I am grateful for the time when my soul has literally muscled in and taken over.

Now I have started to identify its voice, at times I have little choice but to let my soul take the lead. In saying this though, my will and mind were involved in agreeing to this act of submission. My mind took some convincing that this was the right course of action, hence so much study of both the Bible and other books. My heart too had to eventually get on board, just to allow my soul to take the lead more.

Being with God, helps satisfy my soul, as well as helping to free my mind. With my soul in charge I am coming to know what is good, and what is not good for me. Strangely this can result in even more time for the Kingdom of God.

As I allow my soul to take the lead, this affects my heart, my will. My motivations are changing. As my inner life is transforming, so I hope and pray my behaviour will become more in accordance with God's will.

Take for example, anger. I can try my very hardest to 'will' myself not to become angry, and this can work right up until someone annoys me! Alternatively I can commit my will to God to God's Spirit and allow God to work through me. To commit my will, is to give myself over to God in prayer. This includes spending more time with God; through times of confession and repentance, through reading His word and seeking to listen to Him. The main ingredient is spending more time with Him, in His Presence. It then becomes less of my will and more of His. Ever so slowly this seems to be having more of an effect.

There are some people who on the whole can intensely annoy me. Often without meaning to, they can say silly things which build up and before I know it, I become angry. I may or may not direct my anger at them. This is a choice and over the past year I have tried to be less angry with them and at them. Inside however, my anger can still burn.

On the exterior all may look well. Sadly I have learnt to wear a mask well! Inside however, I am knotted up. My head can hurt, my stomach can feel gripped and on occasions I have felt like I was going to burst. In an attempt to release the angst, I took to clenching the muscles in my legs. The pain in my muscles would almost soothe what was building up inside. I am not proud of any of this. As I look back I was attempting to sort things out in my own strength and not in God's.

I was recently with one such person and as I came away, I marvelled that I was not feeling angry. I reflected on our conversations and realised they had still said the usual things which annoy me, but somehow this had not penetrated. I can only attribute this change in myself to God's Spirit and for this I am truly thankful. This was possible through God drawing me to spend more time with Him.

As I come to depend on God more, so my strength is restored and fuelled by God. Within time those around me, are bound to benefit as well. Through being more focused on God, on His ways and His kingdom, so I am becoming more aware of how God originally intended me to be. As a consequence I am less stressed and I am slowing myself down.

The great advantage of allowing my soul to lead is that, it is much kinder on me than any other aspect. My soul encourages my racing mind to quieten down; to breathe. My soul causes my heart to pause and my muchness has had to accept a rest is okay.

As I continued to think these things over, I began to fear however that perhaps I was taking my thoughts to an extreme. After all Jesus as He encouraged us to love Him with our all had uttered some 24 words. Perhaps I was taking it all just a bit far. Above all else I did not want to be reading ideas into the text which were not of God.

As my thoughts continued down this path, I was relieved to find that A.W. Tozer had also had some similar thoughts. Tozer wrestled with the relationship between the Creator and created. He spoke of how our minds and hearts are not always joined up in their being. In speaking of a *'God-above-all position'* (which is not easy to live), Tozer said:

> *'The mind may approve it while not having the consent of the will to put it into effect. While the imagination races ahead to honour God, the will may lag behind and the man may never guess how divided his heart is'.* [lvi]

In speaking of how to live the Christian life, here was a pastor who identified the different aspects of himself as he sought to love the Lord with his all.

I have since come across others who speak of different parts of themselves as separate entities. For example, Jamison in talking of *'praying constantly'*, says:

'The mind can be turned to God in the midst of noise and the heart can be turned to God in the midst of complex mental activity'. [lvii]

It therefore seems there are times when different parts of us vie for attention or dominance.

I realise Tozer and Jamison only spoke of their mind and heart, but as someone who was wanting to love God with their all, I have come to listen to my soul and acknowledge my 'strength'. For too long I had allowed my mind and heart to over-ride my soul. My soul would be left panting, parched, bereft of not being with God. I cannot imagine I am alone in this.

Self-medication with addictions, or patterns of behaviour which are not good for us, can also over-ride our soul. At other times as my inner will has tried to take the lead, my heart has almost told my mind to 'man up' or to 'get a grip'. My will, reminds my mind and my strength of what my whole being is capable of. Now of course, some motivation is good for us, but not always.

On becoming more aware of my soul, I long for it to take more of a lead. This is not just to prepare my soul for being with God in heaven, but because my soul's desire is to be with God here on earth as well. As I listen to my soul, I am aware it has my best interests at heart. My soul is more gentle and far kinder to me than my heart or even my mind.

I believe my soul is also more in tune with God's Spirit which dwells within me. This all said, it is hard to break old patterns, to be freed from former bad habits, to be healed...Even now, I am very aware of how my old ways of 'being' are just below the surface. I may now see them as wrong and unhealthy but they can still quickly rise.

I am now grateful of being able to identify certain ways of being, as unhelpful, as ugly, as disabling. For example, even in the writing of this, sometimes I have become so immersed in it, that I have wanted to write longer in the day than I know is good for me and my family.

I am eternally thankful for the additional time I am able to have to pray, to bring myself, my mind, soul, heart and strength to God. Yet all too often I have found myself wanting to write just one page, or read just one book. The irony of this is not lost on me. Here I am writing a book on loving God with my all and yet it is this very book that sometimes distracts me from doing so!

I did tell you I wrestled a lot! As I say to Jack, you should be grateful you are only being opened up to a bit of my thinking, I have to live with me all the time. Moving on...

Through coming to Jesus, I now know there is something different for me, a better way and although I am far from whole-heartedly living this, I feel I am at least on the right path. I am learning to live with my mind and heart in tension – each vying to take the lead.

For too many years though, I had tried to break these negative traits in my own strength. With my soul in the lead, I now come to depend on God's strength first. This is more than just a battle of wills, it is getting my heart to be willing to surrender and submit to God. As I began to do so, so the words, *'meaningless, meaningless'* dwelt less in my mind, as in God I was finding 'meaning' in all things.

As I seek to strike a balance in life, it is important I am not tempted to do this in my own strength but in God's alone. As I am invited to come to God with my heart, mind, strength and soul, so this involves an inner surrendering of them all.

With God in the lead, His Holy Spirit can open the door of my mind, enter my heart and transform my soul. It is as Paul says:

'Since we live by the Spirit, let us keep in step with the Spirit'
(Galatians 5:25).

It is God who must take the lead and as I love Him with my all, so I am encouraged to follow Him. A prayer of Thomas Acquinas has put all of this into perspective for me:

'Grant me, O Lord my God, a mind to know you, a heart to
seek you, wisdom to find you, conduct pleasing to you, faithful
perseverance in waiting for you, and a hope of finally embracing
you. Amen'.

In allowing my soul a voice and God's Spirit to flow through me, I am getting there - slowly. My mind and heart remain easily able to be dominant and at times I have to quieten them down. I am not there yet and whilst the process is healing it is also humbling. The more I come to love God with my all, the more I am loved by God and the more I can see what is good for me and those around me.

CHAPTER SEVENTY-FOUR:
WHOLE BEING OR WELL-BEING?

As much as I believe God wants me to come to Him with my mind, soul, heart and strength as individual entities, I also know He wants me to come to Him as a whole being. This is after all how we are created. God longs for us to come to Him with our whole being.

Note I do not say our 'well-being', rather I say 'whole being'. The former would perhaps fit better in today's society. It has become a widely used term in the twenty-first century. It encourages us to be healthy and happy in a more holistic sense. I do not think however, this is what Jesus was getting at.

Jesus wants us to be complete in the love of God, He wants us to love God and to be loved by God. This does not automatically result in being healthy or happy as a move toward 'well-being' aims for. We can however, experience 'peace', 'joy' and inherit eternal life, all of which I consider outweighs short-lived good health and happiness.

The testimonies of many of God's followers give voice to this. Are Christians with terminal cancer in a state of well-being? Are those who are persecuted and imprisoned for their faith in a state of well-being? Hardly! And yet they can all love God and be loved by Him with their whole being.

I was humbled to hear of a punishment for persecuted Christians, imprisoned in North Korea. They were banned from looking up, from gazing at the sky, from considering God. Instead they were forced to keep their heads bent down. God calls us, *'to lift up our eyes, to see where our help comes from' (Psalm 121:1)*. My fervent hope and prayer is that they are still able to remember God, even with their heads bowed low. Christians in prison and those tortured for their love of God are hardly in a state of well-being, and yet they can love God with their whole being.

As people seek perfection here on earth to gain 'well-being', (dare I say) it has almost become an idol. Perhaps this sounds odd, after all much of my musings have centred around wanting to get the best of life. Also, surely it is a good thing to want our well-being to be as good as we can.

Please do not hear me wrong, in no way am I devaluing healthy eating or exercise or many things which go along with people seeking a healthy well-being. I am aware many people claim different physical and mental practises, are of great benefit. I am questioning rather, where all of this can eventually lead.

Many practices can become so absorbing, that people are led deeper and deeper into something which they feel promises some wonderful personal goal. My concern is when the practise begins to focus on any goal other than being with God.

To seek merely a healthy well-being, is accepting second best. Certain meditative techniques, to control one's body and mind, can absent God. What sets out to be a good ideal can become our main focus. Our idols today are unlikely to be of stone or gold, but they can be practices which lead us away from God.

I believe God has made us for Himself and He longs to be with us in all things. Having accepted second best for too long, I am unwilling to do so any longer. Living a long, healthy life on earth is only the beginning of the story.

I am now more conscious of our souls. God is for our whole being, not just our well-being. There is more to life than just our time on earth.

***

'Love the Lord your God with all your heart and with all your soul and with all your mind and with all your strength.'

***

CHAPTER SEVENTY-FIVE:
R.S.V.P?

Throughout these pages, on the whole, I have been calling this verse from Jesus, these 24 words, 'an invitation'. Occasionally I may have dropped in that it was a command, but in the main I have referred to these amazing words as being 'an invitation', 'a glorious invitation' even!

Quite honestly, apart from salvation in Jesus, it is the greatest thing I have ever come across. I was being invited to be loved by God and to love Him with my all. Little ole mixed up, tired and weary me.

God still wanted my love and as I loved Him, so He was able to love me all the more. I ran with this for over a year, or rather I walked – still too weary to run! As my strength was renewed with God, so my heart was more resolved to be easier on myself. In turn my mind began to be renewed, and as such my soul was more at peace.

After some time my mind eventually registered Jesus hadn't quite so much invited me to this way of living, as commanded me to it. Deep down, I had known right from the beginning that Jesus referred to loving God as a commandment, but I guess I had baulked at the thought of being commanded to do something.

If I am also really honest, the word invitation sounded, well, quite frankly more inviting. I mean who likes to be commanded to do anything?

As I approached thirty, my call to the Army was so of God - I do not like taking commands, let alone like ironing or camping and at the time I hated running as well.

For several years I took the verse to love God with my all, as an invitation but the more I reflected on this, I had to admit this was not really accurate. With an invitation there is a choice. On receiving one, people can choose whether they accept or not. An invitation though, implies a choice. Did this apply to these words of Jesus? Was there a choice?

I believe God gives us choices in all things. We have 'free will' for a start. We are not robots, but human beings who can make both good and bad decisions. God loves us so much He gives us a choice as to whether we want to be His child. John's Gospel reveals this:

'For God so loved the world that he gave his one and only Son,
that whoever believes in him shall not perish but have eternal life'
(John 3:16).

The words, *'whoever believes'* show we have a choice.

No one is forced into heaven or likewise sent to hell. God longs for us all to become His children and He even sent His Son into the world for that very reason. God loves the world and He loves us.

God longs for us to have eternal life, but He does not force us. On becoming God's child however, He loves us too much for us not to get the best of life. God guides us through His Word (the Bible), through His Holy Spirit and through the wisdom of others who love Him.

Having 'free will' however, means we are still able to make poor decisions and consequently lead more difficult lives, but we are given a choice of how to live *(1 Corinthians 10:23)*. At times it seems God intervenes and powerfully encourages people to turn their lives around BUT He never forces us. Even though I have come to see, it is only through loving God with our all that we are able to live the life intended for us, every day in my very humanness, I still make wrong decisions.

God loves us too much to force us to love Him, but through His Son He has shown us the way. As we become more willing to obey His commands so we are accepting Him as our Lord. This is all for our good.

Our response should not be motivated by trying to earn God's love. Rather as we receive God's love, so we yearn to live the life God longs for us to have. Such a life is more than even an expression of thanks. It is us experiencing the best of life.

God loves us so much He wants us to live the way He created us. Thus we are actually given not an invitation, but a commandment to 'love God with our all'.

To merely invite us to love Him, would be almost cruel. If we R.S.V.P. saying, 'No thank-you', well, we would not be living the best of life. God created us for Himself and He knows loving Him, being loved by Him and loving others is the only way we can have the best of life, on earth before heaven.

God commands us to love Him, so we can be loved by Him. From a place of love, from a state of being loved by God, we can then love – truly love. It's if you like, one less thing to think about. To be invited to love God with our all, may involve us wrestling whether to or not. This is just too important to be merely an invitation. God commands us to love Him with our all.

In raising John, I was conscious I wanted to give him choices. I did not want to be dictatorial. However, at the age of three I realised I had over done this. On more than one occasion he would sigh heavily and say: 'Mumma just tell me what to do'. Too much choice had become a burden for him. Sometimes, for our own good, we just need to be told what to do!

As Sovereign God, as Lord of all, God is the supreme authority and from this position He commands, He gives an order. Obedience to God is only for our good. To be commanded to do something is more than being given a set of laws or rules, which we may or may not choose to follow. The very nature of a command is it is given expecting obedience.

In the Army no commander gives an order/command wondering whether soldiers will follow it or not! In the Army, unless it is an illegal order, you do what you are commanded.

An instinctive response for many people is to depend on their feelings, to let emotions govern behaviour. Unfortunately, feelings at best can be flighty. I have come to see, in being commanded to love God with my all, I am called to obey and not to depend merely on my feelings. I am commanded to obey through making a decision, through determining my heart/my will to follow God's lead. I am called to make a choice.

Through faith, I believe God exists, and I know I am called to be His child. As I come to Him as my Father, as Creator God, so I acknowledge He is my Sovereign Lord, and as such I trust He knows best.

The more I come to God as Sovereign Lord, the more I see Him at work in the world, throughout history and in my own life. With time, experience and faith, so I am more confident that God knows best.

All too often we treat God like an internet search engine. We type in a request and expect a response. In fact, let's be honest, we don't all that often even wait for a response – we just rush on to the next thing!

God is here and He longs for us to communicate with Him, but He has also given us the actual way to be with Him. For God's people pre-Jesus, it was through the Old covenant and the Law and now it is through Jesus, the cross and through His command to love.

Even as Christians, rather than coming to Him, we often put up barriers; we are stubborn. So much so, that we almost prevent God from being able to form a relationship with us.

Imagine if I had given birth to John but then abandoned him. He would still be my child, but we would have had no opportunity to form a relationship. God longs for us to be His child, to have a life-long, life-giving relationship with Him. This cannot be easy for God. Our stubbornness must test God time and again.

I love the imagery of the prophet Hosea, who talking of Israel says:

> *'The Israelites are stubborn, like a stubborn heifer. How then*
> *can the LORD pasture them like lambs in a meadow?'*
> *(Hosea 4:16).*

God longs for us to follow His commands, as He knows this is how to get the best of life. Yet, there is still a choice, because even though God commands it, we have a choice whether to obey or not. Does this make it an invitation after all? Who knows? Perhaps, it doesn't actually really matter. Of more importance is that we come to follow His words and in doing so, come to live our life to the full, on earth before heaven.

The key is, 'love'. The more I come to love God, the more I see He wants the best life possible for me. The more I come to love God, the more I naturally want to obey His commands. A motivation to obey comes from being loved by God and through loving Him.

I believe this is why God doesn't merely call or invite us to love Him rather He commands us to do so. Jesus on more than one occasion encouraged His followers to love one another as He loved them. It is no accident that when Jesus speaks of love, He also refers to obedience:

> *'If you love me, keep my commands... Whoever has my*
> *commands and keeps them is the one who loves me. The one who*
> *loves me will be loved by my Father, and I too will love them'*
> *(John 14:15 and 21).*

Also, in *John 15:10*:

'If you keep my commands, you will remain in my love, just as I have kept my Father's commands and remain in his love'.

We are commanded to love as God loves us. To be commanded to love God is more than to be invited, with an invitation one can accept or decline. We are commanded. Why? Because God knows best.

CHAPTER SEVENTY-SIX:
TO HAVE AND TO HOLD

Before Jack and I got married, we did a Bible study on *Ephesians 5:22-33*. If you haven't come across it, it's the one where wives are told to *'submit to their husbands...For the husband is the head of the wife...'*.

As you may have gathered, I am naturally quite a strong independent person. Jack on the whole is more easy going. At times I had wished Paul had not written this passage on husbands and wives, after all what did he know? He wasn't married and he rejoiced in God, in his celibacy.

As someone who takes the Bible seriously, any passage which is not easy to understand or accept, in my mind, needs all the more wrestling with. As we studied this passage, first separately and then together, I found I was able to say I can submit to my husband. This was a surprise to us both.

As such I was even willing to say in our marriage vows that I would 'obey' him. Little did I know the liturgy had been revised and it was no longer in Common Worship!

As we studied this passage together, the reason I found that I could submit to a husband, is because I was being called to do so, as the church submits to Christ. The husband meanwhile is to love the wife as Christ loved the church. Who has the harder calling? I believe, the husband!

I am able to willingly submit to anyone if they are loving me as Jesus loved the church. After all Jesus died for the church. Jesus loves the church and never asks anything of it, that is not good for it. Jesus wants the church to get the best of life. To submit to my husband, who should always be looking out for the best of me - even to his death, has to be in my best interests. Likewise obeying God's commands because they are for my good, has to be the right thing.

Incidentally, the word *'obedience'* comes from the Latin *'oboedire'*, meaning to pay attention to, to serve. It shares its routes with *'audire'* which is to hear. To obey therefore, is to hear and then to respond to it, to act upon it.

If we hear and do nothing, there seems little point in hearing in the first place. As we come to God we are invited to obey gladly *(2 Corinthians 9:7)*. My obedience to love God with my all, comes from a loving response to God who knows better than me. This submission gives me freedom to live. This does not mean though that there is no work on our part.

In coming to a position of wanting to obey God, it does not take long to see God only has our best purposes at heart. God designed us, He created us in His image and He only wants what is best for us. I am grateful that although we are involved in this, it is all through God's grace. God does offer us different ways of training towards this goal. Such disciplines include prayer, study, meditation, fasting, service, solitude, worship, silence – there are many more. But all of this is wrapped up in God's grace.

However, please hear me - attempting to keep any such discipline DOES NOT make us a better Christian. Rather by engaging with God we make ourselves more available to God for Him to do within us that which we cannot do ourselves. Richard Foster calls it *'growth in grace'*. As he says:

> *'By undertaking Disciplines of the spiritual life that we can do, we receive from God the ability to do things that under our own steam we simply cannot do, such as loving our enemies'*. [lviii]

God longs for us to be in partnership with Him.

CHAPTER SEVENTY-SEVEN:
4+6=10

Back to this commandment of God. As mentioned earlier, I love the Ten Commandments. Now in case you did skip the earlier chapter on it, this is a little re-cap but shorter and lighter.

In many ways the Ten encompass the whole of our life. Inspired by J. John's book: *'Ten: Living the Ten Commandments in the 21st Century'*, I have taken every opportunity in ministry to preach on them. I have always spoken of the *'Ten'* as being God's love letter to us, they are God's best information on how to live life. They are God's way for us to lead a decent existence.

The Ten can be divided into two groupings. The first four, point more specifically to a relationship with God, whilst the latter six, refer more to how we are to live with people. Jesus in stating the greatest command refers to us loving God, whilst the second most important command is to love others. Jesus not only sums up the top Ten, but every one of the other 603 laws.

With one sentence Jesus put love back where it belonged – at the centre of everything. In His command, Jesus offers us a new way of living. Far from Jesus offering restrictions, I see He offers liberation. In keeping God's commands, in embracing God's way of living, I have found freedom. Living God's ways, in accordance with His love, may limit some of our choices, but actually this is only for our good and the good of others around us.

Living life to the full, is not just about not sinning; it is about doing what is right: Paul talks of our becoming, *'slaves of righteousness' (Romans 6:18)*. So often with laws and commands, we look at what we cannot do rather than what we can. Human nature often laments restrictions rather than rejoicing in what is permissible.

This has happened from the beginning of time and I am sure, it will continue until Jesus returns. Adam and Eve were shown by God they could have the fruit of any tree in the garden, all except one *(Genesis 2:17)*. They were free to eat of everything, except one!

Adam and Eve could have rejoiced in this amazing invitation and lived in the Garden of Eden forever. They were only asked not to do one thing. Yet in temptation they did it. God only asked them not to eat from the tree for their own good, but they thought they knew best and as such had to be banished from the garden.

CHAPTER SEVENTY-EIGHT:
KNOWING BEST

Okay, confession time. I like to drive fast, or at least I used to like driving fast. I always thought I knew best. I was vaguely aware speed limits were for our good, but I always thought they were a little stingy on the allowance.

I am not proud of having been pulled over on many occasions, some were my fault, others not. There was a spate one year where yes I did speed a few times. I was duly caught and punished, with points on my licence and speeding fines. On three other occasions when I was pulled over however, I was innocent...

There was great irony one time at midnight when I saw a police car with flashing lights behind me. I was pulled over and questioned because I was driving under the speed limit. As it was so late at night the policeman was sure I had been drinking and thus I was breathalysed! I was innocent.

On another occasion I was pulled over for apparently combing my hair and on another for not wearing a seat belt. I had no comb and my seat belt was on! But there have been occasions when I have been in the wrong...

My stint in Germany with the Army nearly cost me my licence. But hey in Germany they hide speed camera's in dustbins – which I think is just mean! Consequently I became the proud owner of photograph's all around the country. Such photographs were sent free to the administration office in Head Quarters. A poor Lance Corporal, would then have the disliked role of informing officers of their misdemeanour's.

As the only female Padre in Germany (with a dog collar which in a photograph seemed to shine like Jesus on the day of His transfiguration), there was no way I could deny each time of being caught that it was me. As my husband droll-fully reflected one day, if I wanted, he would buy me a dash board camera and turn it round to face me – it would be cheaper.

Such was my reputation with driving, that I was even blamed by my brother when he had an accident and ended up in a ditch, even though I was 100 miles away at the time. Apparently I had taken a specific corner at 60mph, so he thought he could too.

My miss-spent activities of driving were not limited to speeding. In trying to find some soldiers one day, I may have driven onto a firing range. Across the radio came the command: *'cease firing, the Padre's car is approaching!'*.

The most recent occasion of driving in an illegal manner, resulted in my having to attend a 'driving awareness course'. Now, I could blame my speeding on Jack who had forgotten his driving licence and was thus not allowed to drive the hired car that day. I could blame the hire company who gave us a car with little braking ability. I could blame the council for not more clearly highlighting a 30mph zone so I didn't mistakenly think I was in a 60mph one - as I genuinely thought. I could blame the can of drink which had exploded all over the car which distracted me. There were many things to blame but none of them were going to get me out of the course. I had broken the law. 41mph in a 30mph limit.

I have to say, in attending the course, I was impressed with the wide range of excuses which were used by other drivers. Children in the back seat were blamed a lot! One man tried to use his wife's pregnancy. If she had been in the car he may have got away with it. Another claimed that it was necessary to speed because they had nearly run out of fuel and they wanted to get to a service station as quickly as possible.

Everyone on the course had one thing in common - we had all broken the law and been caught. One group were particularly angry though, as there were seven of them from the same wedding party. As the first driver sped along, in an effort to keep up, so all the others also broke the speed limit.

There was more angst however, when a husband and wife, turned up at the same course. They had both been caught but had been trying to keep it quiet - the course leaders made sure they sat on different tables!

I have to say the 'driver awareness course' was amazing, as it has honestly made me a better driver. It has completely convinced me that the rules of the road are there for our sake. Speed limits and signs attempt to make the road safer for all users. In keeping to speed limits nowadays, I also no longer fear flashing lights behind me, or the wrath of an over-zealous back seat driver in the form of my son John.

The course has revolutionised my driving, my attitude and has perhaps saved my life and the life of others. On it I discovered why certain limits were imposed in certain areas. It gave me answers to my growls of, *'what a silly limit, why would it be 40mph here?'*. Thus I would go 60mph...I knew best.

I learned how to read a road better. As it had been 24 years since I had passed my test, I learnt of new laws which had come into being, and I learnt of how the design of many roads had changed. During the six hour course, as well as learning how to become a better driver, God spoke to me about my own life and His command to love Him.

The course at times, tried to use scare tactics to encourage us to slow down. Some people also try and use scare tactics to get people into heaven. Through the threat of hell, some have almost been frightened into heaven. I prefer to remember the marvellous promise that we may *'have the right to sit on the throne'* with Jesus *(Revelation 3:23)*.

God, however longs to love us into His Kingdom. As I heard of the appropriate stopping distances for cars, so I conceded God in my own life was giving me stopping distances – all for my own good. So many warnings in my own life were for my own good.

This course has highlighted my choices, I am now very much aware of how I drive: I can either slow down or not. I have been warned of the dangers of not slowing down, in turn I have been shown a better way of driving.

Some of the advice of the course was practical, such as drivers need to become more aware of what gear they are in, as this affects your speed. Likewise in life with God, I have had to become more aware of the gear I find myself in. At times my will and mind want me to live at a faster pace than is good for me.

My pride also had to be broken during that course. In the past I preferred to drive fast, but now I have slowed down. My family are even helping me to do this, for example, John, no longer refers to motorways as fast roads, as that may incite me to drive faster. The outside lane is now called that rather than the fast lane. The near side lane is no longer called the slow lane, as the very word 'slow' would make me hesitant in using it!

The course has given me a new rule and is developing a new attitude. Being told to drive as though we already have nine points, as another three would result in a ban, has helped. All of these restrictions, all of these laws, rules and advice are only for my good and for the good of others.

In one activity we were asked to make 'risk assessments' of a journey. In a car we are doing this all of the time, whether to pull out or over take. We have to think what gear to use and whether to use the accelerator or brake. Everything we do in the car is affected by making assessments.

I am grateful to God for the risk assessment He has provided. He knows what is best and as I come to love Him with my all, I am becoming more aware of this.

CHAPTER SEVENTY-NINE:
PHARI-SPIES

God gave His people the Law for their own good. It identified a people as His own. The Law brought His people into a relationship with God. The Law was if you like, a mirror in which they could see what holiness was. As they looked, so they would see their sin and realise that atonement was needed.

The Law laid foundations for God's people and gave them a framework for life. Some of these laws, were particularly relevant for God's people's time of living in the desert; they were intensely practical providing for their health and sanitation (for laws on skin diseases just check out *Numbers 5:2* and even take a look at *Deuteronomy 23:12-13* for a law on poo).

It is fair to say criticism has been levied at some of the 613 laws. A few seem rather peculiar to say the least.

Take for example, in *Deuteronomy 25:11-12*, where a woman is warned if she tries to grab another man's genitals, to help her husband when he is fighting another, she'll lose her hand. This was to ensure no man was rendered incapable of re-producing, but at a first glance it does strike one as odd.

Another law required that you ensure no-one would fall off your roof *(22:8)* – this was all before health and safety had gone mad. It was also forbidden to eat a number of animals including owls *(Leviticus 11:13-19)*, and additionally you were required to leave some of your grape harvest behind for the poor to eat *(19:10)*.

It is too easy to look at these and other laws and write them off as ludicrous or out dated. Yet, for God's people, as they entered the Promised land, the Law was given to keep them close to God. It was even supposed to bring them joy. Isaiah spoke of this, revealing how God longed for His people to keep the Sabbath, so they may find joy in the Lord *(Isaiah 58:14)*.

Many of the laws actually make perfect sense to a nomadic people who were entering a new land. To not eat certain animals would help them to keep away from certain diseases and uncleanliness. To leave behind some of the grape harvest was actually a precursor to a state benefits system. Such a law worked towards social justice. The book of *Ruth* is more than a love story; it depicts how such laws benefitted the poor and needy. The book of *Amos* also shows how passionately God longs for justice.

Sadly the Bible however, reveals more people who broke the Law, than those who kept it. In addition time and again we see others who may have looked as though they kept the Law, but actually did not:

> *These people come near to me with their mouth and honour me*
> *with their lips, but their hearts are far from me. Their worship of*
> *me is based on merely human rules they have been taught'*
> (Isaiah 29:13).

Jesus longs for us to love Him with more than our lips. Jesus wants us to love Him with our words yes, but also with our very being, with our actions, our thoughts, with an intelligent love. Through loving Him with our understanding we are invited to intimately know Him.

God always looks at our hearts. The Pharisees at the time of Jesus had been well respected, after all they knew the Law inside out. Yet it was these very people who repeatedly criticised Jesus, not least for breaking the Law; for apparent blasphemy, and for breaking the Sabbath.

On this note, I do wonder how the Pharisees always seemed to know when Jesus was about to break the Law! Jesus' disciples were condemned for picking heads of grain and eating them *(Mt 12:2)*, after all it was on the Sabbath no less! But, just what were the Pharisees doing in that field?

Perhaps of greater alarm should be how some of them brought a lady who was caught in adultery to Jesus *(John 8:1-4)*. Had they themselves, been outside her house, just waiting for the sin to be committed? Did they spend their lives just looking for law breaking? Pharisees or Phari-spies?

Sadly the religious leaders of the day had become so obsessed with the letter of the Law, they had lost sight of the heart of the Law. The very people called to reveal the truth of God had taken away the key of knowledge *(Luke 11:52)*. They had quenched God's Spirit. Hosea understood this as he revealed of God:

'For I desire mercy, not sacrifice, and acknowledgement of God
rather than burnt offerings'
(Hosea 6:6).

Jesus knew this too and quoted *Hosea 6:6* twice *(Matthew 9:13 and 12:7)*. If Jesus says something once it's good to listen to it, if He says it twice, you really need to listen! God was interested in the hearts of people, not just outward observance.

It was perhaps the Psalmist though in *Psalm 119* who understood not only the importance of the Law, but of its life changing ability:

'Oh, how I love your law! I meditate on it all day long. Your
commands are always with me and make me wiser than my
enemies. I have more insight than all my teachers, for I meditate
on your statutes. I have more understanding than the elders, for I
obey your precepts. I have kept my feet from every evil path so
that I might obey your word. I have not departed from your laws,
for you yourself have taught me'
(Psalm 119:97-102).

Through meditating on God's Law, through knowing it, and submitting to its teachings so the Psalmist came to know God. Through allowing his mind to understand it, his heart to follow it, and his soul to live it, so the Psalmist came to love God's Law!

We cannot be entirely sure of the background of this Psalm. Tradition suggests, King David compiled it to teach his son Solomon the Hebrew alphabet. Of this we cannot be sure but the Psalm as a whole certainly sums up the alphabet of life.

Psalm 119, may have been written after the King obediently copied out the Law for himself *(Deuteronomy 17:18-19)*. New leaders were instructed to write out the Law and read it all the days of their life...this was also expected of Joshua.

You would have thought as Joshua was entering the Promised land, (with God's people), the reading of the day would have been battle strategy and tactics. Rather he was encouraged to read and meditate on the Law, day and night *(Joshua 1:7-8)*. James (in the New Testament) knew of the blessing received from doing such a thing and encouraged his readers to not forget the Law, but to live it *(James 1:25)*.

Absence of the Law in the life of God's people only had a negative effect. It was only on finding the Law, reading the Law and keeping the Law that life went well for God's people. We only have to look at the time of Josiah *(2 Kings 23)* and Ezra *(Nehemiah 8)* for this to be confirmed. After a period of not living God's way, in His generosity God taught His people how to get the best of life.

In coming to know God's commands and in obeying them, so we too are able to grow closer to Him. As Dallas Willard succinctly says:

> *'When we keep the Law, we step into his ways and drink in his power'.* [lix]

I love the imagery that as we love God, we are walking alongside Jesus in our life. This is not merely our own strength but in God's.

It is as *John* says:

> *'We know that we have come to know him if we keep his commands. Whoever says, 'I know him,' but does not do what he commands is a liar, and the truth is not in that person. But if anyone obeys his word, love for God is truly made complete in them. This is how we know we are in him: Whoever claims to live in him must live as Jesus did'*
> *(1 John 2:3-6).*

Yikes, now this all sounds a bit like tough love. Yet, sometimes love has to be tough. John is only stating a fact. It is impossible to truly come to Jesus as Lord and then ignore what He says and how He lived. God is either our sovereign Lord or He is not.

I have to trust that God, as my Creator, knows better than me. Through obeying God we are able to prosper *(Deuteronomy 6:24)*. This does not mean prosperity as in monetary gain, but as in living the best of lives, living God's way.

Although keeping God's commands may seem hard, in reality they are not. As John later states: *'His commands are not burdensome' (1 John 5:3)*. At the outset however, God's commands can look so. The fact that John declares they are not burdensome, implies a different way of living - living from God's love rather than living towards it.

Please do not hear me wrong, I am not advocating that we are to start striving in our own strength to attempt to keep every rule in the Bible. As Paul reminds us, we belong to Jesus, to His Spirit. We are no longer subject to regulations, based merely on human commands and teachings *(Colossians 2:20-3:1)*. We belong to God and to His Spirit. We are called to obey God's love which is at the heart of the Law.

CHAPTER EIGHTY:
GPS

Sometimes quite frankly we over complicate matters. We just need to know God's law of love and follow it.

I was once on a road trip. I was in the front beside the driver. I didn't know the area and I didn't have a map. There was GPS in the car but it belonged to someone who sat in the back and I wasn't allowed to touch it! The challenge with this scenario is, the person with the GPS did not like barking out orders as they felt it sounded rude. The consequence of this was that we took more than one wrong turn. I should mention, the roads were long with few junctions. On one occasion after a wrong turn, it took over an hour to turn around, and all because someone did not want to shout, *'LEFT... Take this turn'*.

I love the person I refer to in this story and I respect their choice of not wanting to bark orders – I guess they are just more polite than me.

In a relationship with God, whilst mercifully He does not shout at me, I am learning to just accept His orders, His commands. I need them lest I take a wrong turn. Jesus in His life and words modelled this way of living. Jesus Himself in coming to earth revealed:

> *'Do not think that I have come to abolish the Law or the Prophets; I have not come to abolish them but to fulfil them'*
> *(Matthew 5:17).*

In His life and death, Jesus became the ultimate sacrifice for everyone, because as Paul confesses, all have, *'sinned and fall short of the glory of God'* *(Romans 3:23).*

It is through Jesus we are saved, not through the keeping of the Law or even any command; so why am I even writing this book?

To obey Jesus' command does not make us right with God, only accepting all Jesus has done for us, can do this. Rather obeying Jesus' words, shows us how to live our life for the better. I would never be so crass as to liken Jesus to a GPS, but in love and from love, following Jesus' commands enables us to navigate eternal living.

CHAPTER EIGHTY-ONE:
RED, AMBER, GREEN

On this note of obeying Jesus, a quick skim through the Gospels reveal how Jesus, did not actually command us to do a whole lot. The disciples were asked to follow Him *(Mark 1:17)*, but not commanded to do so. Jesus did command the wind to be still *(Mark 4:39)* and He commanded evil spirits to come out of people *(Luke 4:35-44)*, but He actually commanded very little.

Jesus spoke to people saying, if they wanted to follow Him, they would have to give up their lives. Jesus knew this was the only way they could gain true life *(Mark 8:34)*. Even in this however, they were being given a choice. Jesus set out the best way, but He left people to make their own choice. For those who could not live such a life, He let them go *(John 6:66)*.

On coming to know God's love for us, in becoming followers of Jesus, so we come under His command. In addition to the fundamental command to love God, the only other commands I see are for His followers to *'change their hearts and lives' (Matthew 4:17),* and then to tell others. As they do so they are to be a disciple; someone learning as they go. Jesus before He returned to heaven said:

> *'go and make disciples of all nations, baptising them in the name*
> *of the Father and of the Son and of the Holy Spirit, and teaching*
> *them to obey everything I have commanded you'*
> *(Matthew 28:19-20).*

Jesus commands His followers to love God with their all as He knows this will result in changed hearts and lives. From this His followers can only ever want to share God's great love for everyone. Jesus' commands are few but they are consistent. They are life and world changing.

As Jesus came, so the Ten Commandments which had become 613, became quite simply one, or two if you include love your neighbour as well. For some-one who has a bad memory I am grateful for this. In doing this, rather than condensing the Law, so Jesus revealed what had been at the heart of all of the Law, all along. Jesus said:

> *'Love the Lord your God with all your heart and with all your*
> *soul and with all your mind and with all your strength.' The*
> *second is this: 'Love your neighbour as yourself.' There is no*
> *commandment greater than these'*
> *(Mark 12:30-31).*

All of the Law is summed up in a oner.

I have often wondered though why Jesus didn't go one step further. Why didn't He abbreviate even more, to just; 'Love God. Love others'? This would have surely been even easier to remember.

Perhaps it is because then we would miss out on the richness of allowing the commandment to wash over our whole being, over our heart, our soul, our mind and our strength. Jesus wants us to live this command and to remember it, but not at the expense of missing out on the life changing nature of it.

I believe it is a command, that is for our own good, given because God knows best. I want it to be an invitation, as it is a most glorious one, and yet no, it is a command that is for our benefit. So forgive me for having referred to this as an invitation throughout my wrestlings. Forgive me also for having it as a subtitle for this book! I do not, however, repent of the conviction I have of how important this is for all of God's children.

A last word on the word, 'invitation'. God invites us to invite Him into our lives. I repeat, God invites us to invite Him into our lives. God longs for us to invite Him into every part of our day. God invites us to invite Him into our minds, hearts, strength and soul. All for our own good. This is pretty glorious!

CHAPTER EIGHTY-TWO:
'PHONE HOME...'

I am eternally grateful for having received this command to love God with my all. It has helped me to value my life on earth all the more. I no longer feel I am trudging through life waiting for the good stuff after death. Loving God with my all has helped me to become more aware of God's Presence on earth before heaven. Inspired by those who have gone before, I now long to walk faithfully, on earth before heaven.

This was an important turning point for me as I had always thought, you 'become a Christian' and on doing so, it was almost like you receive a password to get into heaven. Life on earth was to be lived or at times endured, before getting to the good place. I have come to see this really was to waste a lot of time on earth. This at times contributed to me existing and not living.

Now forgive me here, because I am going over some ground already covered within this book, but I consider it is so important, that some re-capping and expanding cannot go a miss. If however, you totally get 'eternal living' and the 'Kingdom of God', please skip this chapter and we'll catch up as we look at 'Aliens'.

In loving God with my all, I have realised on being a Christian, we are called to eternal living. Loving God and loving our neighbour is the Kingdom of God on earth. I am called to be part of the Kingdom of Heaven, the Kingdom of God, here on earth before our souls live in heaven. Life doesn't start in heaven, life in abundance starts now – on earth. Going to heaven is a transition from life on earth to life in heaven. Jesus is more than life after death – Jesus is life now.

Anything other than this, is perhaps as Dallas Willard calls; *'consumer Christianity'*.[lx] To be a Christian merely for what one can get out of it, (namely forgiveness and heaven), misses out on the glorious riches of living with God here on earth. Rather than Christianity being life changing or life forming, it's almost as if it's a 'Get out of jail free card'. Such a belief structure does not allow for inner transformation and offers little commitment to the Kingdom of God.

Every day millions of people, without even really realising it, pray about God's Kingdom. Within the Lord's Prayer there are the words: *'Your kingdom come, on earth as in heaven...'*. In these words Jesus invites us to pray for God's kingdom to be on earth, just as it is in heaven.

Our life on earth is preparing us for our time in heaven, which hey, is for eternity which is a really long time! So, perhaps we should pay a bit more attention.

But, what of all those really bad days? For those days when we don't want to be on earth, when illness abounds, or yet another disaster strikes. I have come to see that on those days it is actually okay to 'wrestle'. This recent acknowledgement has liberated me from feeling guilty about wrestling with life as it is. I desire more than this world.

In the past I would reason with myself that I am a Christian, I am loved by God, so surely life should be perfect! How could I be a good witness to those around me, unless life was great? How could I allow myself to be angry, disappointed and troubled when I was after all a person loved by God? I have come to see life isn't perfect.

Perhaps particularly in the West, we have become so comfortable on earth, that we call this place, 'home'. So much so that many people even consider this is it. This is not it. We are strangers in this world.

As Paul recounts of people of faith in *Hebrews 11*, so he reminds us, life on earth was not all that laid in store for them. These people on the whole were remarkable and they did some extraordinary things for God and yet:

> *'They did not receive the things promised; they only saw them and*
> *welcomed them from a distance, admitting that they were*
> *foreigners and strangers on earth. People who say such things*
> *show that they are looking for a country of their own...Instead,*
> *they were longing for a better country — a heavenly one'*
> *(Hebrews 11:13-15).*

God has placed within us a longing for a better country – a heavenly one. *'Therefore God is not ashamed to be called their God, for he has prepared a city for them'* *(Hebrews 11:16).* When we despair, or are saddened at abuse, poverty, illness, and basically everything which is not right with this world, this is okay. We need to recognise this is a longing which God has given us.

Matt Redman's song; *'One Day (When We All Get To Heaven)'* is a beautiful reminder of how this world is not all there is, and of the hope we have in Jesus. Go on youtube! Using the beginning of *Revelation 21* for inspiration, Matt puts life into perspective and manages to put a thousand words succinctly into one song.

God does not call us to a perfect world in our lifetime, (this is reserved for our soul), but He does promise to be with us on earth. Nowadays, when a newscast troubles me, when yet another person falls ill, or dies, I realise it is okay to feel wretched, overwhelmed or even angry. More than this, as I feel like this, God longs to come alongside me to comfort me. The Psalmist's time and again knew of this and sang of it. One such example is from Psalm 88:

> *'Lord, you are the God who saves me;*
> *day and night I cry out to you.*
> *May my prayer come before you;*
> *turn your ear to my cry.*
> *I am overwhelmed with troubles*
> *and my life draws near to death.*
> *I am counted among those who go down to the pit;*
> *I am like one without strength'*
> *(v.1-4).*

Life isn't perfect – not yet anyway. Our calling on earth is to live with God, to be loved by God, to love God and in His strength to love others. Living in His Kingdom here on earth is real.

For all of those times when I despair at this world being far from perfect, I pray into specific situations - yes, but also in my wrestling I accept God's Sovereignty. I acknowledge all history begins and ends in His hands. But more than this, I recognise we are designed for heaven, to be with God, away from sin. One of the roles of our soul is to remind us of this.

CHAPTER EIGHTY-THREE:
ALIENS

We are in fact all *'exiles' (1 Peter 2:11), 'our citizenship is in heaven' (Philippians 3:20)* and as such we suffer from *'homesickness' (Hebrews 11:13,16)*. Life on earth is not all there is, and contrary to Belinda Carlisle's 1980's song, *'heaven is not a place on earth'*.

Talking of song lyrics from the 1980's, (as I am unashamedly an 80's chick), many songs confused me. Lisa Stansfield sang: *'Been around the world and I, I, I, I can't find my baby'*. As a young girl, I just thought this was at best careless and at worse negligent in the highest form. Had she just left her little child in an airport?

And just every so often, have you misheard lyrics, sung them out loud and wondered why you were attracting attention? Well, in one of Madonna's songs, I honestly thought she was singing, 'I'm not a virgin…whooh'. I was 11 years old okay, and a pretty innocent one at that, so I was always confused at school disco's when I received quite a bit of attention from older boys! Moving swiftly on…

We are exiles, we are currently on earth, we are not in heaven. Heaven awaits and when we feel the world is not all as it should be, this is an appropriate response. We may not always be able to describe what heaven will be, but we are designed to have an ache for it. St Augustine of the fourth century, knew of such an ache but also of the promise for our souls:

> *There we shall see rest and see, see and love, love and praise.*
> *This is what shall be in the end without end. For what other end*
> *do we propose to ourselves than to attain to the kingdom of which*
> *there is no end?'.* [lxi]

When we experience an ache of homesickness, this is a good thing because it reminds us of more…of a home reserved for us with our

Heavenly Father, Jesus Christ His Son and the Holy Spirit.

We may not be able to truly describe heaven or imagine what it will be like, and this is partly because we do not know, but also because it is inexpressible. We may occasionally have a glimpse of it, but this is infinitesimal compared to heaven itself.

The disciple John, in his book of *Revelation* gives us a marvellous picture of the heavenly throne room, of Jesus at the centre, being surrounded by praise and worship *(Revelation 4 and 5)*. We are heaven-bound but this does not mean our time on earth is as boring as being at an airport departure lounge.

Okay I really tried not to pause here to rave about *Revelation 4 and 5* but I just cannot do it. These are amazing chapters and in terms of the rest of the book of *Revelation*, pretty easy to understand. In these chapters we see God at the centre of the most incredible worship.

God is surrounded by thrones, elders, creatures and angels all of whom are worshipping Him. Who needs stage lighting? There are flashes of light and colours galore. There are the sounds of trumpets, harps, thunder, lightning. The scene is nearly overwhelming. And we, yes, we – little ole us, are invited to be part of this. With God at the centre, we are invited to uniquely experience God.

On earth we can be with God, but it is just a foretaste of things to come. It's a pretty short time too, so we should make the most of it.

It is interesting to note that Jesus spoke very little about heaven. His interest was more on the Kingdom of God, of our living our eternal life on earth before heaven.

Life with God on earth can be the most incredible adventure. We are created to be with God on earth as well as in heaven. God longs for us not to miss out on being with Him, of receiving and living the greatest invitation ever given.

The command to love God with all our all, is in fact leading us home. To miss out on loving God with our all only leads to us feeling even more homesick. Thankfully even as we are on earth, we are not left alone.

I have just spent the morning reading about the Olympics with my son and one race has been on my mind.

I do not know if you remember the Barcelona Olympics of 1992 – you may not even have been born! It was the year of Linford Christie winning the 100 metres, with Roger Black, Kriss Akabusi and Sally Gunnell achieving medals. The race I remember most however, was the 400 metre race with Britain's Derek Redmond hoping for a Gold medal.

In the lead, running the race of his life, Redmond looked as though he had a chance for a medal. With the finishing line in sight, as he rounded the turn into the backstretch, with a sharp pain in his leg, Redmond however, fell face first. He had torn his right hamstring. As the medical attendants ran to him, Redmond fought to his feet and began hopping furiously to finish the race.

At the final stretch a large man leapt from the stand. Hurling security guards aside, he ran to embrace Redmond.

'Son, you don't have to do this', said a father to his weeping son.

'Yes I do' said Derek.

'Well' said his father, 'we'll do it together'.

Fighting off security guards, with his head sometimes buried in his father's chest, with the crowd cheering and weeping, Derek made it to the end.

I do not remember who won the race that day. Derek certainly didn't come away with a medal, but assisted by his father, he did finish the race.

Just as Derek's father in the Olympics did not let His son run alone, so our loving Heavenly Father does not let us run our race of life alone. Indeed Jesus left His place in heaven to come to earth to live alongside us. Jesus promises in the Gospel of Matthew:

'I am with you always, to the very end of the age'
(Matthew 28:20).

Whilst on earth, until heaven, I rejoice in God's promise of Him never leaving us on our own. I come to Him as Sovereign Lord, knowing He is always there to call upon.

The apostle Paul knew of this. Called away from his earthly home to be a missionary in lands far and wide, he must have had times of feeling homesick. On being repeatedly beaten, imprisoned and shipwrecked, he must have had times of thinking back to the good old days of being at home with family and friends.

Paul must have wistfully looked back and remembered home cooked meals. Paul must have longingly thought of the days when he was a revered Pharisee *(Acts 23:6)*, of worship in his local synagogue. Yet the homesickness Paul spoke about was not that of home comforts, but of heaven.

As I consider Paul's homesickness, I am convinced that Jesus, surely, was the only one to truly know this 'homesickness'. After all, He had been in heaven before coming to earth. Jesus knew what a perfect place heaven was. Paul had not been there, rather, he was hoping in faith that heaven was perfect. Something dep within Paul just knew - was it his soul? Paul believed and it seems His soul knew of his ultimate destination.

> *'For we know that when this earthly tent we live in is taken*
> *down (that is, when we die and leave this earthly body), we will*
> *have a house in heaven, an eternal body made for us by God... we*
> *long to put on our heavenly bodies like new clothing'*
> *(2 Corinthians 5:1-2).*

As Paul wrote, so he acknowledged how on earth we are left to groan *(Romans 8:22-23)*. Life on earth is not perfect. God designed us to be homesick for heaven. It is God who has *'put his Spirit in our hearts as a deposit, guaranteeing what is to come' (2 Corinthians 1:22)*. We may be God's children and His Spirit may be in our hearts, we may know of our inheritance, but for now we are homesick.

We will never be entirely at peace until we are in heaven with God. Until then we have a guarantee. He has given us His Holy Spirit.

> *'So we are always confident, even though we know that as long as*
> *we live in these bodies we are not at home with the Lord'*
> *(2 Corinthians 5:5-7).*

We were designed not to be entirely satisfied in this world. Our ageing, imperfect bodies even serve to remind us that we are away from God. For God's children, heaven will come soon enough and until then God longs us to live with Him, being loved by Him and loving Him with our all.

Meanwhile on earth, even in its imperfections, God is here. Mother Teresa found God in the slums of Calcutta. Corrie Ten Boom found He was in a Concentration camp. For Jackie Pullinger He was amongst drug addicts in Hong Kong. Nicky Cruz and David Wilkinson discovered God was not absent in the gangs of New York. God is no more or less at home in Canterbury Cathedral, than in an Intensive Care Unit or a prison.

God is omnipresent (God is everywhere) and He longs for all people to come to know of His love and to live in His love. For our part we are called to be part of the Kingdom of God. Life on earth is not all there is. Dietrich Bonhoeffer knew of this and as he was led to his execution, he remarked to a friend, *'This is the end, but for me it is the beginning of life'.* [lxii]

Christians in all conditions on earth can join with Paul who knew of his real home:

> *'Therefore we do not lose heart. Though outwardly we are wasting away, yet inwardly we are being renewed day by day. For our light and momentary troubles are achieving for us an eternal glory that far outweighs them all. So we fix our eyes not on what is seen, but on what is unseen, since what is seen is temporary, but what is unseen is eternal'*
> *(2 Corinthians 4:16-18).*

As I seek to live on earth as an alien, as an exile, I have found it helpful to remember the words of McGrath:

> *'Christians are in exile on earth. They are in the world, but they look forward to going home. They are citizens of heaven, who are exiled on earth'.* [lxiii]

***

*'Love the Lord your God with all your heart and with all your
soul and with all your mind and with all your strength'*

***

CHAPTER EIGHTY-FOUR:
'PLEASE SIR, IS THERE ANY MORE?' ^{LXIV}

As you can observe there are not many pages left...we are nearly coming to the end of this particular journey together. So, perhaps you are thinking you are safe from any more wrestling's...if only!

I have had to ask myself the question, if to love God with our all, with four different parts, is so important, why is it not mentioned more? Why doesn't John quote it specifically? Why are the New Testament letters not full of this command of how we must love God?

Furthermore, why are there are more references to 'loving your neighbour' than to loving God. Being called to love others is important, but Jesus Himself did say, it was the second most important command. To seek to love others is a high task indeed, especially when Jesus extended this to loving our enemies as well (Matthew 5:44), but this is the second command. The first is to love God.

I am grateful that now I appreciate how hard it is to love others in our own strength. It becomes an almost impossible expectation. Loving others is the second command not the first, so why did the likes of Paul and Peter speak more of loving others, than of loving God?

Perhaps the lack of emphasis on loving God, has led to some people skimming over the first part of the command of Jesus straight to the second. Some people even struggle with separating them, as they see them both flowing into the other. On the one hand yes they do; it is surely impossible to love God without loving others. Equally to love others we need to love God first. However, Jesus Himself separated them into two commands and so I follow His lead.

Let's be honest, many people pay more attention to loving their neighbour, than to loving God. With the New Testament writers speaking more of loving our neighbour, perhaps we can be forgiven for thinking that this is the most important command after all.

There are temptations to see the second command as more important. One reason for this could be because the results are more tangible. Through loving others, through social reform and social justice, we can see people's lives being transformed for the better. Some of the results may hold us in better stead with society.

To love others may also make us feel good about ourselves and perhaps before we know it we may even be tempted to receive the praise of people. After all, loving God can almost be seen as a little self-indulgent. Christians singing songs of praise, praying, being quiet with God, reading the Bible, hardly change the world, do they...?

Now please do not hear me wrong, in no way am I advocating that to love others is wrong. Nor am I saying social reform or working towards social justice is a bad thing – far from it. Jesus in His own life lived loving His neighbour: He fed the hungry, healed the sick, raised a man from the dead and finally died on the cross for us. Therefore we are certainly encouraged to love others.

Some people seek to love others, with little regard to God Himself. As they seek to love others with all their heart, mind, strength and soul, it is almost as if they leap frog the source, ('God'). We are commanded to love others yes, but only from loving God.

In being commanded to love God first, not only does it put everything in the right order - God first, humanity second, it also reminds us in whose strength we are called to love others. It is in God's alone.

To put the love of others before God, could lead us back to the place of the Pharisees at the time of Jesus. After all they had become more concerned with how people viewed them, than with how God viewed them.

Furthermore before we know it, we may be tempted to believe it is good deeds which lead to God's favour. This has spurred well intentioned people to do a great many works, but it negates the cross. To believe we come to Jesus through good works only, is against what Jesus Himself preached and lived *(Galatians 1:8-9)*. It is by grace we are saved and not by works *(Ephesians 2:8)*.

We are human and can therefore only truly love others when we are immersed in God's love. As we come to love God with our all, not only are we equipped to love God more, but also it is then impossible not to love others. Human beings are made in God's image and as such His love flows through us onto others.

But back, if I may, to the New Testament and how in it there appears to be little encouragement to love God. Now I am aware that there are some instances of writers of the New Testament recording how we should love God, but to my mind they are rather few. *Romans 8:28, 1 Corinthians 2:9; 8:3, 16:22* and *Ephesians 6:24* do so, but even so they are not in the context of Jesus giving the greatest command.

I have to ask, how could they not have wanted to speak of the command of Jesus more than they did?

But before we get there, I need to have a few words about John's Gospel. After all he doesn't even mention the greatest command. In his defence, I concur John does spend more time looking at love as a whole. *John* devotes two chapters (*14 and 15*) writing of love and following Jesus' commands.

In *John 14:15-31*, John reveals Jesus' extended teaching on the relationship of love and keeping His commands. In just seventeen verses, the word *'love'* is mentioned nineteen times, *'commands'* three times and *'teaching'* twice.

While John does not have Jesus speaking of our heart, mind soul and strength, instead in much greater depth he speaks of loving God as whole. Some highlights which John records of Jesus, are:

'If you love me, keep my commands'
(v.15)

'Whoever has my commands and keeps them is the one who loves me. The one who loves me will be loved by my Father, and I too will love them and show myself to them'
(v.21)

'Anyone who loves me will obey my teaching. My Father will love them, and we will come to them and make our home with them'
(v.23).

We also gain an insight into how loving God is not all our own responsibility, but it is through the working of the Holy Spirit in our hearts.

In his following chapter *(15)*, just in case we haven't quite got the message, John speaks of love and commands again. In his famous text of abiding ('remaining') in Jesus, just as fruit abides in the vine *(15:1-17)*, John shows he did know of Jesus' teaching on love. The love, Jesus speaks of is not some fuzzy feeling. This love is agape, it is love of the will, love of choice, it is a love of action, not least as modelled in Jesus' sacrificial love on the cross.

John uses the word *'remain/abide'* eleven times, the word *'love'* nine times and *'commands'* five times. So important is the word *'μένη'*, *'menē'* *(abide/remain/stay)*, that he uses it 11 times in just 7 verses *(v.4-10)*. John reveals the flow of love. As the Father has loved Jesus, so Jesus now loves us.

We are encouraged to remain in this love:

> *'If you keep my commands, you will remain in my love, just as I*
> *have kept my Father's commands and remain in his love'*
> *(v.10)*.

These commands are not specified, except for the command to love each other *(v.17)* and this is where I have struggled. All too easily this could be taken to mean that the only loving we are required to do, is to love others. Yes Jesus has asked us to remain in His love, which must mean we are to love Him, but why didn't John specify it more as the other Gospel writers did?

It is widely believed John's Gospel was the last to be written, so it could be argued John did not need to waste time repeating what could easily be found in the other Gospels. This said, if this verse from Jesus is so important, surely John could have included a tiny verse of just 24 words. It's hardly going to stretch his word limit, is it?

This wrestling did not sit well with me. Then it slowly dawned, could it be that to love God, was just too obvious to mention? Could it be that all that John was saying was structured around the command of us loving God? More on this later...

CHAPTER EIGHTY-FIVE:
HAM SANDWICHES AND GINGER BEER

As I have already explained, at the time of Jesus, Jews would already have been saying the Shema twice a day. As they did this, so they reminded themselves of their commitment to love God with their all. Perhaps to write specifically of the command to love God, was as obvious as the importance of the Lord's Prayer to Christians today.

Just as an aside (the last one of the book), I was a big Enid Blyton fan, in particular of the 'Famous Five' series. I loved how they always had adventures galore and pic-nic's overflowing. But they never went to the loo! Neither do the Gospel writers speak of Jesus going either.

The Bible does contain one person on the loo, King Eglon, but this didn't work out so well *(Judges 3:24)*. He was murdered and his guards failed to help him, as they thought he was *'relieving himself'*. Generally in books, characters do not go to the loo. I guess there is no need to mention it as it is a given that at some point everyone needs the loo. Sorry, Mother-in-law, I know you are uncomfortable with the image of Jesus going to the loo...but as someone who was fully human He did.

Where am I going with this? Well, perhaps, loving God was so obvious to John and writers such as Paul, Peter and James that they did not feel the need to write of it. To love God with your mind, soul, heart and strength was a given. It was just all too obvious to keep going on about it.

Jews as they recited the Shema knew they were to be loving God with their all. For many years followers of Jesus were labelled followers of 'the Way', which was seen as a Jewish sect. It was not until Antioch that Jesus' followers were first called Christians *(Acts 11:26)*. New disciples are likely to have been encouraged to recite the Shema or/and to love the Lord with their all.

It is interesting to note within the New Testament, how we only know of some things because of mistaken practices. Take for example the Lord's Supper. Yes, Jesus had asked His followers to remember Him in it and the Gospels record this. However, it is only with Paul's directions in *1 Corinthians 11*, that we truly get a picture of what the Lord's Supper should be like.

Why does Paul share this? Because the church in Corinth were getting it all wrong. Paul writes to admonish them for their practices. If the church at Corinth had been behaving well, perhaps Paul would never have given such teaching.

So, perhaps, Loving God was just obvious. Loving their neighbour perhaps was not so, hence the New Testament authors writing of loving others more. The latter was not being done, the former was. To be honest, I cannot be sure, but this is the conclusion I have reached.

The challenge I have as a 21st Century disciple is I do not know what it was like to be a follower of Jesus in the early church. Sure, we get lots of glimpses in the book of Acts and the letters, but day to day we cannot be entirely sure. Sometimes, in faith, we are called to live and walk one step at a time. Living 'loving God' at the centre of my being is helping me to navigate my way through life.

CHAPTER EIGHTY-SIX:
A ROUND UP OF GOD'S LOVE

I have now said many times that we are commanded or invited to love God with our all. I have also repeatedly said, for this to happen, we need to be loved by God first. As we come into this relationship of love, as we experience it for ourselves, so we are able to learn more about what love truly is.

Through being loved by God, through God's Holy Spirit dwelling within us, so our love for God and others flows from God's love within ourselves. God's love comes first. To try and love in our own strength, well...not only is it not perfect love, but it's pretty exhausting if not impossible. God did not create us to love in our own strength but in His. Loving those we naturally choose to love can be tiring, let alone loving our enemies as well. The only way is to love from being loved.

From my own experience I can testify that I have become more aware of God's love and through allowing God's love to flow through me, (rather than depending on myself) loving has become easier.

God's love can flow through us, but we have to be open to being loved first. Second is us loving God, and from here flows our love for others. John in his first letter, has helped me develop my understanding of the flow of love and he says it so much better than I. So, it seems that here I forgive John for not mentioning the actual verse to, 'Love the Lord...' as his letter, is pretty awesome. Some highlights of *1 John 4:7-21* are

'let us love one another, for love comes from God'
(v.7)

'And so we know and rely on the love God has for us. God is love. Whoever lives in love lives in God, and God in them'
(v.16)

'We love because he first loved us'
(v.19).

Okay, who am I kidding? Please go and read it in full...and then again and quite possibly again. If you end up never returning to this book, well hey ho, John in his letter, says it so much better than me.

Jim Borst however, puts it pretty well too:

'It is not we who love but He who loves in us and through us'.[lxv]

Julian of Norwich has a good way with words too:

'God want us always to be strong in our love, and peaceful and restful as he is towards us, and he wants us to be, for ourselves and for our fellow Christians what He is for us'. [lxvi]

All of this brings me to what I can only describe as a new way of living...

CHAPTER EIGHTY-SEVEN:
THE WAY

At the time of my becoming a 'Christian', the phrase bandied around was, 'Have you invited Jesus into your heart?' I didn't really question it. Overwhelmed with God's love for me, I knew I wanted to live with Jesus, so I too adopted the phrase.

I think I probably made a connection with my heart and God's love and I left it there – I was also at University on a teaching practise and writing my dissertation. On reflection however, I acknowledge this is not a phrase found in the Bible.

Interestingly though with my new found understanding of my heart, (of my inner being), in one sense it is as if I had truly invited Jesus into my heart. Accepting Jesus as my Saviour and Lord, I wanted to live the way He wanted me to live, which is directed by my heart. I invited God's Holy Spirit to dwell within me.

After more thought however, I see this is actually to limit the Lordship of Jesus. I now see in becoming a Christian I invited Jesus to be Lord not just of my heart, (my will), but of my mind, my soul and my muchness. To accept or to identify anything else would be to limit God's reign over my life. I wasn't merely asking Jesus into my heart, but into my mind, soul and strength.

I have come to see for eternity my soul belongs to God and while on earth my mind and my all belong to Him, as well as my heart. To consider Jesus dwelling in just one part of me may be better than nothing, but it limits His Sovereignty over all areas of my life. I had failed to see in becoming a Christian I had entered into God's rule, into God's way.

Take for example learning to ride a motorbike. My dad had an old scrambler for a while. I had seen him use it many times. I had watched him and I asked him how it worked.

My dad offered me a manual but I felt I knew enough. The key ignition was broken so I had to jump start it. After ten failed attempts, it eventually started up. In fact it roared down my dad's drive - heading towards his car. I realised at this moment, I did not know how to stop it.

Although I had invited my dad to tell me about starting the bike and he had done so, I had not asked him how to stop. Rather than crash into his car, I turned the bike sharply bringing it down upon myself into the rockery. On reflection it would have been less painful to just crash into the car!

A manual would have been a helpful resource, a proper lesson would have helped. I had gone ahead thinking I knew it all and painfully I was proved wrong.

God does not want this for us. He longs for us to know Him, to be loved by Him, to love Him and to live our lives wholeheartedly for Him. Loving God, should be the most defining characteristic of a Christian disciple. A holiday stick of rock has the same words running throughout the whole stick. Our love for God should flow through every part of us.

The more we come to know God, the more our love and understanding of Him should develop and deepen. Paul in writing to the church in Philippi recognised that love for God was connected with knowledge and in his prayer he hoped that our: *'love may abound more and more in knowledge and depth of insight' (Philippians 1:9).*

The more I have had the privilege of looking at the Bible and Judaism, the more I have come to see the intimacy of the relationship of God with His People. Judaism at its best is not a religion but 'a way of life'. Within Judaism, God, *'is an active, living 'decision making' being who plunges into human history and personally encounters men in their activity'.* lxvii

Just a cursory glance at the 613 commandments illustrate this. No area of their life, it seems is left out! The Mitzvah sees all of life should be ordered in the Presence of God. To abide by such commandments is a form of prayer, as God and His people are in communion together.

Perhaps a criticism which could be levied at the Christian Church today, is how often Christians compartmentalise their lives into the secular and sacred. Even worse, rather than Christianity, many people are living Churchianity! Attending church every so often can be all some people equate a relationship with God as being.

There are also people who say they are 'Christian', even though they may or may not spend any time with God or go to church. They may be 'Christian' by name, but not their heart, or their mind or soul. To be a 'Christian' by name only is to miss out on a glorious relationship. It seems to me almost a shame that the term Christian even came about!

It was first used in Antioch *(Acts 11:26)* and it may have first been used almost as an insult. Before this time, it seems followers of Jesus were called, *'followers of the way' (Acts 22:4)*. In this, there is a clear link to Jesus' own words about Himself: *'I am the way, the truth and the life' (John 14:6)*. Also, the term, *'followers of the way'* would have reminded Christians that they were following a way, a way of life.[lxviii]

Jesus never told us to make 'converts' or even 'Christians'. He commissioned us to make *'disciples'*. His followers are now commonly called Christians but I believe this is not enough. We are called to be disciples, to learn from Him, to follow His way.

Today we are surrounded, if not bombarded by choice and information. Sadly only a cursory look at our western world reveals rather than wanting to learn, or change, we often just want to escape. At the touch of a button, internet search engines can supply us with knowledge.

As I look to Jesus as my teacher, I see Him less as a person who can impart knowledge, (although His teaching is amazing), and more to a way of being. A great teacher to my mind, is someone who can make a significant change in the life of their hearers. Jesus lived His life and longs for us to live His way of life. We are as Paul says, to be clothed in Christ *(Galatians 3:23)*.

I realise the word, Christian, has Jesus *Christ's* name in the title, but it also has the name 'Ian'. I have nothing against the name Ian, but sadly some people who claim to be Christians do so, without wanting much to do with Christ. Are they following the way of Ian?

Too many people seem to want to go to heaven and may even call themselves, nominal Christians or woolly Church of England, without actually giving much thought to Jesus or God themselves.

Such a distinction of claiming to be something, but not letting it affect your life, is not really recognised in the Hebraic religion. The Sovereignty of God reigns over all things.

God is seen as the absolute Lord over all, and all must come under His sovereign rule. In living with God daily, so His people have the opportunity of a unique life of spiritual adventure.

Some years ago now, the phrase WWJD? (what would Jesus do?) was popular. I remember wearing a bracelet with it on and I tried hard in different circumstances to consider what Jesus would do in that instant. For a while it was helpful.

If I was watching something that I felt uncomfortable with I would wonder if Jesus would stay and watch it. Equally these were my University Clubbing days, so at times I would think would Jesus have just one more drink? Would He go to that particular club? If I considered the answer was no, then I would try and act accordingly.

Over a period of time though, considering WWJD? became yet another thing, to work at, another thing to do and strive towards. Inevitably I repeatedly failed and at times I felt even worse about myself.

I am currently trying to live kind of along these lines but with a slightly different take. Rather than thinking how I can live my life if I were Jesus, I am thinking how would Jesus live my life, if He were me. From this I am learning to live my life the way Jesus would if He were living my life on earth right now. He was a human once and lived His life on earth. Looking at His words and actions are a good start in terms of seeking to model myself on Him.

More than this though, I am learning to come alongside someone who lived loving God with His all. Jesus' starting place however, was always being loved by God Himself. All of His actions and words flowed from this and of course He loved God. If we could get to living just a fraction of our lives like this, just imagine how much better our lives could be.

A cursory look at the book of Acts reveals just how this is possible. Luke, in his book, follows the lives of a group of despondent, fearful people becoming quite extraordinary. How? Because through the power of the Holy Spirit, Jesus' disciples grew more dependent on God's love.

The disciples had lived with Jesus for three years and they had heard of His teaching, to change their hearts and lives. Yet even while Jesus was on earth we saw on more than one occasion when they either misunderstood Jesus or plainly messed up. It was only when the disciples were filled with the Holy Spirit that they began to live a different life. Extraordinary miracles, amazing sermons and words of wisdom all flowed from lives which were filled with God's love and Holy Spirit.

We too today are invited to be filled with the power of the Holy Spirit to lead a God led life. The Holy Spirit, I believe, works in a relationship with our heart, soul, mind and strength. For too long I had tried to serve God out of 'spiritual bankruptcy'. [lxix]

The Holy Spirit in partnership with ourselves can renew our minds, transform our actions and behaviour and keep our souls safe. To try to change merely in our own strength is surely setting ourselves up for an inevitable failure - God longs to be our strength. Our role is to be available, to be in the right place with God, so His grace may be able to work within us.

CHAPTER EIGHTY-EIGHT:
LIVING THE LIFE WE ARE CREATED FOR

So, back to the beginning: I discovered I was being invited to love God and after some wrestling I found this was not just another thing to do. It is if you like, the only thing to do. From this everything else flows.

Being in love with God, means all I want to do is to be with God. Everything else at the same time seems both insignificant and all the more significant. In loving God we are able to become the person we are created to be.

As I have allowed Jesus' command to speak to me, so it has re-ordered my life, my very being. My prime reason for being is to be loved and to love God. I am not created merely to do. I am born to love God.

Through breaking down this command of:

'Love the Lord your God with all your heart and with all your
soul and with all your mind and with all your strength'
(Mark 12:30).

...word by word, I have been given an opportunity to live and to heal. My mind quite literally needed to be wrung out and my strength restored. My heart needed inner transformation, so my soul could lead the way.

Rather than merely existing I am now living. I have been given a better way of being and from this state, all other things can and do flow. It is more than just 'being' and not 'doing'. I have come to see how our 'being' influences our 'doing'.

We still have to 'do' some things, of course we do. Unless you have very few needs and servants galore, 'doing' is part of life. However, just perhaps, if our 'doing' flows from our 'being', from loving God and of being in His Presence in all things at all times, well...it may just be our 'doing' becomes easier. More than just easier, our doing comes from a place of love, from God Himself.

We do not need to live in a state of permanently doing, which eventually often results in abject exhaustion. We can live from a position of blessing (and even stillness), rather than living from a state of perpetual, all-consuming busyness.

In other words...actually no, let it not be my words but those of John. In his first letter *(1 John 4)* he succinctly reveals:

> *'This is how God showed his love among us: He sent his one and only Son into the world that we might live through him. This is love: not that we loved God, but that he loved us and sent his Son as an atoning sacrifice for our sins'*
> *(v.9-10).*

Jesus longs to give Himself to us. Jesus does not call us merely to live as He did, but to be as He was. We can only do this as we dwell in Him.

When I seek to 'do', when I seek to love, I am now starting from a position of strength. This is not my own strength but it is God's. I had got it all topsy-turvy for too long.

On my final day at theological college, as I sat in the college chapel in my final service, I was given a picture which I sensed was from God. College had not been a high point of my life and at times it had felt like I was trudging through mud. The picture I received was of a seed, which had been in the soil for a long time. During this time the seed had been in the dark. At times it was cold, often wet, and on occasions a worm and other insects would pass by. But one day I sensed the seed was beginning to poke through the soil and was going to flower.

At the time I thought this referred to my going off into ministry, to serve my curacy. The picture gave me a sense of liberation, of freedom, to go and to serve. Time spent at college had not been wasted. After all a seed needs to die in order to become something else. The dark times, the times of being cold and wet, well they were actually all for my good. The theological term is 'spiritual formation'. I was being equipped for service and now I was free to go...

As I look back however, the trouble was, I was so eager to go and do, that I often did so from a position of me, rather than from God and with God. This had only been sustainable for so long. I was now receiving a second chance, an opportunity to be loved by God and to love Him.

Rather than 'flourishing' after years of ministry, I had almost started to retreat back into the soil. It was only on fully acknowledging I am loved by God and I am being commanded to love God with my all, that I have become able to live life to the full.

I now sense this picture is speaking to me once again. Except rather than 'go' and 'serve', I am being required to be that seed once more. During my times of brokenness, I have literally been 'dying' again. I am far from shooting forth out of the ground and yet I know in God's timing I will. And this time, when I do, the plant will be stronger and have firmer foundations. It will be more nourished in God's love.

Coming to Jesus as 'the way' is not a formula or a ten step program. It involves all of me, all of the time. Paul knew of this:

> *'And whatever you do, whether in word or deed, do it all in the*
> *name of the Lord Jesus, giving thanks to God the Father*
> *through him'*
> *(Colossians 3:17).*

For too long (as I have said), I had seen Paul's words as yet something else to do. Now I see his words as encouraging me to follow Jesus, to live His way, to live in Him and to allow Him to live through me.

> The only way to live a life worth living, is to
> live the life we are worthy of.

Our worth comes from being made in the image of God and through being saved by Jesus. From here, in God's love and in keeping His command, we can live the life given to us by God.

Loving God and following the way of Jesus leads to an inner transformation. God blesses us with *'fruits of the spirit' (Galatians 5:22-23).* *'love, joy, peace, forbearance, kindness, goodness, faithfulness, gentleness and self-control'* are not to be earned or awarded but grow within us. They are not trophies to be awarded along the way. God's gifts are given for us to live the life He longs for us to live, and they equip us to love others.

This invitation has been lived out by God's people from the beginning of time, from the first walk of Adam in the garden of Eden, to Moses who first received the words 'loving God', and supremely Jesus lived out these words in spirit and truth.

Throughout the Bible I have come to see how when God's people lived wholly loving God and being loved by God they lived life to the full. The

329

very best of life was lived. Even during times of despair, grief and hardship, when God was being loved first, life was a lot better than when they ignored Him.

To not put God first, was actually to sin, as humanity was then no longer living the life they were created for, which is to know God, to love God and to be with God.

***

'Love the Lord your God with all your heart and with all your soul and with all your mind and with all your strength. **The second is this: 'Love your neighbour as yourself.'** **There is no commandment greater than these.'**
(Mark 12:30-31)

***

CHAPTER EIGHTY-NINE:
LOVING OTHERS

I have spoken over eighty chapters about loving God and although I have acknowledged Jesus' second command, *'love your neighbour'*, I have not done so at any great length. This however, has been on purpose.

As I stated earlier, too often we can be tempted to leapfrog loving God just so we can get on and love our neighbour. The second command is important, of course it is, but I really wanted to spend time focusing on loving God first. As only from here can our love for others flow.

For me personally loving God first, has radically changed how I am with Him. Considering *'Walking with God'* as Enoch did *(Genesis 5:24)* and becoming more aware of God's Presence in all things is causing my life to 'slow down'. Silence and meditative prayer, not least for a Charismatic evangelical, has not come easily, and yet this is how it seems God wants me to be with Him.

To truly love others has to come from an inner transformation, blessed by God. To do otherwise may lead to the temptation of seemingly loving others, merely to impress, or to gain rewards. Alternatively we may be motivated to help others, out of trying to please others or from some inner guilt.

In talking about loving our neighbour, people often begin to look for effects on earth. Before we know it, we can become like the religious leaders of Jesus' day. We can become more interested in praise from people than that of God. Pharisees looked at trying to keep the Law, they became law-keepers, rather than becoming the kind of person whose deeds naturally conform to the Law.

To try to love others without loving God first, can therefore lead us to try and love others with the wrong motivation. Some people however, may argue so long as people are being loved and helped, does the motivation really matter?

All I can say, from my own life is YES it does matter. To love from a source other than God can be draining, it can eat you up inside, and you can begin to live like a hypocrite. To be motivated by personal reward can make our love of others selective.

We can begin to only love those who are easy to love. We can attempt to only love those who may help us in return. This is not loving our enemies. This is limiting our love for others, rather than widening our love to everybody.

Jesus invites us to focus less on the externals and more on the internal flowing out. Now do not hear me wrong, many people do love their neighbour and I know many people who do this without any reference to God at all. Some atheists are the nicest people I know.

For me however, loving God has to come first and it is from here alone that my love for others can flow - in God's strength and not merely my own. Other forms of love have a shelf life! Loving in God's love can lead to even more than sacrificial love, as even this form of love can self-motivated. Altruistic love is rarely spoken of and perhaps even less lived. It is a totally unselfish love, purely for others.

I need to point out here, I am not even close to living this form of love. This said, though, as I give time to consider that all people are created in the image of God, so I am coming to want what is best for them. I have never prayed so fervently for people's souls as in recent months. I was quite overwhelmed recently in a train station as I saw people 'scurrying' around. My heart quite literally went out to them, as I stopped to pray for them all.

Accepting second best for myself or for others no longer seems an option. God longs for us to love our neighbour. Love is an action. Paul emphasises this. It's worth quoting in full:

> 'Let no debt remain outstanding, except the continuing debt to love one another, for whoever loves others has fulfilled the Law. The commandments, 'You shall not commit adultery,' 'You shall not murder,' 'You shall not steal,' 'You shall not covet,' and whatever other command there may be, are summed up in this one command: 'Love your neighbour as yourself.' Love does no harm to a neighbour. Therefore love is the fulfilment of the Law' (Romans 13:8-10).

'*Love is the fulfilment of the Law...*' marks the movements of God's Kingdom here on earth: first through God's own love for us, through the life and actions of His son, and then through God's children living God's love.

In loving our neighbour, we can be confident that we are doing what God longs for us to do. We are given an opportunity to be God's love in human form. But even this should not be done in our own strength but with and in God's Holy Spirit. Jesus was fully human and He knows how hard it is for us to keep His commands of loving our neighbour. Jesus invites us to follow Him and His ways: to rely on His advocate, the Holy Spirit.

I wonder, when do you most like yourself? For me, it is when I am with John, he quite simply brings out the best in me. He encourages me in every way to be a nicer person, to be patient, to be genuinely loving and caring. Instinctively I long to put him before myself.

Some environments and some people simply bring out the best in us. Others do not...Jesus commands us to love our neighbour, to be His Kingdom on earth. To do so, is through becoming more like Jesus. The foremost way of doing this is through being with Jesus more.

For every person this will be lived slightly differently. God invites us to be with Him through, His word, music, prayer, art, church, reading, listening and doing. Perhaps how we spend time with Jesus is less important, than actually living with Him.

As we are invited to be with God, the more we are able to become a person who naturally loves our neighbour. This is less about achievement and accomplishment and more about abiding with God, being with Him.

As our inner life, our heart, our mind, soul and strength belong more to God, so our life can flow from the Kingdom of God, rather than trying to strive towards it.

Consider the flow of a river. As I said before, it is very hard to change its direction. One summer, John and I spent ages in a stream. Through forming dams, we tried to change the flow of it. Could we change the ultimate direction of the river? No! Water typically flows with gravity, downhill.

In June 1969, for several months, U.S. engineers diverted the flow of the Niagara River away from the American side of the falls. The plan was to remove the large amount of loose rock from the base of the waterfall. If you have been fortunate enough to visit the falls, you will appreciate the incredible task of this. To try in effect to stop and change the flow of the river was a mammoth task. Due to expense, in the November of that year, the idea was eventually abandoned.

God longs for us to be His Kingdom on earth, to be like Jesus, to love our neighbour - not through trying to keep laws, but through being more like Jesus and through allowing God's love to naturally flow out of ourselves. We must allow God to transform the inner life of the soul and from this more Godly-behaviour will naturally flow.

Nineham expresses this well saying:

> 'true love of the neighbour springs from the love of God, and on the other hand there can be no true love of God which does not express itself in the love of the neighbour'. lxx

CHAPTER NINETY:
INTENTIONAL DISCIPLESHIP

Okay, before we part ways, I sense you would like something tangible, something actual, something to take away. You have probably heard enough of loving God, yet, you may still not be sure how to do this, and actually, you may just want to skip to loving others.

Allow me to share a phrase I have heard from Dallas Willard, who speaks of this so much better than I. Do consider checking out the book 'The Divine Conspiracy'. It's definitely in my top 5 of books I have read. It can be hard going, but wow it is amazing, life changing even.

If I am honest it is a book which took me a long time to read, because it is so deep. Often I could only read one paragraph at a time, after which I would need a long time to grapple with what he was saying. Dallas advocates that we are not being called to 'consumer Christianity', rather we are being called to 'intentional discipleship'.

To be 'intentional' is to have calculated the pro's and con's, it is to deliberately lead a particular way of life. To be an 'intentional disciple' is someone who has recognised God's love for them and longs to love God in return, but there is more. Jesus' parable of the sower (Mark 4:1-20) serves to show not everyone who says they will follow Him will continue to do so. It is too easy to be distracted by the ways of the world. As Jesus further says, not everyone who says to Him, 'Lord' truly means it (Matthew 7:21). An intentional disciple has weighed up the cost and follows Jesus in all things (Luke 14:25-34).

Too often discipleship is seen as going and doing. This actually refers more to an apostle, than a disciple. The former was someone who was sent out, the latter was someone who quite literally was to sit at the feet of their master. Yes, I know that often a disciple became an apostle and Jesus does send us out into the world, but not without being a disciple.

Being a disciple in the first instance is less about doing and more about being. The doing can come soon enough but when it does, it is in the right spirit, with the right motivation. Being a disciple is to be a life student of Jesus. This is not easy, but Jesus never says it will be.

Time and again, after a conversation with Jesus, we see people who realised that what He was asking was too much for them. Some of them wanted to keep their riches, others their status in society. Jesus warned again and again, that true discipleship meant putting Him first in all things. This is a matter for our mind and heart to wrestle with, before we decide whether we can indeed truly follow Jesus.

This can seem incredibly daunting and perhaps more than we envisage when we first see the command, 'Love your neighbour'. Perhaps it should be daunting though. After all, to truly love others is massive. Time and again religious leaders of Jesus' day were trying to limit who they could be a neighbour too. Jesus on the other hand threw it as wide open as possible.

Luke records how Jesus followed up the verse of 'Love God...Love others', with the parable of the Good Samaritan *(Luke 10:25-37)*. The expert in the Law wanted to see who his neighbour was, so he knew who to love and who not to love. In effect he was looking to limit his love.

The expert in the Law wanted to do as little as possible for the greatest gain. Jesus however, rather than limiting who our neighbour is, extended it to mean everyone, even our enemy.

A Samaritan being a good neighbour to a Jew was not just surprising to Jesus' first hearers, it was shocking; it was unheard of. Jesus however, was less interested in who our neighbour is. He was more interested in, to whom we can be a neighbour to.

Note also which incident Luke records after Jesus encourages us to love our neighbour, (even our enemy)...it is that of Mary and Martha *(Luke 10:38-42)*. In this episode we see how Mary chose a better way, a way less about 'doing' and more about 'being'. Mary in effect, as she sat and listened to Jesus, was becoming His disciple. There would be time enough another day, for doing.

On that day, with Jesus in her house, Mary knew it was time to take a risk. It was the opportunity of a life time. Even though she shouldn't have even been in the same room as this great teacher, she risked social convention. She ignored the protocol of male and female separation and she sat at the feet of Jesus.

In coming to know and love Jesus, we are invited not to pick up a badge or a label of being a Christian, rather we are invited to a new way of life, a new way of being. We are invited to be a life-long disciple.

One aspect I love about the Bible is how real it is. In many instances it is completely topsy-turvy. If you were making up a religion you certainly wouldn't let the Bible be your publicity tool.

Jesus too often turned everything on its head. Having been baptised and sent into the desert to be tempted, one of the first things He does is choose some disciples. If you were Jesus, where would you start? More than likely, the synagogue, or some religious school.

In thinking of who would make a good disciple, it is unlikely you would have trawled the shores for fishermen, searched the back streets for a tax-collector or allowed a zealot to join your team!

Paul too, chose a crazy bunch. One day Paul set himself the task of coming up with a top ten list of people of faith. I think I would have thought twice about including a drunk, a people pleaser, a deceiver, a murderer and an adulterer. Those people who fear easily or allow themselves to be dominated by their wife need not apply, let alone anyone who would not fight without a woman at his side. Yet Paul regards Noah, Abraham, Jacob, Moses, David, Gideon, Samson and Barak as being people of faith.

Was this really God's best?! Jesus called people who no other Rabbi would have short listed. Paul heralded people who had just as many bad days as good. Yet these were God's people, loved by God, used by God; disciples, apostles, His children. Perhaps all of these people can actually give us hope.

Time and again we see God loves everyone and chooses to use some complete miss-fits. The Bible is all about God working through people, by the power of His Holy Spirit. No-one in God's book, 'need not apply'. Any or no C.V. is good enough. All that is required is an ability to be loved by God and to love Him in return. God can handle everything else.

The book of *Acts* is a wonderful invitation to see just what can be done in the power of His Holy Spirit. We see God's love and patience for His people, who time and again fail and mess up. We see God empowering His people one step at a time to love others. It's always more about God and less about the people. God is love, God is the source.

In seeking *'intentional discipleship'*, which I believe incorporates loving others, I have realised I need to be with God all the more. I need to be prepared to learn. Sadly too often, our lips may say we want to be a Christian, but we are prepared to learn from almost anyone but Christ Himself. There will be good days and bad days. There will be days to rejoice and days where we are called to grow.

As I come to love God, so then I know God will encourage, guide and teach me. It is only in this relationship, I am truly being shown how to live life to the full. Becoming a disciple with a capital 'D' does not mean life is any easier, but it does create a desire of living *'wholeheartedly'* *(Romans 1:9)*.

Jesus spoke of this life and it is lived and revealed throughout the New Testament. A life where our hearts and lives are changed *(Luke 13:3; Acts 3:19; Romans 2:4)*. For too long I thought this referred to actions first.

Could it however be referring more to repentance and to our interior, to our heart, mind, strength and soul? Surely it is in our hearts and minds where our thoughts, our desires and our motivation lies? As our thinking evolves, changing to be more like that of Jesus, so our hearts (our wills), will be motivated to live as Jesus did.

Now, I know I promised we were coming to land, but perhaps before we take an aerial view of where we have been, let's have another look at the best tour guide going...

***

'The most important one,' answered Jesus, 'is this: 'Hear, O Israel: The Lord our God, the Lord is one. Love the Lord your God with all your heart and with all your soul and with all your mind and with all your strength. The second is this: 'Love your neighbour as yourself.' There is no commandment greater than these'
(Mark 12:29-31).

***

CHAPTER NINETY-ONE:
JESUS

Throughout our journey together, I know I have mentioned Jesus but perhaps not enough. For this chapter, I invite you to consider Jesus - fully human and fully God.

Now, I am aware that being fully God gives Him a huge edge on the rest of humanity. Who else can perform such miracles, remember Scripture so well and be such an amazing person?

But just perhaps every so often, in His humanity He may have preferred not to have been fully God. Please do not pick up a stone ready to throw it at me – let me try to explain.

In being fully God, Jesus knew where He came from and what life on earth was going to involve. At no point was He naïve. He knew the Scriptures, He knew the score. Jesus knew of *Isaiah 53:12*:

> *'he poured out his life unto death, and was numbered with the transgressors. For he bore the sin of many, and made intercession for the transgressors'.*

Jesus even quoted it *(Luke 22:37)* and now He was going to have to live it.

Jesus knew He was going to be despised, rejected, ridiculed, let down and become a man of sorrows *(Isaiah 53:3)*. He knew He was going to have to die for humanity in unimaginable pain. Being fully God meant He could never gloss over the ending and hope for a better end.

Have you seen the film, *'The Perfect Storm'*? I hope it is no spoiler to say, the ending is not good – they all die! I went to see the film with a couple of friends who somehow did not know this. As the film ended they sat in shock. They even waited until the credits had rolled, to see if somehow there was another ending. The car journey home was somewhat sombre.

Jesus knew what coming to earth truly meant for Him. In being fully human for some thirty three years, Jesus was given an insight into what it was like to live on this earth. Rather than just watching the nature of humanity, He lived among it. Yes there was some good, but also there was a lot of bad that entered hearts.

Jesus saw at first-hand how these bad things translated into ill-speaking and despicable actions. Jesus witnessed and endured just how badly human beings could ill-treat each other. Jesus knew humanity for what it was and yet still He did not give up, He had hope. Jesus still commanded us to Love God with our all and to love our neighbour. Yet as He said these words, He also knew they were actually impossible to live, unless of course you were Jesus.

To love God with our all, all of the time, almost seems like we are being set up to fail. Even the best of people after all have bad days, where they may put themselves or others before God. We question, was Jesus commanding us to do something which is unachievable; if so, was Jesus just not being pretty mean?

From everything else I have read and know about Jesus, I cannot imagine He was setting us up for a fall, for a fail. It seems completely out of character and against His very nature. Now I realise He Himself in His very being, did live the commands of God every day, but Jesus also knew He was fully God. We are only human. Hmm, maybe this is a good excuse. Do we get a waiver after all?

It seems not. Perhaps we need a better lawyer, as Jesus will not take us being merely human as a good defence. Luke records Jesus as saying after the verse of loving God and loving others, 'Do this and you shall live' (Luke 10:28). I am left thinking then, that as no-one can actually do this, perhaps heaven will be rather empty.

In such thoughts I am brought back to Jesus. Yes, in our strength alone - to love God and our neighbour is actually impossible. Thankfully though, our salvation is not dependent on our fulfilling these commands. Salvation comes from Jesus Himself. The defeat of sin on the cross and an invitation to have eternal life with Him, enables us to become His children.

Jesus' command of us loving God and others is for our life here on earth in the Kingdom of God before heaven. Yet still, where does this leave us? Saved yes, but often floundering when we mess up, again and again! Is this any way to live? The answer has to be in Jesus' life itself.

Reading a Gospel through in a oner can be a wonderful way of becoming more aware of Jesus' life on earth. Through four different authors, with different reasons to write, we can piece together a picture of Jesus' life on earth.

Putting down a chick flick, over the last summer, I read and re-read the Gospels. Reading the Gospel of Mark can take less than an hour and in doing so, we can see how Jesus lived His human life on earth.

The first time I read through a Gospel in a oner, (with a cuppa in hand), I was actually surprised at what I saw. Now, yes, Jesus was without sin *(1 Peter 2:22; Hebrews 4:15; 1 John 3:5)*, and He did always do things which were pleasing to God *(John 8:29)* but He was still human – very human.

Just a skim through the Gospel of Mark alone, reveals, Jesus was at times, stern *(1:25)*, filled with compassion *(1:41; 6:34)*, angry *(3:5; 11:15)*, deeply distressed *(3:5)* and overwhelmed with sorrow *(14:34)*.

Jesus faced people disbelieving and doubting Him *(6:1-6)*. If being told nothing good came out of Galilee, was not mocking enough, even His own family considered Him to have lost His mind *(3:21)*.

At times, perhaps out of frustration or sadness, Jesus sighed deeply *(7:34; 8:12)*. John records how Jesus wept *(11:35)* and His heart was troubled *(12:27)*.

As I read of Jesus within all four Gospels, I encountered His humanness. Within this I saw Jesus Himself was made up of a heart, mind, soul and strength. In His life on earth, as a human He too was called to love God with every part of Him. And even though He was God, being a human nevertheless was not always easy. In fact at times because He was God, life was perhaps made all the harder.

If Jesus hadn't been God's Son He would not have forgiven others for their sins *(Mark 2:5-7)*, nor would He have called God His Father. Consequently He wouldn't have been accused of blasphemy and got into trouble with the religious authorities, time and again *(John 10:30-33)*.

If Jesus hadn't been God's Son, it is unlikely He would have healed so many people, let alone on the Sabbath. For centuries people had indeed been stoned to death for any small act of work. Other prophets it seems obeyed this – Jesus meanwhile healed on the day of rest.

I have to confess here though, Jesus did not attempt to appease the opposition. Sometimes in reading the Gospels, (for example *John 9:14*), it seems Jesus only healed on the Sabbath! Either Jesus went out of His way to deliberately provoke discussion or He was healing so many people, that this included even on the Sabbath.

Now in no way am I suggesting Jesus was perverse, but it does seem that Jesus was not afraid of confrontation. Perhaps, at times, He did go out of His way to make the greatest impact. Take for example the clearing of the temple. *Mark* tells us *(11:11)* that Jesus visited the temple on the day He arrived in Jerusalem, but as it was already late, He left, only to return the next day.

Jesus returned the following day when there were more people present. Jesus over turned tables and threw out the money changers at a time when it was more busy. Was this partly for a greater affect? The religious authorities were sure to hear of it and they did *(11:15-18)*.

Furthermore, if Jesus had not been God, then the Devil is less likely to have seen Him as such a threat. Whilst at times many human beings have been under the eye of the Devil (not least Job), as fully God, Jesus is likely to have come under even more scrutiny. It is unlikely, if He was merely an ordinary person, that the Devil would have tempted Jesus to such an extreme.

The temptations of Jesus demonstrate how the Devil tempted Him in His very humanness *(Matthew 4:1-11)*. Jesus was tempted to turn stones into bread, to throw Himself down from the temple and to bow down and worship the Devil. All of these things would have given Jesus great status within Israel.

Many people are likely to have heard of Him, of His message and more than likely followed Him. Hearing Jesus' words in response to the third temptation, further encourages my desire to love God with our all, showing its supreme importance. Taken from *Deuteronomy 6:13*, Jesus answered the Devil saying, *'Worship the Lord your God, and serve him only' (4:10)*.

CHAPTER NINETY-TWO:
HEAVEN SENT

Being fully God often brought Jesus more ridicule. Jesus at times was mocked and misunderstood for the very reason that people wrestled with whether He was actually truly God. If Jesus were merely a man, would the soldiers at the cross have mocked Him for being the King of the Jews and yet not being able to help Himself? If Jesus had not been God, it is unlikely the criminal next to Him on the cross, would have questioned whether Jesus was the Messiah and ironically queried if He could save them both.

Perhaps the place where we see being fully God and fully human at its most poignant, was the day before the cross. As fully God, Jesus knew of the *'baptism He had to under-go'*, the death which awaited Him *(Luke 12:50)*. As fully human, this 'baptism' troubled Him. Jesus longed for this suffering to be taken from Him. Yet He knew that He had to bow to an authority, dare I say, to a love greater than Himself. Hence Jesus, in His obedience and love, spoke out the refrain; *'not my will but yours'*.

What of Jesus' day on the cross? As God's Son, Jesus knew the intimacy of their relationship and yet at the very moment He needed His Father most...He experienced being forsaken, being abandoned, being separated from God's love at His greatest time of need.

Jesus was heaven sent. Jesus knew what it was like more than any other human being to know God's love. Jesus alone knew of the peace and perfection that comes with being with God. And yet in the most painful of deaths, not only was His body stretched to its full capacity, not only was His strength taken from Him, He faced the anguish of separation. The heart of Jesus was truly tested that day.

When those around Him mocked and ridiculed, encouraging Him to come down from the cross *(Luke 23:35-39)*, was not every part of Jesus' mind and heart being tested? Was His strength not tested? Perhaps it crossed His mind that it would be okay to jump down – after all no-one else had leapt down from a cross. Perhaps that miracle alone, would be enough to encourage more people to come to know God.

Did not every part of Jesus (His heart, mind and soul), just want to leap down from the Cross? Not just to escape the pain, but to prove He was indeed the Son of God. We cannot imagine what it was like for Jesus on that day. But let's once again return to the day before...

In the Garden of Gethsemane, Jesus reveals not only His true humanness, but what human beings in the strength of God, can achieve. As I have said earlier, Jesus' strength and body was tested, His sweat was like drops of blood. Jesus' heart and mind, were tested as He asked His Father to take away this cup of suffering.

Jesus knew what lay ahead and He earnestly asks His Father to remove it. Not just once does He ask, but twice *(Mark 14:36-39)*. He was experiencing so much stress, anguish and turmoil that He asked His disciples to keep watch.

This the disciples could not do – they fell asleep. It wasn't as if Jesus didn't know this was coming though. Even at the time of the transfiguration His disciples had sneaked forty winks *(Luke 9:32)*. Peter, James and John were not well known for their prayer warrior stints. No 24/7 prayer for them!

Okay, on the night of Jesus' arrest, the disciples were probably tired and stressed out. From entering Jerusalem with the applause of the crowd, Jesus had been teaching and healing non-stop. His disciples were with Him and would have been tired. Jesus had also shared the Lord's Supper with them. This must have been playing on their minds. What did Jesus mean by lifting up bread and wine saying, remember me, this is my body and blood?

As the disciples approached the garden that evening, they knew Jesus was not Himself, He seemed troubled. There is nothing more unsettling, than when your teacher or the person in charge is out of sorts. The disciples had been busy, they were tired but Jesus had asked them to stay awake.

In addition, Jesus, their Lord, their teacher had had the humility to share with them His distress and trouble. Jesus, God's Son, who had previously been transfigured with Moses and Elijah on a mountain top; Jesus who had performed miracles galore; Jesus who had even commanded the winds and waves to stop; this same Jesus was having such a bad day, that He asked His disciples to stay awake.

Perhaps Jesus wanted their fellowship in prayer, maybe He yearned for their companionship, or their support in His sorrow, before the soldiers arrived to arrest Him. Perhaps He just wanted them to see how, at the most difficult time of His life so far, He was modelling prayer. Whatever the reason, Jesus wanted them to stay awake.

As Jesus made His request, so He poured out His everything. He said; *'My soul is overwhelmed with sorrow to the point of death' (Mark 14:34)*. Here we see, not only was Jesus' mind, heart and body in turmoil, so was His soul.

In fact Jesus' soul was in effect tortured by the knowledge of all He would have to go through. Jesus confessed the 'sorrow' He was experiencing. Jesus was allowing the very people who had spent the last three years revering Him, to see Him having the worst of days. Jesus knew His flesh was weak but thankfully for us His spirit was strong *(Mark 14:38)*. In spite of all of this, His disciples fell asleep.

Within the last twenty four hours of His life, Jesus allowed Himself to be betrayed *(Mark 14:45)* and to look defeated *(15:20)*. He faced the turmoil of mental anguish *(15:34)*, had a broken heart, and lived with a soul which was overwhelmed with sorrow.

All of this was wrapped up in the most unimaginable physical pain, of flogging *(15:15)* and crucifixion *(15:24)*. Jesus would not have cried lightly, the words: *'My God, my God, why have you forsaken me?'*.

Having known the closest of all relationships, having been in heaven, in union with God His Father, how much more must it have hurt that day...to be forsaken. We may at times feel forsaken, but I think Jesus knew it with a capital 'F'. Yet He still went through it all. Perhaps all the more remarkable is that Jesus did so - fully human.

Jesus in His humanness endured many things which we also do. He had a mind and a heart which must have been hurt when people misunderstood Him. How must it have felt the day His family came to 'take charge' of Him, as they thought He was out of His mind? Jesus knew what it was like to be hunted down. At times things grew so intense, He had to escape their grasp *(John 10:39*, compare also *7:19)*.

Jesus loved and felt compassion – He had a heart and longed for things to be better than they currently were. Mark in his account of the feeding of the 5000, remarks: *'Jesus...had compassion on them, because they were like sheep without a shepherd' (Mark 6:34)*. Jesus had compassion on a widow who had lost her son, so much so He raises the young man to life *(Luke 7:13)*. Time and again, the heart of Jesus went out to people; He had compassion

(Matthew 9:36; 14:14, 20:34).

Jesus had compassion on those who had little voice in society. Jesus listened to the blind, to lepers, to adulterer's, to Gentiles, to a lady with menstrual problems, to those with demons, to tax collectors, to fishermen, to centurions. In fact a glimpse at the Gospels shows how He seemed to spend more time with those who had no voice, rather than with those who had one!

Yet in all of this, every day, Jesus loved God with all of His heart, mind, strength and soul. In the Garden of Gethsemane, yes Jesus pleads with His Daddy to take away the cup of suffering, but this is followed by: *'Yet not my will, but what you will' (Mark 14:36).* Even in His lowest moment, He loved God with all His will, with all His heart.

Even though He was overwhelmed, in anguish and unimaginable physical and mental pain, He still loved God with His all – with His very all. Jesus knew it was for this very moment, He had been sent to earth:

> *'Now my soul is troubled, and what shall I say?*
> *'Father, save me from this hour'?*
> *No, it was for this very reason I came to this hour'*
> *(John 12:27).*

In this verse we see how even in Jesus' life, different parts of Him at different times, took the lead. His soul was troubled and yet His heart (His will), knew He was called to love God with His all. Jesus let His heart take the lead and He was supremely obedient.

Jesus' revelation of His humanness, of asking God to spare Him, actually gives me more hope for myself. Jesus' call upon His Father in His dying breath of saying, *'Why have you forsaken me?'*, strangely gives me hope too. In all of this I see Jesus (fully God and fully human), was tested to the hilt, tempted to give in and yet He did not.

Jesus, filled with the Holy Spirit, (with God's love flowing through Him), loved God with all of His mind, heart, strength and soul. As He did so, Jesus shows what it is like to be human. Jesus in the Garden, reveals what it was like to have a wobble, to want an easier way. Even Jesus at times wanted out...but as He did so, He also lived and breathed loving God with His all.

Jesus lived His life fully obeying the commands He gave us; He knew this was the way to get the best of life. More than this, Jesus went through all of this for me and for you. Jesus offers not only salvation but the way to live life the best we can. As we are invited, commanded, called to live to love God with our all, so we too can live the life we are created for.

Tom Wright sums this up better than me:

> *Jesus really did believe that through His kingdom-mission, Israel's God would enable people to worship and love Him and to love one another, in a new way, the way promised in the prophets, the way that stemmed from renewed hearts and lives'.* [lxxi]

Jesus knew God's commands and He knew His mission on earth, and He kept to both. Everyday Jesus spoke in Aramaic, He was reminded Israel was no longer the nation it once was. Speaking an adopted language of Babylon, Jesus was reminded daily of Israel's exile. Every day Jesus saw a Roman official, so He was reminded that He was living in an occupied territory.

Jesus must have faced the temptation daily to become the political Messiah the Jews had been looking forward to. It must have crossed Jesus' mind that He could become the 'hero' who freed His people from Rome's dominion. Yet, He knew there was more than just this earth to consider. Jesus came to build a new Kingdom, one that would last forever. Jesus came for souls. Jesus kept to His mission of preaching the Good News. He did this through living God's commands of love.

At those times when we feel our own strength will fail, that our minds may break and our hearts may lead us away from God, with God's Spirit and His love flowing through us, we can follow Jesus' way. This is hard but even in this we need not rely on ourselves but on Jesus. We can remember to put on a new self, that of Jesus, which is renewed through God our Creator *(Colossians 3:10)*.

In the garden of Gethsemane Jesus cried out to His Father, and even though the mission of dying for the world was not taken from Him, His Father heard and *'An angel from heaven appeared to Him and strengthened Him'* *(Luke 22:43)*.

If Jesus needed God's help and an angel to strengthen Him, how much more do we? The first step is recognising it, the second, as Jesus did, is to bring ourselves in love, to God. We were created for a relationship with God and nowhere does Jesus reveal this more powerfully, than as He approached the cross. As Price says:

> *'True love is a fruit of the Spirit, not a fruit of the determined Christian. The Spirit of God is alone its source...Unless we are*

Jesus it seems, as He called upon His Father knew the limit of His own ability and in turn was strengthened by an angel. If Jesus had to rest in the sufficiency of God alone, how much more do we have to?

As we consider Jesus and the journey to the cross however, I would like us to go back even further...perhaps to a conversation in heaven when Jesus was first sent to earth. We are told Jesus was indeed sent: *'(God) loved us and sent his Son as an atoning sacrifice' (1 John 4:10).*

As Jesus and His Father had a chat, just how did it go? We, of course, do not for sure but I wonder, as God revealed His plan to save humanity, whether Jesus Himself had some different ideas. The plan and travel itinerary must have seemed pretty bizarre to say the least.

Jesus, (heaven sent), was to go to the womb of a young unmarried peasant girl. The Son of God was to be born in an obscure town and laid in a food trough. His family, as they fled to Egypt were to become immigrants, only to return sometime later to Nazareth – and we all know nothing good comes from Nazareth *(John 1:46)*!

For thirty years, living in the ordinary, Jesus was to support His family, working hard with wood. After this, He was to have no real home to speak of and no money of His own. He was to eat with sinners, prostitutes, lepers and outcasts.

Where was the Son of God's great ministry to begin? In Capernaum and Bethsaida, at the north end of the sea of Galilee, in the furthest outposts of Jewish life.

Jesus was to be hunted down, judged, put on trial, crucified and laid in a borrowed tomb. There was at least a return ticket, but for thirty or so years Jesus was bound to feel like He was on the longest road trip ever.

How did Jesus react? He said, 'yes' and He came to live among us. Jesus left heaven to be with us, to become one of us.

And yet before He did so, His cousin, John (the Baptist) went before Him, preparing the way. John the Baptist was the leading religious figure of his day and was recognised as a prophet according to the Old Testament pattern. Jesus in His humility, even allowed a relative to prepare the way for Him.

With the travel arrangements in mind, as Jesus looked upon earth, what must have run through His mind, His heart, His soul and His strength? He knew humanity, He knew what we are like, of our own hearts being hardened *(Mark 10:5)*, of all the evil which comes out of our heart *(Mark 7:2-23)* and yet still He came to earth.

More than this, as a baby, born in the natural way, He came to be one of us, living amongst us. Paul as he speaks of Jesus, sums it up well:

> *'Who, being in very nature God, did not consider equality with God something to be used to his own advantage; rather, he made himself nothing by taking the very nature of a servant, being made in human likeness. And being found in appearance as a man, he humbled himself by becoming obedient to death - even death on a cross!'*
> *(Philippians 2:6-8).*

In being sent to earth, Jesus was separated from the close communion He had enjoyed with His Father in heaven. Jesus continued to be without sin and yet still He was separated from God. On leaving heaven, all be it for just thirty three years, He embarked on the longest road trip ever.

On the very day Mary was alarmed at being told she was to be a mum, so Jesus was preparing Himself to enter our world. It was on this day, just as on His last, that Jesus gave His all. On His first day just as on His last He gave everything to God - His all; His heart, mind, body and soul *(Luke 23:46)*.

We may look to the cross as a place where Jesus was separated from His Father, but actually in a real sense, every day Jesus lived on earth He was separated from God. No wonder perhaps, we see Him so often withdrawing from the crowds, to places of silence and solitude, to be with His Father.

I find it fitting that the first words Luke records of Jesus are: *'Why were you searching for me? Didn't you know I had to be in my Father's house?'* *(Luke 2:49)*. As a young boy, Jesus knew His Father God. Just as Jesus had dwelt with His Father in heaven, so as best as He was able; Jesus dwelt with God in the temple courts *(Luke 2:46)* and in quiet lonely places *(Luke 5:16)*.

Jesus who had once been in the manifest Presence of God in heaven, knew on earth, the only way to live was to also be in God's Presence. Such times strengthened Him. If Jesus needed this, how much more do we? Time to be with God in His Presence.

Jesus lived and breathed loving God with His all. Jesus knew of our design as human beings. He knew we are created and designed for God alone. Jesus knew He had to take care of His soul and His whole person so He could indeed live life to the full.

In loving God with His all, Jesus knew He was trusting someone other than merely Himself to take care of His whole being. As I seek to love and follow God it makes sense that I should follow the ways of someone who knew Him better than anyone.

Jesus, heaven sent, will return. Until He does He longs to be Lord of our heart, soul, mind and strength. On earth, we saw Jesus was able to be Lord over every aspect of life. He restored minds, healed bodies, refreshed souls and longs to be Lord of our heart. Jesus longs for this to be a reality for all of us.

CHAPTER NINETY-THREE:
WE ALL NEED A LITTLE MORE OOMPH!

I was all set to send this off to be edited when I was invited to speak to a group of ministers. A friend, after I had shared a little of my journey, rather than giving me a sympathetic look and a hug, just said: *'I sense hope'*. He promptly then gave my name to someone, who wanted a speaker to encourage a group who were ministering in smaller contexts!

In the past, in preparation for such a talk, I would have just spun out some words, prayed a little and hoped for the best. On this occasion however, I really wanted to say what God may be wanting this group to hear. This was a privilege but quite a challenge. In the end after much prayer and mulling over what to say and what not to say, I journeyed nearly a 100 miles to this small gathering.

After I had shared what I fervently hoped God had wanted them to hear, I was encouraged by their feedback. Although I had gone off-piste from the topic I had been asked to speak on, it seemed my words had been right for many of them. I was relieved, but also silently pleased, not least that I had been listening to God correctly.

As I journeyed back, I had a list of chores to accomplish before returning home. I was praying as I drove, but I admit in my haste, I may have gone over the speed limit a little. As I journeyed, I sensed some spiritual attack. All that week as I had mulled over what to say, I had been praying for protection, but I now felt some onslaught. With this, a light flashed on the dashboard and my car suddenly lost all of its oomph!

I cautiously pulled over from the third lane onto the hard shoulder. The car had reduced from over 70mph to just over 30mph. I then remembered our car has an over-ride so that when there is a fault, our car reduces speed. There was only 2.5 miles left to go on the motorway so I reasoned, with hazard lights flashing, it may be better to pull out into the near side lane to limp to a safer spot.

My prayer became all the more urgent and I ended up praying in tongues as I had no words other than *'help me God!'*. As I limped those few miles, I noticed an enormous white lorry in my rear mirror! It was behind me when I went onto the hard shoulder, but then also as I pulled back out. It remained with me until I turned off the motorway.

I do not know who they were and I am unable to thank them in person but I sense the lorry was sent by God. Many vehicles had begun to get cross and understandably they had been trying to overtake me. The lorry on that day was providing me with some protection, a guardian angel if you like!

I eventually made it off the motorway and I turned into a supermarket car park. I marvelled as I parked at how I was feeling, in the past I would have been livid and very grumpy, at the car playing up. On this occasion I was only thankful, for the day and the safe passage.

Inside the supermarket however, things which might have irritated me continued...an excessively noisy mother had everyone on edge. I felt compelled to pray for her and the poor man who bravely tried to rebuke her for how she was treating her children! I only had a few things to get, but I kid you not, quite literally there were empty shelves for the items I required! And of course I had an excessively wonky trolley!

Thankfully I bumped into a 'prayer warrior' from church and I asked her to pray for the car and for my safety. Long story short, and all be it very slowly, I made it home that evening, narrowly missing an accident on the way.

The next day was not good however. Having to rush into the day as it was a particularly busy one, I did not make much time to be with God. My husband and I suffered for it. All day I felt as I once had; angry, defeated, fed up and grumpy. It was not until the evening that I even reflected on the whys and how's!

Initially I had blamed my husband for my bad mood. He had asked how the talk had gone, but he was clearly more concerned about our broken car. I returned like for like so before I knew it, his grumpiness had manifested within me! He went to his study to work and I took an early night.

I am not saying that either God or even the devil caused our car to break down...I cannot say for sure that I was being tested or attacked. All I do know is I was able to go from being thankful in the midst of adversity, to being grumpy. The next day this developed into being even more bad tempered. Both days had frustrations but in relying on my strength one day and on God's strength the other the outcomes were very different.

I am designed and created to live life flowing from God's love. For me personally this can only happen when I live in God's love and spend significant time with Him. God loves us so much He does not want us to live a second rate life. God longs for us to live our lives from His love, from His strength, from God Himself. On those occasions when I rush into the day, my day is always the worst for it.

As I later reflected on the car, for too long I had depended on my own strength and this was fine until I lost my oomph! When my heart, mind and strength had ceased to live, my soul did an over-ride on myself. Rather than needing a mechanic I needed this verse of 24 words and a new way of living. For this I am eternally grateful.

Now, I am not likening God to an enormous lorry, however, God was and is always there for us. Sometimes perhaps, we just have to use our rear mirror to see this.

For those interested in the car...we took it to the garage, the light went out and it started to function normally once again!

CHAPTER NINETY-FOUR:
LET'S LAND

So dear friend, (I believe we have journeyed together long enough for me to call you that), thank you for sticking with me. I know at times I have taken us on massive detours. On occasions we even kept revisiting a particular place of interest and for a period you may have even thought we were lost. Hopefully along the way we have both learned a little more, not just of God, but of ourselves.

You have heard it before, but as I come to the greatest command as defined by Jesus, I am grateful for this second chance. Loving God with my all, can only occur as I am being loved by Him first.

For too long I had tried to love others, God a little and if there was time, I had allowed God to love me. I had read God's word topsy-turvy.

From God's love and through His love, so I am able to love God all the more. This I believe, is enabling me to live the life I am designed and created for. God's agenda - all for our own good.

God is love and He has created each of us for an exclusive relationship with Him. I had accepted second best for too long. I had tried to be a Christian in my own strength. God loves us too much to let us do this for long.

God longs to be in a relationship with us. Through allowing God's Holy Spirit to dwell all the more in me and for me to dwell in God's love, so I am able to live life – truly live life. It is from God I am drawing life.

I had tried to live like Jesus outwardly, instead of inwardly. Too often I had thought, just as soon as I got my external world sorted so my inner world would be filled with peace and joy. I have come to learn, God is inner out, not outer in.

Through the life of Jesus and the power of the Holy Spirit, I am being turned inside out – all for my own good, (I hasten to add). No longer is life about doing, it is now about being. Far from this meaning nothing now gets done, rather anything which is now achieved flows from a position of love. The motivation is better and on the whole so is the outcome.

From this state of being, flowing from the source of love, so I am *becoming* the person I am designed to be. Jesus came to save souls and I am grateful that He has helped me to identify the part of me designed for eternity.

Through recognising each different part of me, my heart, soul, mind and strength, so I believe I can love God more fully. The more I come to do so, the more I am loved by Him. In this love, I am being renewed and transformed, all for good.

There are still plenty of flaws. Believe me, I can identify them as well as anyone. However, I give God thanks and all the glory for things which are all the better in my life, and I wait in expectant hope for even greater things.

Flowing from God's love, we are able to gain a purity of heart, a transformation of our minds, a renewal of strength and a refreshed soul. God chooses to work within and through the faculties He gave us. All for His glory and to enable us to love Himself and others.

I didn't know best after all. I have come to trust and put all of my hope in the One who created me in His image. Amongst many pilgrims, I journey on this earth, living in God's Kingdom, until I am called out of exile to my ultimate home.

Far from this being an individualised quest for perfection, it is a journey to help me love God and in turn others. I believe the latter can be done all the better flowing from God's heart of love. I am not just called to love God *with* my being, but I am called to love God *from* my being; from my heart, mind, soul and strength. This can only occur when God's love is flowing through me first.

Walking faithfully in His Presence and doing so wholeheartedly is a life long journey and I am thankful for the time to do so. Eternal living starts now. Until I am called 'home', to my true home in heaven, I hope as an exile to do more than muddle through. I hope to do more than survive. I would love to flourish and live life to the full. Come what may, I hope to live the best of life on earth before heaven. As I do so, I pray the words of Solomon into my life:

'Let love and faithfulness never leave you... Trust in the Lord with all your heart and lean not on your own understanding; in all your ways submit to him, and he will make your paths straight. Do not be wise in your own eyes; fear the Lord and shun evil. This will bring health to your body and nourishment to your bones'
(Proverbs 3:3a, 5-8).

An answer to this prayer of mine to not merely lean on my own understanding has been God giving me many people to learn from. No-one is more surprised than me, that I have been drawn from a busy evangelical life to one more of silent reflection.

In the company of others I have been in awe at the precious wealth of material there is to assist me on such a journey. From those in the Bible, such as Jacob and the Psalmist, to Christians from the medieval period, to modern day influences such as Frank Laubach and Mother Teresa, I have been drawn to, *become more aware of the Presence of God*. This is helping me to be loved by God, to love Him with my all and in turn to love others.

No longer am I living in my own strength, from an ever depleting source. Rather it is God who strengthens me in all forms of life.

Finally, (I promise), I am a child of God, a disciple of God and a servant of God. I am a mum who is enjoying being part of John's local school and I have been blessed with new friendships. I have been given a second chance, a different way of being with God and for this I will always be thankful.

As well as writing and editing books, I have been convinced by God of just how much of my life also needs 'editing'. No matter what I end up doing, in my being and all that I am, I hope to love the Lord my God with all my heart, soul, mind and strength. As I do this, I hope to be strengthened by God's love to love others. As I become more aware of God's Presence, I know I am forever wrestling and yet forever resting...

May,

'The LORD bless you and keep you; the LORD make his face shine on you and be gracious to you; the LORD turn his face toward you and give you peace'
(Deuteronomy 6:24-26).

FATHER'S LOVE LETTER

An intimate message from God to you.

You may not know me, but I know everything about you. Psalm 139:1 I know when you sit down and when you rise up. Psalm 139:2 I am familiar with all your ways. Psalm 139:3 Even the very hairs on your head are numbered. Matthew 10:29-31 For you were made in my image. Genesis 1:27 In me you live and move and have your being. Acts 17:28 For you are my offspring. Acts 17:28 I knew you even before you were conceived. Jeremiah 1:4-5 I chose you when I planned creation. Ephesians 1:11-12 You were not a mistake, for all your days are written in my book. Psalm 139:15-16

I determined the exact time of your birth and where you would live. Acts 17:26 You are fearfully and wonderfully made. Psalm 139:14 I knit you together in your mother's womb. Psalm 139:13 And brought you forth on the day you were born. Psalm 71:6 I have been misrepresented by those who don't know me. John 8:41-44 I am not distant and angry, but am the complete expression of love. 1 John 4:16 And it is my desire to lavish my love on you. 1 John 3:1 Simply because you are my child and I am your Father. 1 John 3:1 I offer you more than your earthly father ever could. Matthew 7:11 For I am the perfect father. Matthew 5:48 Every good gift that you receive comes from my hand. James 1:17

For I am your provider and I meet all your needs. Matthew 6:31-33 My plan for your future has always been filled with hope. Jeremiah 29:11 Because I love you with an everlasting love. Jeremiah 31:3 My thoughts toward you are countless as the sand on the seashore. Psalm 139:17-18 And I rejoice over you with singing. Zephaniah 3:17 I will never stop doing good to you. Jeremiah 32:40 For you are my treasured possession. Exodus 19:5 I desire to establish you with all my heart and all my soul. Jeremiah 32:41 And I want to show you great and marvellous things. Jeremiah 33:3 If you seek me with all your heart, you will find me. Deuteronomy 4:29

Delight in me and I will give you the desires of your heart. Psalm 37:4 For it is I who gave you those desires. Philippians 2:13 I am able to do more for you than you could possibly imagine. Ephesians 3:20 For I am your greatest encourager. 2 Thessalonians 2:16-17 I am also the Father who comforts you in all your troubles. 2 Corinthians 1:3-4 When you are broken hearted, I am close to you. Psalm 34:18 As a shepherd carries a lamb, I have carried you close to my heart. Isaiah 40:11 One day I will wipe away every tear from your eyes. Revelation 21:3-4 And I'll take away all the pain you have suffered on this earth. Revelation 21:3-4

I am your Father, and I love you even as I love my son, Jesus. John 17:23 For in Jesus, my love for you is revealed. John 17:26 He is the exact representation of my being. Hebrews 1:3 He came to demonstrate that I am for you, not against you. Romans 8:31 And to tell you that I am not counting your sins. 2 Corinthians 5:18-19 Jesus died so that you and I could be reconciled. 2 Corinthians 5:18-19 His death was the ultimate expression of my love for you. 1 John 4:17 I gave up everything I loved that I might gain your love. Romans 8:31-32 If you receive the gift of my son Jesus, you receive me. 1 John 2:23 And nothing will ever separate you from my love again. Romans 8:38-39 Come home and I'll throw the biggest party heaven has ever seen. Luke 15:7 I have always been Father, and will always be Father. Ephesians 3:14-15

My question is... Will you be my child? John 1:12-13

I am waiting for you. Luke 15:11-32 Love, Your Dad

My Child,

Almighty God © 1999 Father Heart Communications - FathersLoveLetter.com - Please feel free to copy & share with others.

BIBLIOGRAPHY

Abrahams, I. *Studies in Pharisaism and the Gospels* (1924: Cambridge Uni Press).

Augustine, *City of God* (2003: Penguin Classics).

Augustine, *St. Ennarrationes in Psalmos* xciii 18.

Banks, R.J. *Jesus and the Law in the Synoptic Tradition* (1975: SNTS Monograph 28. Cambridge University Press).

Barclay, W. *The Gospel of John, Vol 1* (1975: Edinburgh: The St Andrew Press).

Barclay, W. *The Gospel of Luke* (1975: Edinburgh: The St Andrew Press).

Barclay, W. *The Gospel of Mark* (1975: Edinburgh: The St Andrew Press).

Barclay, W. *The Gospel of Matthew, Vol 2* (1975: Edinburgh: The St Andrew Press).

Barclays Bank website. *From the Archives: The Evolution of the Cheque* (available from https://home.barclays/news/2016/08/evolution-of-the-cheque/ accessed 18 November 2018).

Barrett, C.K. *The Gospel according to St John* (1955: London: SPCK).

Beasley-Murray, G.R. *Word Biblical Commentary, John, Vol 36* (1987: Texas: Word Books).

Becker, L.C. ed. *Encyclopedia of Ethics, 2 vols* (New York: Garland, 1992).

Bernard, J.H. *The International Critical Commentary on the Gospel according to St. John, Vol 1* (1928: Edinburgh: T & T Clark).

Bloesch, D. G. *God, the Almighty: Power, Wisdom, Holiness, Love* (2006: Downers Grove, IL: InterVarsity Press).

Bonhoeffer, D. *Life Together* (1954: New York: Harper and Row).

Borst, J. *Coming to God in the Stillness: Discovering the Power of Contemplative Prayer* (2004: Kevin Mayhew Ltd).

Bourne, Edmund, J. *The Anxiety and Phobia Workbook, 5th Ed* (2010: Oakland, CA: New Harbinger).

Browne, R. *The Message of Deuteronomy* (1993: Bible Speaks Today).

Caird, G.B. *The Pelican New Testament Commentaries: Saint Luke* (1963: Penguin Books).

Cho, D. Dr. and Hostetler, H. *Successful Home Cell Groups* (2012: ReadHowYouWant).

Christensen, D. and Metzger, B.M. *Deuteronomy 1:21:9, Volume 6A; Second Edition* (Word Biblical Commentary). (2014: Zondervan).

Craigie, P.C. *Deuteronomy: The New International Commentary on the New Testament* (1976: Eerdmans).

Cruz, N. and Buckingham, J. *Run Baby Run* (2003: Hodder & Stoughton).

Dickens, C. *Oliver Twist* (2000: Wordsworth editions).

Dray, S. *Discovering Matthew's Gospel* (Crossway Bible Guides) (1998: Crossway Books).

English, D. *The Message of Mark* (The Bible Speaks Today) (1992: IVP; New Edition edition).

France, R.T. *The Gospel of Matthew: The New International Commentary on the New Testament* (2007: Eerdmans).

Foster. R. *Celebration of Discipline* (1980: London: Hodder and Stoughton).

Foster, R. *Prayer: Finding the Heart's True Home* (2008: London: Hodder and Stoughton).

Foster, R. *Sanctuary of the Soul* (2011: London: Hodder and Stoughton).

Foster, R. *Streams of Living Water* (2017: London: Hodder and Stoughton).

Got Questions website. *What Is the Human Soul?* (available from: https://www.gotquestions.org/human-soul.html cited 18 November 2018).

Green, J.B. *Matthew: The New International Commentary on the New Testament* (1997: Eerdmans; Sixth Impression edition).

Gundry, R.H. *The use of the O.T. in St Matthew's Gospel* (1967: SNT 18.

Leiden: E.J. Brill).

Hagner, D.A. *Word Biblical Commentary, Vol. 33B: Matthew 14-28* (1995: Thomas Nelson).

Herberg, W. *Judaism and the Modern Man* (1983: Pennsylvania: Atheneum).

Heschel, A.J. *The Sabbath: Its Meaning for Modern Man* (1951: Farrar, Straus and Giroux, New York: The Noonday Press).

Ignatius of Loyola (Saint) and Hughes, G.W. *Spiritual Exercises of St. Ignatius of Loyola* (2004: Gracewing).

Jamison, OSB, Father Christopher. *Finding Sanctuary: Monastic Steps for Everyday Life* (2010: W&N; New Ed edition).

John. J. *Ten: Living the Ten Commandments in the 21st Century* (2000: Kingsway Publications).

Johnston, W. *Exodus* (1990: Sheffield: JSOT Academic Press).

Julian of Norwich. *Showings* (1978: Paulist Press).

Kempis, Thomas A. *The Imitation of Christ* (2005: Hendrickson Christian Classics).

Kolodiejchuk, B and Mother Teresa. *Mother Teresa: Come Be My Light: The revealing private writings of the Nobel Peace Prize winner* (2008: Rider).

Lucado, M. *Anxious for Nothing* (2017: Thomas Nelson Publishers).

Lucado, M. *You'll Get Through This* (2013: Thomas Nelson Publishers).

Luther, M. in Ebeling, G. *Lutherstudien II: Disputatio de homine, Text and Hintergrund* (Tubingen: Mohr, 1977), pp. 31-43

Macarthur, J. *Slave: The Hidden Truth about Your Identity in Christ* (2010 by Thomas Nelson).

McGrath, A. *Beyond the Quiet Time: Practical Evangelical Spirituality* (1996: SPCK).

Meyer, F.B. *Gospel of John* (1970: London: Lakeland).

Michaels, J.R. John: *The New International Commentary on the New Testament* (2010: Eerdmans; Sixth Impression edition).

Neusner, J. *The Mishnah: A New Translation* (1991: Yale University Press).

Nineham, D.E. *The Pelican New Testament Commentaries: The Gospel of St Mark* (1963: Penguin Books).

Nolland, J. and Hubbard, D.A. *Word Biblical Commentary Vol. 35B, Luke 9:21-18:34* (1993: Thomas Nelson).

Ortberg, J. *Know Doubt* (2009: Zondervan: Reprint with A New Title edition).

Ortberg, J. *Soul Keeping: Caring for the Most Important Part of You* (2014: Zondervan).

Ortberg, J. *The Me I Want To Be Curriculm Kit – Becoming God's Best Version of You* (2010: Zondervan).

Painter, J. *Mark's Gospel* (1997: London and New York: Routledge).

Price, C. Matthew: *Focus on the Bible* (1998: Christian Focus Publications).

Pullinger, Jackie. *Chasing the Dragon* (2006: Hodder & Stoughton).

Ryle, J.C. *Expository thoughts on Mark* (1985: Edinburgh: The Banner of Truth Trust).

Strong, James H. *Strong's Exhaustive Concordance. Complete and Unabridged* (Reprinted 1989, Baker Book House, Grand Rapids, Michigan).

Swinney, J. *Through the Dark Woods: A Young Woman's Journey Out Of Depression* (2006, Monarch Books).

Ten Boom, C. *The Hiding Place* (2004: Hodder & Stoughton).

Ten Boom, C. *Amazing Love: True Stories of the Power of Forgiveness* (2018: CLC Publications).

Tinsley, E.J. *The Gospel according to Luke (Cambridge Commentaries on the New Testament)* (1965: Cambridge University Press; Fourth Printing edition).

Tozer, A.W *Hungry For God?: The Pursuit of God* (2017: CreateSpace Independent Publishing Platform).

Underhill, E. *The Cloud of Unknowing* (2007: Kessinger Publishing Co).

Upchurch, John. Bible Study Tools website. *7 Daily Steps to Trust in the Lord with All Your Heart* (available from https://www.biblestudytools.com/bible-study/topical-studies/7-daily-steps-to-trust-in-the-lord-with-all-your-heart.html accessed 18 November 2018).

Wilcock, M. *The Saviour of the world: The message of Luke's gospel (The Bible speaks today)* (1979: IVP)

Willard, D. *The Divine Conspiracy: Rediscovering Our Hidden Life in God* (2014: Harper Collins).

Willard, D. *The Great Omission: Jesus' Essential Teachings On Discipleship* (2014: Monarch Books; 2nd Revised edition).

Wright, C. *Deuteronomy* (1996: New International Biblical Commentary; Massachusetts: Hendrickson).

Wright, C.J.H. *Living as the People of God: The Relevance of Old Testament Ethics* (1983: Leicester: IVP).

Wright, N.T. *The New Testament and the People of God* (1992: London: SPCK).

Wright, Tom. *John for Everyone: Part 2* (The New Testament for Everyone) (2004: Westminster John Knox Press; 2 edition).

Wright, Tom. *Luke for Everyone: Part 2* (The New Testament for Everyone) (2004: Westminster John Knox Press; 2 edition).

Wright, Tom. *Mark for Everyone: Part 2* (New Testament Guides for Everyone) (2001: SPCK Publishing; First Edition edition).

Wright, Tom. *Matthew for Everyone: Part 2* (New Testament Guides for Everyone) (2002: SPCK Publishing; First Edition edition).

NOTES

i. Randall Arnold, a business man, frustrated at the local council for the condition of the roads outside of his frozen food depot, reluctantly paid his rates bill, all be it with a 150lb halibut fish. At the time (1978) it formed a legitimate cheque. Why did he do it? Well imagine the smell of a fish being kept in a bank vault for seven years! (https://www.home.barclays/news/2016/08/evolution-of-the-cheque.html - accessed 17 November 2018).

ii. Rollinson, P. and Kelly, D.F. *The Westminster Shorter Catechism in Modern English* (2012: Presbyterian and Reformed).

iii. Compare, Abrahams, I. *Studies in Pharisaism and the Gospels* (1924: Cambridge Uni Press) and Banks, R.J. *Jesus and the Law in the Synoptic Tradition* (1975: SNTS Monograph 28. Cambridge University Press).

iv. Writers after Jesus became more familiar with the linking of these texts, such as Philo of Alexandria a Jewish philosopher at the time of Jesus (Look at Banks, *Jesus and the Law in the Synoptic Tradition* (1975: SNTS Monograph 28. Cambridge University Press), p.170-171). Also look at the writings of the Pseudipigrapha, such as the *Testament of Issachar* (5:2) and the *Testament of Dan* (5:3).

v. Nineham, D.E. *The Gospel of St Mark* (1963: Middlesex: Penguin Books), p.324. It is widely accepted that Rabbis spoke on this.

vi. Nineham, D.E. *The Gospel of St Mark* (1963: Middlesex: Penguin Books), p.324.

vii. Wright, Tom. *Matthew for Everyone: Part 2* (New Testament Guides for Everyone). (2002: SPCK Publishing; First Edition edition), p.93

viii. Gundry, R.H. *The use of the O.T. in St Matthew's Gospel* (1967: SNT 18. Leiden: E.J. Brill), p.22-24. Gundry suggests it could be a misreading, that is, Matthew used *dianoia* 'thinking' and not *dynamis*, 'strength'. Personally I cannot equate this with Matthew who not only takes such care elsewhere, but he would also have known the quote from Deuteronomy too well to have made a mistake.

ix. Wright, C. *Deuteronomy* (1996: New International Biblical Commentary; Massachusetts: Hendrickson), p.98.

x. Tozer, A.W *Hungry For God?: The Pursuit of God* (2017: CreateSpace Independent Publishing Platform), p.26.

xi. *Father's Love Letter.* (Available from http://www.FathersLoveLetter.com/text.html accessed 18 November 2018).

xii. Tozer, A.W *Hungry For God?: The Pursuit of God* (2017: CreateSpace Independent Publishing Platform), p.26.

xiii. Donne, John. *1624 MEDITATION XVII Devotions upon Emergent Occasions.*

xiv. Julian of Norwich. *Showings: Shorter text.* (1978: Paulist Press), p.167.

xv. Tozer, A.W *Hungry For God?: The Pursuit of God* (2017: CreateSpace Independent Publishing Platform), p.71.

xvi. Augustine, St. *The Confessions of St. Augustine*, trans. R.S. Pine-Coffin (Baltimore, MD: Penguin, 1961), I.1, p.15, as quoted in Foster, R. *Streams of Living Water* (2017: Hodder and Stoughton), p.199.

xvii. Wright, Tom. *Matthew for Everyone: Part 2 (New Testament Guides for Everyone).* (2002: SPCK Publishing; First Edition edition), p.178.

xviii. For more on this, do look at Foster, R. *Streams of Living Water* (2017: Hodder and Stoughton), p.389, footnote 61.

xix. Matt Redman's Song; *'Gracefully Broken'* (2017) inspired this phrase for me.

xx. Barclay, W. *The Gospel of Matthew, Vol 2* (1975: Edinburgh: The St Andrew Press), p.278.

xxi. France, R.T. *The Gospel of Matthew: The New International Commentary on the New Testament* (2007: Eerdmans), p.319

xxii. Willard, D. *The Great Omission: Jesus' Essential Teachings On Discipleship*

(2014: Monarch Books; 2nd Revised edition), xiv and the whole book!

xxiii. If you would like to explore more about Christianity and mental health, you may be interested in the website, http://www.mindandsoul.info/

xxiv. Bourne, Edmund, J. *The Anxiety and Phobia Workbook, 5th Ed.* (2010: Oakland, CA: New Harbinger), xi.

xxv. Lucado, M. *Anxious for Nothing.* (2017: Thomas Nelson Publishers), p.7.

xxvi. Kempis, Thomas A. *The Imitation of Christ* (2005: Hendrickson Christian Classics), p.158.

xxvii. Willard, D. *The Divine Conspiracy: Rediscovering Our Hidden Life in God* (2014: Harper Collins), p.355.

xxviii. Lucado, M. *Anxious for Nothing* (2017: Thomas Nelson Publishers), p.32

xxix. Willard, D. *The Divine Conspiracy: Rediscovering Our Hidden Life in God* (2014: Harper Collins), p.29

xxx. Thomas, Ben. The Man Who Tried to Weigh the Soul. Discover: Science for the Curious, 03 November 2015. (Available from http://blogs.discovermagazine.com/crux/2015/11/03/weight-of-the-soul/ accessed 18 November 2018).

xxxi. Ignatius of Loyola (Saint) and Hughes, G.W. *Spiritual Exercises of St. Ignatius of Loyola* (2004: Gracewing), #169.

xxxii. Julian of Norwich. *Showings* (1978: Paulist Press), p.163.

xxxiii. Julian of Norwich. *Showings* (1978: Paulist Press), p.164.

xxxiv. Julian of Norwich. *Showings* (1978: Paulist Press), p.165.

xxxv. Foster, R. *Prayer: Finding the Heart's True Home* (2008: London: Hodder and Stoughton), p.22ff.

xxxvi. Teresa, Mother. ed. Le Joly, E. and Chaliha, J. *Stories Told by Mother Teresa* (1999: Element Children's Books).

xxxvii. Kolodiejchuk, B and Mother Teresa. *Mother Teresa: Come Be My Light:*

The revealing private writings of the Nobel Peace Prize winner (2008: Rider).

xxxviii. Caroll, L. *Alice's Adventures In Wonderland* (2010: Createspace Independent Publishing Platform).

xxxix. 1980s Ready Brek *'Get Up and Glow'* Advert. https://www.youtube.com/watch?v=9Xii0_7nMaA (accessed 17 November 2018)

xl. Goodreads: Quotable Quotes website. George MacDonald. (Available from https://www.goodreads.com/quotes/889692-we-don-t-have-a-soul-we-are-a-soul-we accessed 18 November 2018).

xli. Augustine, St. *The Confessions of St. Augustine,* trans. R.S. Pine-Coffin (Baltimore, MD: Penguin, 1961), I.1, p.15, as quoted in Foster, R. Streams of Living Water (2017: Hodder and Stoughton), p.199

xlii. Lutes, Chris. *The Secret that Will Change Your Life.* Christianity Today 2018. (Available from https://www.christianitytoday.com/iyf/hottopics/faithvalues/8c6030.html accessed 18 November 2018).

xliii. Flavel, J. *On Keeping the Heart* (2010: CreateSpace Independent Publishing Platform).

xliv. Eva F. Kittay, in Becker, L.C. ed. *Encyclopedia of Ethics, 2 vols* (New York: Garland, 1992). vol. 1, pp. 582-87, explores this in much greater detail.

xlv. St Augustine, *Ennarrationes in Psalmos* xciii 18

xlvi. Ten Boom, C. *The Hiding Place* (2004: Hodder & Stoughton). Ten Boom, C. *Amazing Love: True Stories of the Power of Forgiveness* (2018: CLC Publications).

xlvii. The author remains anonymous. Translated by, Underhill, E. *The Cloud of Unknowing* (2007: Kessinger Publishing Co), Chap lxiv, p.245

xlviii. The author remains anonymous. Translated by, Underhill, E. *The Cloud of Unknowing* (2007: Kessinger Publishing Co), Chap lxiv, Chapter xli, p.199

xlix. Cho, D. Dr. and Hostetler, H. *Successful Home Cell Groups* (2012: ReadHowYouWant), p.19

l. Moon R. *Founder of World's Largest Megachurch Convicted of Embezzling*

$12 Million. Christianity Today International 2014. (Available from https://www.christianitytoday.com/news/2014/february/ founder-of-worlds-largest-megachurch-convicted-cho-yoido.html accessed 18 November 2018).

li. Swinney, J. *Through the Dark Woods: A Young Woman's Journey Out Of Depression* (2006, Monarch Books).

lii. Macarthur, J. *Slave: The Hidden Truth about Your Identity in Christ* (2010 by Thomas Nelson), studies this in greater detail.

liii. Wright, C. *Deuteronomy* (1996: New International Biblical Commentary; Massachusetts: Hendrickson), p.99.

liv. Tozer, A.W *Hungry For God?: The Pursuit of God* (2017: CreateSpace Independent Publishing Platform), p.74.

lv. Luther, M. in Ebeling. G. *Lutherstudien II: Disputatio de homine, Text and Hintergrund* (Tubingen: Mohr, 1977), pp. 31-43.

lvi. Tozer, A.W *Hungry For God?: The Pursuit of God* (2017: CreateSpace Independent Publishing Platform), p.74.

lvii. Jamison, OSB, *Father Christopher. Finding Sanctuary: Monastic Steps for Everyday Life* (2010: W&N; New Ed edition), p.56.

lviii. Foster, R. Streams of Living Water (2017: London: Hodder and Stoughton), p.88. See also, Foster. R. Celebration of Discipline (1980: London: Hodder and Stoughton).

lix. Willard, D. *The Divine Conspiracy: Rediscovering Our Hidden Life in God* (2014: Harper Collins), p.159.

lx. Willard, D. *The Divine Conspiracy: Rediscovering Our Hidden Life in God* (2014: Harper Collins), p.134.

lxi. Augustine, *City of God.* (2003: Penguin Classics), Book 22, paragraph 29.

lxii. Bonhoeffer, D. *Life Together* (1954: New York: Harper and Row), p.13.

lxiii. McGrath, A. *Beyond the Quiet Time: Practical Evangelical Spirituality* (1996: SPCK), p.62.

lxiv. Dickens, C. *Oliver Twist* (2000: Wordsworth editions).

lxv. Borst, J. *Coming to God in the Stillness: Discovering the Power of Contemplative Prayer* (2004: Kevin Mayhew Ltd).

lxvi. Julian of Norwich. *Showings* (1978: Paulist Press), Chapter 25. p.170.

lxvii. Herberg, W. *Judaism and the Modern Man* (1983: Pennsylvania: Atheneum), p.62.

lxviii. Not least from ,Willard, D. *The Great Omission: Jesus' Essential Teachings On Discipleship* (2014: Monarch Books; 2nd Revised edition).

lxix. Foster, R. *Prayer: Finding the Heart's True Home* (2008: London: Hodder and Stoughton), p.177.

lxx. Nineham, D.E. *The Pelican New Testament Commentaries: The Gospel of St Mark* (1963: Middlesex: Penguin Books), p.326.

lxxi. Wright, Tom. *Mark for Everyone: Part 2* (New Testament Guides for Everyone) (2001: SPCK Publishing; First Edition edition), p.171-172.

lxxii. Price, C. *Matthew: Focus on the Bible* (1998: Christian Focus Publications), p.256.

MEET THE AUTHOR

Tracey is grateful for a recent change in circumstances which has allowed a bit of scribbling. Life started as a farmer's daughter in Somerset. Tracey loves that so much of her family and school friends still live in the local area. At University whilst training to be a Primary school teacher, she became a Christian. If however, she had known this would have resulted in her wearing a collar and joining the Army, she wonders if the conversation with God would have been a little longer...

On becoming a Christian, she remained at the University College of St Mark and St John, Plymouth as a Pastoral Assistant. This led onto her becoming a youth worker for Sway and Brockenhurst in the New Forest. Whilst there, she longed to communicate God's love to all ages and ended up being ordained into the Church of England. It is fair to say she wrestled with this enormously, but God is bigger than any of our plans.

At Trinity theological college, Bristol she met and married Jack. They moved shortly afterwards to Iford, Bournemouth as she served her curacy. She loved her time there, learnt lots from Andy and picked up a bestie.

If becoming 'collared' was a surprise, her joining the Army was even more of one. Jack was a tremendous support and encouragement as he quite literally accompanied her around the world. Tracey enjoyed every minute of serving with 26 Royal Artillery in Germany (during which she was deployed to Iraq) and the 1st Batallion of the Royal Regiment of the Fusiliers. During this time John, their son, was born. After a particularly long night of prayer it soon became clear it was time to leave.

Tracey re-entered parish Ministry as a Bishops' Missioner and Priest for a few years, during which time Jack started at theological college himself.

To support and encourage her husband, Tracey has recently stepped back from serving God with a collar. She is really enjoying serving God as a Christian in the local area, most recently with running Active Church. As a family they love days out, cycle rides, walks and every so often you may even find Tracey on a golf course or a vineyard.

373

KEEP IN TOUCH

www.foreverwrestling.org.uk

I have succumbed to Facebook just for you – that is love!

Printed in Great Britain
by Amazon